God's Bargain with the Jews

And How They Kept It

Robert Strauss

Simeon Press
2017

A SIMEON BOOK

First Printing: 2017

ISBN: 978-0-578-19048-8

Simeon Press
7 Read Road
Hanover NH 03755

Dedicated to Judith, my wife and best friend.

Acknowledgements

I have had the opportunity to prepare and present a dozen ILEAD (Institute for Lifelong Education at Dartmouth) courses on the Hebrew Bible and the history of the Jewish Diaspora. Dartmouth College's Baker-Berry Library has made it possible for me to track down hundreds of obscure citations. I am sincerely indebted to bibliographers William Fontaine and Reinhart Sonnenburg.

My research was aided by Jacob Neusner, Distinguished Service Professor of the History and Theology of Judaism at the Bard College Institute of Advanced Theology (sadly now deceased), who was most generous in discussing the finer points of the rabbinic period and difficult passages in several of his many books.

I would also like to thank the following for their considerate review of specific portions of this book: Mark Lilla, Professor of the Humanities at Columbia University and James Van Cleve, Professor of Philosophy at the University of Southern California for the philosophers of the Enlightenment, and Gene R. Garthwaite, Professor of Asian Studies at Dartmouth College, for his review of the Arab Period.

Equally important to the integrity of the manuscript was the proofing work of my good friend and Hebrew scholar Bruce Pacht. I would also like to thank my brother Richard Strauss who has helped me talk through some of the trickier areas and who suggested on numerous occasions particular sources for information, as well as Kelly Ahlfeld who prepared the index. And one more, the editor of the book, Bill Craig without whose help the book would never have been finished.

Much of the material in this book began life as a Bible study program at St. Thomas Episcopal Church where I had helpful interaction with a faithful group of parishioners.

January 24, 2017

Preface

This book is intended to provide the reader with an understanding of the vast sweep and impact of the Jews' bargain with God, the Covenant. A reader who wishes to probe more deeply is encouraged to consult the sources referenced in the end notes of each chapter.

When quoting from the Hebrew Scriptures, I use *TANAKH: The Holy Scriptures* (Jewish Publication Society). The Hebrew Bible is not identical to the Christian Old Testament (OT), for reasons that will become clearer as we read through the early chapters of this book.

When quoting from the Christian New Testament (NT), I use the New Revised Standard Version (NRSV) for its familiarity and wide acceptance. All quotations from the Christian Apocrypha are from *The Harper Collins Study Bible* (NRSV), Wayne A. Meeks editor.

All quotations from the Eastern Christian Septuagint (LXX) are from *The Septuagint with Apocrypha: Greek and English*, Sir Lancelot C.L. Brenton translator, Hendrickson Publishers, 1995.

All quotations from Qur'ân are taken from the widely available *The Koran (Everyman's Library)*, J.M. Rodwell translator, Orion Publishing Group, 1994. Other English translations differ in verse designations. On occasion, I use *The Noble Qur'ân in the English Language*, Dr. Muhammad Muhsin Khan, Darussalam Publisher, 1996.

When it has been appropriate to use a scriptural source other than these, the variance is noted.

All of the scriptures quoted in this book are in the English language, not in the language in which each was originally written. That translation results, of course, in a less finely nuanced, perhaps less accurate, reading.

I have followed the current convention of designating the periods before and after the life of Christ as BCE (before the common era) and CE (common era).

I invite the reader to come into this study with an open mind. As colleagues in this enterprise and fellow travelers on the journey, I further invite the reader to contact me at bobstrauss15@gmail.com

Table of Contents

God's Bargain with the Jews

And How They Kept It

Chapter One
The Covenant

In my grace, I have summoned you,
and I have grasped you by the hand.
I covenanted you, and appointed you.
A covenant people, a light of nations.

Isaiah 42:6

     The premise of this book is that the ancient covenant (*bĕrît*) received by Moses from God at Mt. Sinai and accepted by the Israelites more than three thousand years ago is a reality still in force today. Reviewing the history of the Jewish people with that premise in mind raises the following questions: What does the covenant bargain imply? What exactly did that bargain demand of the Israelites? How have the Jewish people carried out that bargain? What can we discern from the historical record?

Background

     Legend tells that the twelve tribes of Israel are named for the sons of Jacob who was renamed by God as Israel. In birth order, they are Reuben, Simeon, Levi, Judah, Dan, Naphtali, Gad, Asher, Issacher, Zebulun, Joseph, and Benjamin. Each tribe probably formed around the founding father. Their territory was the east bank of the Mediterranean Sea, which moderated the hot weather of summer. The time of their founding cannot be determined accurately, but it probably was contemporaneous with the beginnings of agriculture and animal husbandry.

     The tribes were small groups, compared to the growing populations of Egypt and Babylonia. They lived a relatively calm and undisturbed existence. The religion of the people who would become the Israelites was consistent with that of other Canaanite tribes living in the general area of present day Lebanon and Israel. The Israelite gods El and Yahweh were existing cult figures in religions that could be either monotheistic or syncretistic.

Moses

Let's start by reviewing the biblical background of Moses. The name "Moses" was commonly used in Egypt, as can be seen in the names of at least two pharaohs: Ahmose and Thutmose. In addition, a 13th-century BCE papyrus speaks of "Amen-em-Opet son of the steward Mose," and a stele of the same age notes a priest, "Pa-ser, son of Mose."

The legendary birth of Moses is framed by Pharaoh's order to the midwives to kill each newborn Israelite son. This is a preliminary condition to the nativity of Moses, whose life-threatening situation at birth parallels ancient myth.

The births of many savior figures throughout history have been associated with mythic elements such as the mother's previous infertility, divine signs of the life to come, naming of the child by God, peril to the infant (including abandonment), miraculous intervention, brilliant youth and triumphant life. In the Bible, we see some of these elements in the lives of Jacob and Esau, Joseph, Samson, and Samuel. Outside of the Bible, we note elements of the same pattern in the lives of Horus (Egyptian), Cyrus (Persian), Oedipus, Cronus, Hercules and Telephus (Greek), and Romulus and Remus (Roman).

If this entire scenario brings to mind the nativity and early life of Jesus, it is not a coincidence. Matthew's gospel testimony to the Jews likens Jesus to Moses and makes every effort to show the concurrence of the two stories. We will keep this in mind as we follow the story of Moses. Let us look for a moment at the first two chapters in the life of Jesus as told by Matthew.

DIVINE SIGNS OF THE LIFE TO COME

> ... *an angel of the Lord appeared to Joseph in a dream and said, "Joseph, son of David, do not be afraid to take Mary as your wife, for the child conceived in her is from the Holy Spirit.* (New Revised Standard Version, Matthew 1:20)

NAMING OF THE CHILD BY GOD

> *She will bear a son, and you are to name him Jesus.* (Matt. 1:21, 1:23)

MIRACULOUS INTERVENTION

> ... *an angel of the Lord appeared to Joseph and said, "take the child and his mother and flee to Egypt and remain there until I tell you..."* (Matt. 2:13)

PERIL TO THE INFANT

When Herod saw that he had been tricked by the wise men, he was infuriated, and he sent and killed all the children in and around Bethlehem who were two years old or under. (Matt. 2:16)

Compare the nativity of Moses to that of Jesus, as told in the Bible and by Josephus.

DIVINE SIGNS OF THE LIFE TO COME

One of the sacred Egyptian scribes who were very sagacious in foretelling future events, said there would be a child born to the Israelites who would bring the Egyptian dominion low, and would raise the Israelites; that he would exceed all men in virtue, and obtain a glory that would be remembered through all ages. (Flavius Josephus, *Antiquities of the Jews*)

PERIL TO THE INFANT

The King of Egypt spoke to the Hebrew midwives ... saying "When you deliver the Hebrew women, look at the birthstool; if it is a boy, kill him. If it is a girl, let her live. (Tanakh, Exod. 1:16)

MIRACULOUS INTERVENTION

The daughter of Pharaoh came down to bathe in the Nile... She spied a basket among the reeds and sent her slave girl to fetch it. When she opened it, she saw that it was a child, a boy crying. She took pity on it and said "This must be a Hebrew child" (Exod. 2:5-9)

NAMING OF THE CHILD

When the child grew up, she brought him to Pharaoh's daughter who made him her son. She named him Moses, explaining "I drew him out of the water." (Exod. 2:10)

We have no specific information that would tie Moses early years to a particular time in Egyptian history. One can theorize that he was influenced by the actions of Pharaoh Akhenaten (c. 1353-1336 BCE) who radicalized the well-established pagan Egyptian religion by placing his faith in the Sun God only. This period in Egyptian history set the court against the priests and carried over into the period immediately following the death of Akhenaten and his wife.

The first important pharaoh to follow the unfortunate reign of Akhenaten was Seti I (1290-1279) whose main objective was to rejuvenate the ancient deities and establish the theological credentials of what was to become the Ramesside Dynasty. It was early in the long reign of Ramesses II (1279-1213) that the Egyptians fought the Hittites, their enemies from the north, to a draw in the historic battle at Kadesh (Qadesh) in Northern Syria. It became apparent that fortifications were necessary to secure the northern border of Egypt. This would have been about 1274 BCE, when Ramesses undertook a massive building program centered on a new, fortified city at the base of the Nile delta.

Meanwhile, back along the eastern shore of the Mediterranean Sea, the Israelite tribes were being uprooted from the more temperate zone by the sea and forced into the hill country by the Philistines, invaders from the north and enemies of Egypt. There the Israelites had to find forage for their grazing animals, a problem in the hot, dry summer season. It became the habit of the Israelites tribes to move their sheep and cattle to the delta region of Egypt, which was fertile following the flooding of the Nile each spring. This was a win-win situation for the Israelites and the Egyptians, because the animals helped fertilize the ground while the Israelites fattened their domestic stock.

It was during the period 1274 to 1259 BCE, when the Hittites negotiated a peace treaty with Ramesses, that the Israelites found themselves, essentially, political prisoners. The pharaoh busied his people in nonstop construction to such a great extent that he had to employ the Israelites as well. The once-peripatetic Israelites were forced to labor at construction year-round. (Exod. 3:7) At some point, Moses was prodded to negotiate their release. Perhaps he obeyed this subconscious urging because he had some prior knowledge of a universal God.

The biblical text that describes events in the life of Moses, from the burning bush to the exodus, theophany, the law, and his death has been subject to much redaction, but scriptural analysis shows that this process began during the period of oral transmission, which implies that the story of the exodus, the covenant, and the law predate the scriptural record, which came into existence about 900 BCE. It appears that Moses was a real figure who, very early in the history of the Israelite tribes, took on mythic stature.

God's Bargain

Returning now to the story of the covenant, we should note that in the biblical world, covenants were the means by which relationships were ordered. The operable covenant words between God and the Israelites are contained in the Book of Exodus:

> *You have seen what I did to the Egyptians, how I bore you on eagles'*
> *wings and brought you to Me. Now then, if you will obey Me faithfully*
> *and keep My covenant, you shall be My treasured possession among all*

the peoples. Indeed, all the earth is Mine, but you shall be to Me a
kingdom of priests and a holy nation ... And all the people answered as
one saying: "[And] All that the Lord has spoken we will do!" (Exod.
19:4-6, 8)

This passage, because of its impact on the life of Israel, is one of the
most carefully analyzed in the Bible. The theophany at Mt. Sinai, which called
the Israelites into covenant with the Lord, and the giving of the law are the
basic tenets of Judaism. Had there been no covenant with God, the religion
and society of the Israelites would not exist today. But what does it mean?

The term *treasured possession* expresses God's special covenant
relationship with Israel and Israel's love for God. *Kingdom of priests* speaks to
Israel's national sovereignty under God. A kingdom (nation) is indispensable
for the proper fulfillment of Israel's mission. This nation is not to be an
ordinary one; it is to be set apart from secular nations. Israel, now being in
league with God, must judge all its actions against God's standards. It must be
prepared to fail, and possibly to be punished.

As a *holy nation*, the Israelites will differ from all other people by what
they are and by what they will become under God. Being in covenant with
God, they will reflect God's holiness and attests to God's attributes. To
achieve God's objectives, the people must understand that individually they
must respect God's morality. Taken together, the phrase *kingdom of priests and a*
holy nation relates to a mission that encompasses God's purpose.

You shall be called "Priests of the Lord" and termed "Servants of our
God." (Isa. 61:6)

Taken as a whole, the institution of an agreement between God and
this particular people (God's Chosen) represented the beginning of institutional
monotheism in this world. It gave God a relationship through which to teach
basic societal mores: respect for all people, peaceful outcomes of all disputes,
supportive communities and the importance of learning about God and God's
society.

Monotheism

The Israelites' affirmative response to God's request marks the "birth
of Israel" as Yahweh's people, and their bond to God by virtue of the law to
which, in the legal sense, they have acknowledged as binding. "There is no
compromising or temporalizing of this promise." The covenant having been
affirmed (Exod. 19:8, 24:3), God blessed the people of Israel and promised to
preserve them:

> *But hear, now, O Jacob My servant, Israel whom I have chosen! Thus*
> *said the Lord, your Maker, your Creator who has helped you since birth:*
> *Fear not, My servant Jacob, Jeshurun whom I have chosen, even as I*
> *pour water upon thirsty soil, and rain upon dry ground, so will I pour*
> *My spirit on your offspring, My blessing upon your posterity.* (Isa. 44:1-
> 3)

Because this work is going to take time, God promises to preserve the chosen ones for countless generations. Thus, each individual Israelite/Jew continues to be obligated to perform the law even if he or she disassociates from the community.

> *I make this covenant, with its sanctions, not with you alone, but both*
> *with those who are standing here with us this day before the Lord our*
> *God and with those who are not with us here this day.* (Deut. 29:13-
> 14)

The promise of God to future generations is declared in the following passage from the Prophet Jeremiah:

> *Thus said the Lord who established the sun for light by day, the laws of*
> *moon and stars for light by night, who stirs up the sea into roaring*
> *waves, whose name is Lord of Hosts: If these laws [the covenant] should*
> *ever be annulled by Me — declares the Lord — only then would the*
> *offspring of Israel cease to be a nation before Me for all time.* (Jer.
> 31:35-36)

This passage essentially confirms the everlasting nature of the covenant between God and the Chosen People. As Childs has explained: "Exodus 19 remains as a witness that God did enter a covenant with a historical people at a particular time and place ... the covenant remains a witness for all ages of the ultimate seriousness of God's revelation of himself and his will to the world." The historicity of this event should not be taken as folklore. From all we know today looking back, it was not only real but momentous to the Jewish people.

Moving from a polytheistic religion to a monotheistic religion is a frightening step to take. In polytheism the various gods are immediately available (*i.e.*, "immanent") and ready to do the bidding of the supplicant. If the prayer is not fulfilled, the one who prays can always choose another god. In monotheism there is only one God. If the supplicant's need is not met, God, being omnipotent and distant (*i.e.*, "transcendent"), cannot be blamed. The supplicant must look into his own heart. Therefore, monotheists must adhere to standards in order to insure that they are doing what God would want.

Covenant Terms

The covenant between God and the Israelites and their promise to keep that covenant and *obey God faithfully* therefore requires the performance of certain duties that will be made clear to them by the prophets of God.

> *I [God speaking to Moses] will raise up a prophet for them [the Israelites] from among their own people, like yourself. I will put My words in his mouth and he will speak to them all that I command him.* (Deut. 18:18)

The Prophet Isaiah speaks of these duties in the following passages:

> *I will also make you a light of nations, that My salvation may reach the ends of the earth.* (Isa. 49:6)
> *Harken to me My people, and give ear to Me, O My nation. For teaching shall go forth from Me, My way for the light of peoples.* (Isa. 51:4)

These passages make two points: first, the covenant implies that Israel as God's servant is to demonstrate God's ways to the world. Did God give the Israelites any guidance as to what methods they should use to carry out this work? The Bible offers clear instructions, which we can paraphrase as:

> Love the Lord and Observe His commandments
> Treat all with justice especially the widow, orphan, stranger, poor,
> the oppressed and needy.
> Speak the truth and deal loyally and compassionately with one another.
> Share what you have with those in need.
> Love your neighbor as yourself.

Second, the covenant commands Israel to bring all nations to a belief in the redeeming love of God, *"Opening eyes deprived of light, rescuing prisoners from confinement, from the dungeon those who sit in darkness"* (Isa. 42:7). Fulfilling the covenant means opening the eyes of those who do not know God, rescuing those whose way in life is so confining that they cannot work for God's kingdom, and bringing back an appreciation of the marvels of life on earth to those who have no inclination to contemplate the miracle of life. Look up to the heavens and see God's glory; seek to understand God's way.

Just before his death, Moses reminded the Israelites of the agreement that they have made with God and its significance in their life:

> *Take to heart all the words with which I have warned you this day.*
> *Enjoin them upon your children, that they may observe faithfully all the*
> *terms of this Teaching. For this is not a trifling thing for you, it is your*
> *very life.* (Deut. 32:46-47)

> *You shall be holy because I am holy.* (Lev. 11:45)

The Israelites have only the one God to pray to who may be there for them or not, but more than that they could get pushback from God. There was a bargain to be carried out. Punishment could follow a disinclination to observe the terms of the bargain. However, the bargain is not one-sided. If Israel does do God's work, then the following can be expected to occur:

> *You shall prosper in peace and security, enjoy the wealth of the nations*
> *and revel in their riches; but, do not glory in your wisdom, strength, and*
> *riches but only in earnest devotion to God.* (Isa. 61:66)

> *Remember that it is the Lord your God that gives you power to get*
> *wealth in fulfillment of the covenant that he made on oath with your*
> *fathers as is still the case.* (Deut. 8:18)

It is quite likely that without this assurance from God, the Jewish people would not have survived. But a covenant, particularly one between unequal parties, is not a gift. Stipulations accompany the acceptance of the covenant along with penalties for failure to keep the covenant. The penalties may be severe, for this is a matter of the gravest consequence. Israel's election has meant that these people must observe a personal relationship with God, and since the entire nation pledged to do everything God asks, the nation as a whole is also responsible.

From this time forward, whether Israel is ruled by judges, kings or priest, whether it governs itself or is dispersed among the nations, the sources of its political authority are the covenant and these laws. This doctrine of "special election" has become a byword for the Jewish people and their strength in adversity. The means of assessing whether the terms of the covenant were kept will be the study of encounters between the Israelites/Jewish people and other peoples throughout their history. Did they succeed in spreading the name of God throughout the world? Did they treat all people with justice and love, speak the truth and deal loyally and compassionately with one another, and share what they had with those in need? Did they refrain from glorying in their wisdom, strength, and riches while remaining devoted to God? What does each encounter tell us about the ability of the Jews to continue to uphold the covenant?

As it turned out, for the first five hundred years the Israelites paid no attention to the terms of the covenant, and continued to live just as they had. They gave no heed to the plight of the poor and needy. They ignored Gods rules, even as the first prophets reminded them and warned them what it meant to disregard the covenantal terms. And what did God want from the Israelites?

First, a people He could count upon to work His will on earth.

At base, the meaning of the covenant is there is only one God of this world. Polytheism does not bring people closer to godly morality. Therefore, the most important prayer in Judaism, and we might say in Christianity and Islam as well, is the *Shema*:

Shema Yisroel Adonai Elohenu, Adonai Ehud
Hear O Israel the Lord our God the Lord is one.

Notes for Chapter One

MOSES

Much has been written about Moses' encounter with God. However, if we place Moses in the prehistory of Israel we do so only on the basis of supposition since scriptural writing did not appear for several hundred years later. For insight on Moses mythological birth read Jonathan Cohen's
The Origins and Evolution of the Moses Nativity Story, E.J. Brill, 1993

The naming of Moses can be found in W. Gunther Plaut, *The Torah a Modern Commentary*, Union of Hebrew Congregations, 1981, 389, 517. Also Sarna, Nahum, *The JPS Commentary Exodus*, The Jewish Publication Society, 1991, 10. For mythological aspects of the birth read Leach, Margaret ed. *Dictionary of Folklore Mythology and Legend*, Funk and Wagnells, 1950, 750.

For the view from the early first century CE, read *The Works of Josephus* translated by William Winston, 1987, Hendrickson, *Antiquities of the Jews*, 2.9.2.

EXODUS

The story of the exile from Egypt and the trek through the desolate lands is probably passed down from the itinerant poets. However, this description is recounted in the first three chapters of the Book of Deuteronomy which overall is intended to provide a summary of God's deeds in Israel's behalf and an approved legend of Israel's founding as a covenantal nation under God.

For a detailed description and exclamation of Deuteronomy read
Everett Fox's *The Five Books of Moses, Schocken Books, first copyright 1983, 983-et seq*

The rationale for the entrapment of the Israelites in Egypt is the
extended drought in the countries on the north shore of the Mediterranean and
their mass movement to their south so well laid out by Trude and Moshe
Dotham in *People of the Sea: the Search for the Philistines,* Macmillan Publishing Co.
1992. The emigration of people from the north, sometimes known as "People
of the Sea," has been verified from Egyptian hieroglyphics. It appears people
of the Aegean region and Anatolia arrived in large numbers along the eastern
shore of the Mediterranean and in northern Egypt likely in search of habitable
land. Apparently, their home region was suffering an extended drought.

It was God's doing that the Israelites were able to outfox the powerful
Egyptian army. Although we know that tides in the Sea of Reeds could
fluctuate depending on the direction of the winds, to do so at the exactly right
moment to spare the Israelite stragglers and drown the Egyptian soldiers,
seems more than ordinary good luck. In any case there are lots of books about
this miraculous event:

Nahum M. Sarna, *The JPS Torah Commentary, Exodus,* The Jewish Publication
    Society, 1991, 104
John I. Durham, *Word Biblical Commentary,* Word Books, 1987, 262-3
Brevard S. Childs, *The Book of Exodus: A Critical Theological Commentary,* The
    Westminster Press, 1974, 342, 367, 380-4
Terence E. Fretheim, *Exodus Interpretation,* John Knox Press, 1991, 208-214
David Noel Freedman, *The Anchor Bible Dictionary,* 1992, Vol.2, 699, Article by
    Nahum Sarna.
Patrick Dale, *The Covenant Code Source,* Vetus Testamentum, Vol. 27, Fasc. April.
    1977 145-157
Carol Meyers, *Exodus,* Cambridge University Press, 2005, 146.

GOD'S BARGAIN

Nahum M. Sarna, *The JPS Torah Commentary, Exodus,* The Jewish Publication
    Society, 1991, 102
Joseph B. Soloveitch, *The Lonely Man of Faith,* Doubleday, 1992, 107-8.
Simone Chambers and Will Kymlicka, *Alternate Conceptions of Civil Society,*
    Princeton University Press, 2002, 15.

MONOTHEISM

Michael D. Coogan *Caananites: Who Were They and Where Did They Live?* Bible
    Review, 09:03, June 1993, 44-5
Philip J. King and Lawrence E. Stager, *Life in Biblical Israel,* Westminster John
    Knox Press, 2001,119, 123

Mark S. Smith, *The Early History of God*, HarperSanFrancisco, 1990. 22

David Noel Freedman, *The Anchor Bible Dictionary*, 1992, Vol. 3, Article by Robert G. Boling, 1107 et seq.

The naming of Moses can be found in W. Gunther Plaut, *The Torah a Modern Commentary*, Union of Hebrew Congregations, 1981, 389, 517. Also Sarna, Nahum, *The JPS Commentary Exodus*, The Jewish Publication Society, 1991, 10. For mythological aspects of the birth read Leach, Margaret ed. *Dictionary of Folklore Mythology and Legend*, Funk and Wagnells, 1950, 750.

COVENANT TERMS

Paul D. Hanson, *Isaiah 40-66*, John Knox Press, 1995, 40-66.

Adele Berlin and Mark Zvi. *The Jewish Study Bible*, Oxford University Press, 2004, 867.

W. Gunther, *The Torah a Modern Commentary*, Union of American Hebrew Congregations, 1987, 1673.

Mark Lilla, *The Still Born Guard: Religion Politics and the Modern West*, Alfred A. Knopf, 2007, 30.

Chapter Two
The Hebrew Bible

[W]hat great nation has laws and rules as
perfect as all this Teaching that I set before you this day?

Deuteronomy 4:8

Of all the writings produced by the Jewish people, none is more important than the Hebrew Bible.

> *Observe them [the laws and rules of the Bible] faithfully, for that will be proof of your wisdom and discernment to other peoples, who on hearing of all these laws will say, "Surely, that great nation is a wise and discerning people." (Deut. 4:6)*

The Bible is the bedrock of Judaism, the center of Jewish life, and the pathway to understanding God's plan for the Jews.

For the Jewish People, it is improper to speak of the "Hebrew Bible." The appropriate terms are "The Holy Scriptures" or, simply, "The Bible." However, throughout this book, it is necessary to use the terminology "Hebrew Bible" to distinguish it from the Christian Old Testament.

The Hebrew name for the Bible is Tanakh, which is an acronym of three Hebrew words: Torah (The Teaching), Nevi'im (The Prophets), and Kethuvim (The Writings). The Hebrew word "Torah" is usually reserved to describe the first five books of the Bible often known as the "The Five Books of Moses" and alternatively "Pentateuch" from the Greek for five or "Chumash" from the Hebrew for five. One other term, used occasionally, is "Masorah," referring to the text of the Bible with vowel signs and accents.

It is proper for liturgical purposes to use the terminology "Torah" in the synagogue because the weekly Bible readings are only taken from the first five books of the Bible, although an appropriate reading from the Book of Prophets generally concludes the weekly reading of Torah. The second reading is known as *haftarah*, or "conclusion."

Basic Bible Questions

First question: What is the Hebrew Bible about? Answer: Basically it is all about the covenant: how it came about, how the people disregarded God's commandments and rules for living a holy life, how the prophets tried to bring them back to an observance of God's ways, and how God, infinitely forgiving, coerced the Israelites to return to their assigned task. Without the covenant, there would be no Hebrew Bible.

Second question: Is the Jewish calendar related to the biblical history of the Jews? Since the Bible relates one event to another by the passage of years, it is possible to relate the Bible to our present (Gregorian) calendar. The most famous attempt to do this was made by the Anglican Bishop James Usher in 1658. His calculation placed the date of creation at 4004 BCE. However, the Bible is far from consistent in its statement of time differentials; other calculations of the beginning are possible. By Jewish calculation the date of creation was 3760 BCE. Hence, to the present year in our Gregorian calendar one must add 3,760 to get the correct Jewish year. For example: 2016 is 5776 in the Jewish calendar. The year changes at sundown on the start of Rosh Hashanah.

Third question: how and when was the Hebrew Bible written? The Hebrew Bible has been edited and re-edited so often that it is dangerous to simplify its original construction. King Solomon built the first Temple in Jerusalem c.950 BCE; about the year 930 BCE, the Holy Land divided into Israel in the north and Judah in the south. The Temple was located in the south. There emerged soon after a definite north-south tension over which priestly group had control of the Bible. At this juncture the seminal event in the story of the Israelites occurred: God's visit to planet Earth and specifically to Moses.

It is well accepted by Bible scholars that there were four primary groups responsible for writing the first five books of the Hebrew Bible.

Bible Textual Divisions

These so called "textual divisions" are as follows:

E — for the **ten** northern tribal communities characterized by the use of the divine name "Elohim," and written between c.950 and c.700 BCE. The priestly writings of E are focused on those religious aspects that would confirm Israel as a *kingdom of priests and a holy nation*. It contains orally transmitted epic traditions that predate writing. For the E writer, the sacred mountain is Horeb and the primary cult person is Moses. The E writers came under the protection of the south after the fall of the Northern Kingdom to the Assyrians in 722

BCE and the dispersion of the ten [lost] tribes of that nation throughout the Middle East.

J — for the southern tribal communities characterized by the use of the divine name "Yahweh," and written between c.920 and c.700 BCE by the priests of the south. This closing date is a primary controversy in biblical circles. J's writings are focused on the early history of humankind and the Exodus. For the J writer, the sacred mountain is Sinai and the primary cult person is Aaron. The Temple is often referred to as "The House of God." J's writings also contain orally transmitted epic traditions in many cases the same as those of the north but presented differently. The intent here is to suggest that the J writers worked in a theological climate of their own making until the time when the northern kingdom fell in 722 BCE It was then likely that they were joined in the scriptorium by the northern writers. This is not to suggest that the merger occurred in a single spontaneous meeting; such an integration would have been "touchy" and tentative for some time.

P — for concern with priestly matters and the centralization of worship in the Temple, and written originally no later than 700 BCE and completed about 590 BCE by priests of the south. P writings make up essentially the entire book of Leviticus. The primary focus of the original P writer was the holiness of the sanctuary, while later priestly tradition extended the importance of holiness to all Israel. *For I the Lord am your God: you shall sanctify yourselves and be holy, for I am holy.* (Lev. 11:44). The later writings also are concerned with social justice. Starting in 597 BCE and continuing through 586, the Babylonians took full control of the southern kingdom of Judah exiling royalty, priests, and scribes to Babylonia and then destroying Solomon's Temple. The P writer is silent from the start of the Exile, as judged by the writings of Ezekiel (627-c.580 BCE) himself a priest of the south.

D — for Deuteronomic writings in which the law of Moses is set down for the second (*deuteros*) time. Written between about 700 and 560 BCE in three stages: the book of Deuteronomy in the first half of the seventh century BCE, the editing of Joshua through Kings in the first half of the sixth century BCE, and the writing of the prose sermons of Jeremiah (a member of a priestly family) in the second half of the sixth century BCE. Deuteronomy, which was publicly revealed in 622 BCE, is written as a farewell speech by Moses. The D writer never subscribed to the widely held belief that God literally dwelt in the Temple. Rather, the expression *"A dwelling for His name"* was consistently used. The sacred mountain is Horeb exclusively in the Books of Deuteronomy and Kings, excepting one use of Sinai in Deut: 33 which appears to be an old appended J story. The D writer, known as "the Deuteronomist," can be seen as the inheritor of the old E (northern) tradition.

As for the combination of these four biblical strands into its present order, the sequence probably was conducted in two stages: J and E were combined about 700 BCE and the other two aspects, based on the framework in P, were integrated in post-exilic times. The redactor(s) of Torah used much of the prior versions combining them in different ways, sometimes providing two separate stories of the same event, and on occasion, even alternating lines from each strand to provide one integrated story. However, "the redactor of JE must have cut substantial portions of each off the sources in order to produce the desired combined work."

History of the Bible

While we are on the subject of biblical roots, let's take a moment to review what most scholar believe are the oldest parts of the Hebrew Bible, some of which was based on the recitations of the wandering poet-orators before the tenth century BCE. When transcribed directly into ancient Hebrew, the rhythmic and repetitious nature of the oral presentation, necessary for memorization, was preserved. Of course, these passages do not come across with the same poetic clarity when translated into modern English. The first of two such passages is in the Book of Exodus at Chapter 15 and celebrates the successful crossing of the Red Sea. This event is believed to have occurred in the second half of the 13th century BCE. The second is the Book of Judges, Chapter 5 — a victory song by the Prophetess Deborah over the kings of Canaan sometime in the 12th century BCE. The transcription of these passages probably occurred in the tenth century, when narratives were first put onto parchment.

The Ten Commandments as presented in the Book of Exodus is also likely to have been of ancient origin. The original form of the Decalogue (Greek for "ten words") must have been brief in order to make use of the mnemonic method of presentation. For purposes of memorization, one would count off the statements using ten fingers. We can surmise that the brief form would be somewhat like the following:

1. You shall have no other gods before Me.
2. You shall not make for yourself an idol.
3. You shall not profane the name of God.
4. Remember to observe the Sabbath Day.
5. Honor your father and your mother.
6. You shall not commit murder.
7. You shall not commit adultery.
8. You shall not steal.
9. You shall not bear false witness.
10. You shall not covet.

The evidence indicates that the brief form of the Decalogue probably changed over the years.

The work of combining the four biblical strands (EJPD) ultimately became the province of the Deuteronomists. They also took on the editorial work of shaping up the entire history of the Israelites from Moses through Joshua, Judges, Samuel, and Kings. In doing so, they placed their particular theological stamp upon that narrative which would become known as the Deuteronomistic history.

In compiling the Book of Kings, the northern writers pronounced their subjective evaluation on each northern king (of Israel), finding all of them wanting. In the words of the Bible, *they did what was displeasing to the Lord.* Neither were the Bible redactors pleased with the achievements of the southern kings of Judah, holding the reign of sixty percent as *displeasing to the Lord* (in various degrees) and the remainder *pleasing to the Lord* (also in various degrees.) The Book of Kings as we know it today contains a condensed version of the reigns in both kingdoms interspersed more-or-less chronologically. The Deuteronomistic strand that runs through Kings strongly points to the writing of the northern priests who saw themselves as the defenders of the true faith.

On the other hand, the southern writers, unaffected by the Assyrian invasion, were intent on the centralization of the cult in the Temple. In order to legitimize the southern priests' entitlement to the Temple, the J writers included in the First Book of Samuel a passage which appears to disqualify the line of northern priests, but which concludes with an interesting passage:

> *I [God] will raise up for Myself a faithful priest, who will act in accordance with My wishes and My purposes. I will build for him an enduring house, and he shall walk before My anointed evermore.* (I Sam. 2:35)

The line of the *faithful priest* will descend from Zadok, King Solomon's chief priest. Although this was intended to affirm the right of the southern priestly line to be the sole legitimate Temple officials, this passage will later be claimed by a northern group not yet a part of Israelite history. These distinctly different tones between north (represented by the Deuteronomists) and south will continue to reverberate throughout Judaism for almost five hundred years.

In the fateful year 586 BCE, southern Israel and with it the holy city of Jerusalem fell to the Babylonians. Since most of those who lived in the south were of the tribe of Judah, the survivors who were forced into Babylonian exile came to be known as the Jews. Some escaped and traveled to Egypt there to join their brethren in an ancient Cairo synagogue. The Jews in exile who chose not to be assimilated into Babylonian society included many of the priests and scribes who continued work on the Bible, and brought the writings of the north and the south together.

When some of the exiles returned from Babylonia to Jerusalem, beginning in 537 BCE, they went to work repairing the Temple. The religious returned about 517 BCE carrying with them the Bible as it stood at that time. Whether a copy remained in Babylonia (likely) is not known, but it would certainly have been prudent to do so considering the dangers of traveling between the two cities, and what the loss of the Bible would have meant. Fortunately, the returnees were not harassed en route. At the dedication of the Second Temple in Jerusalem (516/515 BCE), the southern priests took over their prior assignment to conduct the sacrificial rites while the northern priests appear to have been given editorial charge of the evolving Bible.

The Deuteronomists in Jerusalem went to work on the copy from Babylonia adding new material and, in some cases, revising existing material. An "approved" version of the Bible in Jerusalem came out of that redaction a copy of which may have been sent to Cairo, Babylonia and Damascus. But most importantly, the chief priest Ezra had it read to the public c.440 BCE (Nehemiah 8:1-3). This copy is known as the "Nehemiah Version" for the then governor of Jerusalem.

Ezra had impeccable credentials having descended from Aaron (brother of Moses) the first chief priest (Ezra 7:1-5). It is believed that only the first five books were available. They were called at that time: "The Book of The Law." The reading of the law under the direction of Ezra has given him a reputation as the "restorer of the law" of Moses. The people at the reading wept when they finally heard the Law, and as a community they bound themselves to it. It had not been the prior habit of the Temple priests to conduct Bible readings.

But note, the master copy of the Bible, now the Nehemiah Version, is the one that resides in the Temple at Jerusalem the center of Judaism. Ezra's reading of The Book of the Law (Torah), memorable though it was, constituted a public release. And public disclosures breed unintended consequences as we shall see. To insure uniformity throughout Judaism, copies would have been sent to the major centers outside of Jerusalem — Cairo, Damascus, and Babylonia — shortly after the beginning of the fourth century BCE. Once out of reach of the redactors in Jerusalem, those export copies were destined to take on a coloring of their own. The copy sent to Babylonia caused modifications and additions to be made to their copy of the Nehemiah version of the Bible which may have undergone unique revisions since The Return began. About two hundred and fifty years later, when the Jews successfully revolted under the Maccabees and reestablished an independent country in Palestine, a major influx of Jews from Babylonia, Egypt, and Syria returned to the Holy Land with their biblical scrolls. The differences between their version of the Bible and the one in Jerusalem were then detected.

The Deuteronomists in Jerusalem, now working beyond the Book of the Law, pretty much wrapped up the prophetic writings in the last part of the fifth century BCE (The Book of the Prophets); Joel may have been added a few decades later. The text variations were resolved and final selection and order of the canon was determined. The third element of Tanakh, the writings, would not be completed until the second century CE.

Deuteronomists and Temple Priests

The Deuteronomists' editorial hold on the Bible was loosened when they felt compelled to go beyond their job description and write contemporary commentary. Here was the situation. Nehemiah, the Persian governor in Jerusalem, was called back to report to Persia's ruler in the year 432. Upon Nehemiah's return about a year later, he found that the Temple priests had slipped back into patterns of disobedience with regard to interracial marriages, violations of the Sabbath, failure to contribute to the maintenance of the Levites, and suspected looting of Temple tithes. All matters that would not have occurred had either Ezra or Nehemiah been present. Nehemiah immediately corrected the injustices and punished those responsible (Neh. 13:4-30). However, after Nehemiah died, conditions probably reverted to their former corrupt state.

Ongoing corruption in the administration of the Temple aroused the displeasure of the Deuteronomistic priests and the Levites (the Temple managers). It appears that the Deuteronomists, then still holders of the biblical editorial pen and self-appointed keepers of the true faith, wrote the Book of Malachi to elucidate their displeasure some time between the governorship of Nehemiah (447 BCE) or soon thereafter (c.445-435 BCE). Although they included this book in the scroll of the Minor Prophets, Malachi most likely means "messenger of God" (*i.e.*, a prophet); it is not the name of a prophet. The title may have come from Malachi 3:1a, *"Behold, I am sending my messenger to clear the way before me."* Without ancestral information and no definitive home location for the prophet, Malachi is unlike the other prophetic books.

Malachi is purely and simply a condemnation of the prevailing priesthood at the Second Temple, presented as a court case before the prophet (Malachi) acting as high priest. The tone of the book is prescient of the later writings of the group we know today as the "Essenes." It also clearly represents the viewpoint of the venerable Deuteronomists. In the first chapter, Malachi speaks of the blind, sick and lame animals offered for sacrifice and asks rhetorically, *Just offer it [a defective animal] to your governor: Will he accept you? Will he show you favor? Said the Lord of Hosts.* (Mal. 1:8) It is quite likely that the "governor" in this case is Nehemiah.

In Chapter 2, Malachi declares, "You [the priests] have made the many stumble through your rulings; you have corrupted the covenant of the Levites — said the Lord of Hosts" (Mal. 2:8b). The first part probably refers to the priests who stated that defective animals were ritually pure, while the second refers to the failure of the priests to contribute the allotted amount of sacrificial food to the Levites, a complaint enumerated in Neh. 13:10. Further, at Malachi 3:9b, 10a: " ... you go on defrauding Me ... Bring the full tithe into the storehouse, and let there be food in My House ... " This passage refers to the stealing of tithes from the storeroom as described in Neh. 13:4-9. In conclusion, the prophetic book reminds the priests to be mindful of the Teaching of My servant Moses, whom I charged at Horeb with laws and rules for all Israel. (Mal. 3:22). A hallmark statement of the northerners. Another phrase in Malachi bears review: [L]et no one break faith with the wife of his youth. For I detest divorce—said the Lord (Mal. 2:15b-16a). Divorce could be obtained readily under Torah (Deut. 24:1) This may be a reference to those who divorced their Jewish wives and married Gentiles. Interfaith marriages, would in due course, produce children who were not of pure Jewish blood, and, therefore, not true inheritors of the covenant.

From the accusations in Malachi, it appears that the Deuteronomists, who had agreed, about two centuries earlier to be in charge of Bible redaction and to let the southern priests take care of the Temple rites, were so appalled by the action of the priests as to warrant negating that deal. This probably would have occurred in the last quarter of the fifth century BCE. The outcome seems to have been that the southern priests took control of the Bible as well as the Temple. Most likely, their first order of business would have been to expunge Malachi from the Bible. But, they were probably too late for that, as the Deuteronomists, again, most likely, had sent that addendum to Cairo, Damascus and Babylonia. It was a new age of Bible security, Jerusalem was no longer the sole source. So the southern priests wrote the Book of Chronicles to express their case. This marked the end of the centuries-long biblical influence of the Deuteronomists.

The Book of Chronicles is a third telling of Israelite history which moderates the strongly conservative Deuteronomistic viewpoint. However, it covers only the Southern kingdom which at its writing was the last remaining Israelite stronghold. With biblical editorial control now in the hands of the southerners, they did not hesitate to praise their viewpoint. The Deuteronomists would certainly have been in no position to oppose this reading. Their only alternative was to leave.

These dramatic events in Jerusalem must have caught the attention of the Bible keepers in Cairo, Damascus and Babylonia. The issuance of the Nehemiah Version, the addition of the Prophet Malachi and then the Book of Chronicles were unusually rapid revisions to what had been a staid book.

At this point in biblical history, approaching the end of the fourth century BCE, biblical conjecture is starting to collide with reality. In the hills of Israel surrounding the Dead Sea, a cache of ancient scrolls was found between 1947 and 1956 CE They are known to us today as the "Dead Sea Scrolls," the oldest of which date to about 250 BCE It is apparent that at least four versions of the Hebrew Bible were fermenting: the one in Jerusalem (also known as the Palestinian version), the Cairo version, the Babylonian version, and the Damascus version. There could have been other variations as well representing the diversity of opinions that was sure to have existed on this most important of all Judaic matters. Vermes notes: "that no two copies display the same text ... In my view, the phenomenon would better be described as scribal creative freedom."

The Essenes

Why were some 900 manuscripts found in the area of the Dead Sea almost two thousand years after they were hidden? To answer this question, it is necessary to follow the fate of the former Deuteronomists. A remnant of the Deuteronomists abandoned their position in Jerusalem and migrated to Damascus. There, they struggled to rebuild the ranks of true believers. Eventually, they formed a new community of devotees whom we call the "Essenes." The name is a Latin transliteration of an Aramaic word meaning "the pious ones."

Our first indication of an active Essene sect comes from a Dead Sea Scroll, *The Damascus Document*. This document states that a remnant of Israel was saved from the depredations of the Babylonians in 597-586 BCE and 390 years thereafter (*i.e.,* c. 200 BCE), God visited them "and caused a plant root to spring from Israel and Aaron to inherit His Land ... yet for twenty years they were like blind men groping for the way ... and God observed their deeds ... and He raised for them a Teacher of Righteousness to guide them in the way of His heart" (c. 180 BCE). Thus, early in the second century BCE, the Essenes, perhaps self-appointed successors to the Deuteronomists, were reorganizing for another assault on the Temple hierarchy in Jerusalem.

The members of the New Covenant Community (the Essenes' own name for their sect) kept the Sabbath day according to exact interpretation, and the feasts and the Day of Fasting according to the finding of the members of the New Covenant in the land of Damascus. In their *Book of Jubilees*, they advocated for a solar calendar. As a result, God *"built them a sure house in Israel whose like has never existed from former times until now."* This phrase refers to that passage from the First Book of Samuel the southern priests wrote to ensure their unbreakable hold on the Temple hierarchy:

> *And I [God] will raise up for Myself a faithful priest, who will act in accordance with My wishes and My purposes. I will build for him an enduring [sure] house, and he shall walk before my anointed evermore.* (I Sam 2:35)

The members of the New Covenant Community, heirs to the Deuteronomistic culture of scriptural composition and textual management and defenders of the covenant, here lay claim to the title of Temple priest, and declared their intent to carry forward the only line of true believers. In essence, this passage in essence tells the Temple priests, "You seized control of the Bible; we will now claim your priestly role."

With their purpose clearly in mind, they relocate to the community of Qumran in Judea about 150 BCE determined to take over Temple operations from the corrupt priesthood.

> *Behold, I am sending My messenger to clear the way before Me, and the Lord whom you seek shall come to His Temple suddenly. As for the angel of the covenant that you desire, he is already coming. But who can endure the day of his coming, and who can hold out when he appears? For he is like a smelter's fire and like fuller's lye. He shall act like a smelter and purger of silver; and he shall purify the descendants of Levi and refine them like gold and silver, so that they shall present offerings in righteousness. Then the offerings of Judah and Jerusalem shall be pleasing to the Lord as in the days of yore and in the years of old.* (Mal 3:1-4)

The line: he shall purify the descendants of Levi and refine them like gold and silver, so that they shall present offerings in righteousness takes us right back to the corrupt priests so distasteful to Nehemiah and Ezra and so deplored in Malachi.

Although controversy exists to this day on just where the Essenes lived, the Roman writer Pliny the Elder (23-79 CE) locates the Essenes to the west of the Dead Sea, then Ein Gedi below the Essenes, and Masada south of Ein Gedi. This location in the same area as Qumran is most intriguing. Philo of Alexandria (c. 20 BCE and 50 CE) also wrote of "those people called Essenes" and their peaceful and observant ways. When Herod the Great was king of the Jews (36-4 BCE), Josephus (c. 37-100 CE) described the sympathy and respect that Herod had for the Essenes. The reason for this, he said, was the special relationship that Herod had developed with Menahem the Essene leader. However, upon the death of Herod, the relationship of the Essenes to the rulers of Palestine deteriorated.

In talking about the Essenes, it is not unusual for someone to ask whether Jesus or John the Baptist were Essenes. In the case of John, there is merit to this supposition. Less so with Jesus.

When John felt prepared to minister to the Israelites, he took his direction from the Essenes' *Community Rule*, which quotes from the Prophet Isaiah:

Clear in the desert a road for the Lord! Level in the wilderness a highway for our God! (Isa. 40:3)

This is the same passage quoted in the gospels to introduce the ministry of John (Matt. 3:3, Mark 1:2-3, Luke 3:4, John 1:23). During his ministry, John the Baptist remained faithful to the Essene laws of purity in both body and soul. He dressed simply and subsisted on locusts and honey (Matt. 3:4, Mark 1:6).

The substance of John's ministry is also directed by the Essenes' *Community Rule.*

For it is through the spirit of true counsel concerning the ways of man that all his sins shall be expiated that he may contemplate the light of life. He shall be cleansed from all his sins by the spirit of holiness uniting him to His truth, and his iniquity shall be expiated by the spirit of uprightness and humility. And when his flesh is sprinkled with purifying water and sanctified by cleansing water [baptism], it shall be made clean by the humble submission of his soul to all the precepts of God.

John railed against the crowds who came to him for baptism, because they had not first sought expiation, of what John considered to be, their sins (Matt. 3:7-9, Luke 3:7).

An argument in opposition to the apparent identification of John the Baptist as an Essene is that he is never identified as such by Josephus or by the gospel writers. It is not that Josephus fails to identify other Essenes by name (he does so several times), but that Josephus does not explicitly say so in his description of John's ministry (*Antiquities* 18.5.2). However, Josephus does call him "a good man," which in biblical times carried a weightier connotation than it does today (*e.g.,* Matt. 19:16-17). There is a question, of course, as to whether John the Baptist undertook his ministry outside of Qumran on his own initiative or with the authorization of the leaders of the community. This is an important consideration. From the Qumran documents analyzed to date, no such specific authority is known. The Essenes are not mentioned in the New Testament.

Jesus and the Essenes held several theological positions in common such as: the sanctity of marriage and the needs of the poor as well as corruption in the Temple. The Bible specifically permits divorce for meaningful reasons, but also for trivial reasons:

A man takes a wife and possess her. She fails to please him because he finds something obnoxious about her, and he writes her a bill of divorcement, hands it to her and sends her away from his house. (Deut. 24:1)

The school of Hillel (the Pharisees) says: "He may divorce her even if she spoiled a dish for him, for it is written — because he has found some indecency in her." The Essenes were the only Jewish group at this time to take a dim view of divorce. They, like the followers of Jesus, considered marriage a sacred union. (Matthew 19:4-6, Mark 10:10, I Corinthians 7:10). But, recall, the Deuteronomists also deplored divorce (Deut. 22:19, 29). As for the poor, Jesus spoke feelingly about their need at Matthew 5:3 and 9:21, Mark 10:29, Luke 4:18.

And with regard to the Temple, Jesus

drove out all who were selling and buying in the temple and he overturned the tables of the money changers and those who were selling doves. He said to them: "My house shall be called a house of prayer; but you are making it a den of robbers." (Matt. 21:12-13)

But Jesus took no interest in the corruption of the priesthood, a major concern of the Essenes.

It is important to understand that the Essenes continued their ancestral practices of copying biblical scrolls (on commission), writing their own materials, and maintaining a storage area for scrolls. When the Jews of Jerusalem rose in revolt against their Roman overlords in 66 CE, it is likely that the Essenes secreted their scrolls in the remote and generally inaccessible hills surrounding the Dead Sea and assisted others who wished to hide their scrolls until the revolt was over.

The scrolls were found in eleven caves near the Dead Sea. The total count is difficult to make because so much is in fragments of which it is estimated there were 25,000. It is known that there are presently some 900 separate texts. So far as differentiating the biblical texts, the best information is from the authors of the *Dead Sea Scrolls Bible*. At the time they published this work, the estimated number of biblical manuscripts was 225. The most frequently represented biblical scrolls were: Psalms-37, Deuteronomy-30, Genesis-24, and Isaiah-21. The Essenes, being meticulous record keepers, would have kept a list of names of those who dropped off their scrolls for safe keeping. Vermes' listing of the Dead Sea Scrolls shows a document entitled "List of persons."

Unfortunately, the Essene community was decimated by the Romans in 68 CE and there were no survivors to point out the storage caves. But the Essenes had preserved biblical history as it existed in their day, and almost two thousand years later the scrolls were found revealing the true story of our biblical heritage.

Notes for Chapter Two

BIBLE ORIGINS

The priests of the north take on the task of preparing a book in the new Hebrew script of tales that compose the scattered record of the distant past that constitutes the origin of Israel's history. They don't have much to rely on: the memorized tales of the itinerant poets, legendary depictions of tribal battles, and the oft repeated stories of the escape from Egypt as guided by God and Moses. The early development of the Bible is thoughtfully described by Richard Elliot Friedman in *Who Wrote the Bible*, Summit Books, 1987. Also includes Bible structure. The orthodox believed that God wrote the Bible: R. Avrohom, *Pirkei, The Wisdom of the Fathers* Noble Book Press, 1995, See also Eugene Ulrich The Dead Sea Scrolls and the Origins of the Bible, Wm. B. Eerdmans Publishing Co. 1999

Not everything fitted comfortably into one scroll; the material probably had to be assigned to one of the several developing scrolls. Since they were now living and writing in "real time," not historical times, it will take almost two millennia before Brevard Childs can declare there is no difference theologically between the Bible and God's covenant in his book, *The Book of Exodus*, The Westminster Press, 1976

To know how the Israelites worshiped before the covenant, read Mark S. Smith's book *The Early History of God*, HarperSanFrancisco, 1987. This book is highly researched and quite technical.

What was the relationship between God and the Deuteronomists, the writers of the Bible? God didn't write the Bible, but in some way God conveyed what was to be written. In the prophetic stories, it seems prophets appeared in Jerusalem to upbraid the king and his court as well as the people. What a prophet said was probably in his own words, but the general content came from above. Over the years, many styluses worked over the Bible, especially the God-speaking sections.

The Dead Seas Scroll Bible by Martin Abegg Jr, Peter Flint, Eugene Ulrich,
    HarperSan Francisco, 1999. Alternative reading:
Philip R. Davies, George J. Brooke, Phillip C. Callaway, *Complete World of Dead
    Sea Scrolls,* Thames and Hudson, 2002
Frank Moore Cross, *Understanding the Dead Sea Scrolls*, Random House, 1992

BIBLE HISTORY

The Bible was always subject to revision based on what was happening to the Israelites and how the people changed their ways. Some commentaries on Bible history:

Shannon Burkes, *God, Self, and Death: The Shape of Religious Transformation in the Second Temple Period*, Leiden, 2003.
The Torah, A Modern Commentary, Union of Hebrew Congregations, 1981
Robert R. Wilson, *Prophecy and Society in Ancient Israel*, Fortress Press, 1984

DEUTERONOMISTS AND THE TEMPLE PRIESTS

The feud between the northern scribes and the southern priests which simmered for three hundred years and finally resulted in the addition of two angry new books to the Bible is carefully chronicled and written in Sara Japhet's book, *I and II Chronicles: A Commentary*, Westminster/John Knox Press. This book is recommended for its careful analysis of this highly charged feud which is not otherwise well covered.

ESSENES

The Essenes are finally getting the respect they deserve. Their arrival in Israel from Damascus about 150 BCE was fortuitous as Jerusalem was being reoccupied by Jews returning after the Maccabees' conquest. Synagogues were springing up all over Palestine and they needed Bibles. Making Temple scrolls was the business of the Essenes. During their more than two-hundred-year stay in Jerusalem, they supplied hundreds of scrolls to synagogues, many of which were stored in the caves during the revolt.

Because of the preciousness of the sheep skin materials used to make the parchment scrolls and the intensiveness and long hours of the scribes, scrolls were expensive; therefore, the usual buyers were synagogues.

However, parchment had a very unique advantage for the Dead Sea Scrolls identification. Remember those 25,000 fragments? Because they were animal matter, they could be DNA scanned and separated into piles. Then using back lit photographic devises, they took pictures of each fragment including the writing there on and put that information into an electronic memory. When all the pieces were cataloged, the camera assembled them for each identified DNA strand by matching edge pieces. Scholars then confirmed the assembly work by checking the flow of the text.

Geza Vermes, *The Complete Dead Scrolls in English*, Penguin Books, 2004, (See Community Rule VIII 13-15)
Maxine Grossman, *Reading for History in the Damascus Document*, Brill, 2002
Lawrence R. Schiffman and James C. Vandercam, *Encyclopedia of The Dead Sea Scrolls*, Oxford University Press, 2000.

Chapter Three
Jewish Proselytism

I am not one to neglect myself, either while reading in private
or during strolls in the portico [thinking such thoughts as]
"Here's a thing to delight my friends with... " Then I ponder
the matter, lips pressed together, and mull it all over; when
leisure time offers, then I start marking up paper with poems.
It's one of those lesser vices of mine that I mentioned before.
If you cannot condone this practice, an army of poets stand
ready to lend me support — we are, after all, the majority
these days, outnumbering critics. And, like the Jews, we will
simply compel you to be one of our circle.

Horace (65-8 BCE)

With some understanding of how the Hebrew Bible developed, let us
now consider the part that the Bible played in the missionary life of Judaism. In
order to have a clear picture of this role, it is necessary to understand the
influence that Greek society had on Judaism. Much happened in the civilized
world during the two-century span which began with the Persian domination
of the Middle East in 539 BCE and ended with the death of Alexander the
Great in 323 BCE. Of particular note was the rise of Athens, which defeated
the invading Persians three times in the first half of the fifth century (with
Spartan aid). The Athenian Golden Age of Pericles and Socrates ended with a
disastrous defeat by Sparta at the conclusion of the fifth century, but was
followed by a rising tide of Greek cultural influence throughout the civilized
world.

Greek Influence

In Jerusalem the Second Temple period (516/515 BCE to 70 CE)
coincided with the rise of Greek culture which had a remarkable affect upon
much of the Jewish population. The interchange of learning in the areas of
religion, literature, philosophy, science, medicine, and economics between

contemporary civilizations of the time was significant. Great Greek names in world history lived during this period: the dramatist Aeschylus (525-486), the statesman Pericles (c.495-429), the dramatist Sophocles (496-406), the historian Herodotus (c. 484-425), the dramatist Euripides (480-406), the philosopher Socrates (469-399), the physician Hippocrates (460-370), the historian Thucydides (c.460-395), the play write Aristophanes (448-388),and the disciples of Socrates: Plato (427-347) and Aristotle (384-322).

One of the misguided acts of that period was the death sentence imposed upon Socrates in 399 BCE for his alleged corruption of Greek youth and the introduction of new divinities. During the trial, at which Socrates was permitted to discourse at length in his own defense, he spoke of his belief in God and of his contemplation of the afterlife. The speech was reconstructed by Plato in his *Apology*.

> Strange, indeed, would be my conduct ... when I was ordered
> by the generals ... to remain where they placed me, like any
> other man, facing death — if now, when, as I conceived and
> imagine, God orders me to fulfil the philosopher's mission of
> searching into myself and other men, I were to desert my post
> through fear of death or any other fear; that would indeed be
> strange, and I might justly be arraigned in court for denying
> the existence of the gods, if I disobeyed the oracle because I
> was afraid of death, fancying that I was wise when I was not
> wise. For the fear of death is indeed the pretense of wisdom,
> and not real wisdom, being a pretense of knowing the
> unknown; and no one knows whether death, which men in
> their fear apprehend to be the greatest evil, may not be the
> greatest good.
> ... Men of Athens I honor and love you; but I shall obey God
> rather than you, and while I have life and strength I shall
> never cease from the practice and teaching of philosophy,
> exhorting any one whom I meet and say to him after my
> manner: You, my friend ... are you not ashamed of heaping up
> the greatest amount of money and honor and reputation, and
> caring so little about wisdom and truth and the greatest
> improvement of the soul, which you never regard or heed at
> all?

Socrates' words reflect a deeply held belief in God and an acceptance of individual responsibility in this life. It is evident that Socrates was more than a philosopher. In biblical lexicon, he would have been considered a prophet.

During the period 399-323 BCE, the arts and sciences were advancing in Greece while the Jewish world apparently changed little. But surrounded by

Greek cities and Greek culture in Judea, the Jews could not help but be influenced. That influence can be seen in the art and architecture of the Jewish world at the time, and in its business practices, diplomatic language, and technological advances all of which were based on Greek models. Greek architectural styles were also borrowed for funerary monuments and tombs.

People of the Book

The center of Hellenistic culture within the Jewish world was the new city of Alexandria in Egypt founded in 331 BCE. Here, the Hebrew Bible was translated into Greek for the edification of a Jewish population no longer familiar with Hebrew, and for the archives of the great library at Alexandria, the collection of which would eventually exceed 700,000 scrolls. This attitude on the part of the Jews to flock to a new city as soon as it is feasible to do so, will be their pattern in the centuries to come. New York City today is the Alexandria of yesterday.

The Egyptian copy of the Nehemiah Bible probably became the basis for the first translation of Hebrew into another language. This translation into Greek has become known as the Septuagint, a Latin term referring to the seventy translators purportedly assigned to this task. The translation was an official undertaking by Jewish authorities in Egypt for liturgical and instructional purposes of Greek-speaking Jews. The translated work, prepared perhaps fifty years after the founding of the city, became known as the "Alexandrian Version" of the Hebrew Bible. Once it became permissible to translate the Bible, a translation into the Aramaic vernacular in Palestine was made since Hebrew was then only commonly used in worship or in school. That translation is known as The Targum. Aramaic remained the vernacular in Palestine.

The Nehemiah Version of the Hebrew Bible had been in Egypt for more than two centuries during which time it had undergone its own original changes. It is doubtful that the Jewish authorities in Jerusalem had much to say about the underlying version of the Alexandrian Bible since the temples in Egypt and Jerusalem observed distant relations. The Jerusalem authorities, however, had a lot to say about the translation *per se*. In all likelihood, they would have been appalled. After all, one of the sacred features of the Holy Scriptures was its transcription in Hebrew, the "holy language." Who knew what mischief might result from a Greek version of the sacred book? They would soon find out. However, prior to the coming of Christianity, the Greek translation preserved the vitality of Judaism and gave Jews the designation "People of the Book" throughout the civilized world.

The appellation "People of the Book" has special meaning in Judaism. From the time of Ezra, each member in the Israelite community was obliged to become familiar with the text through oral presentations and discussion, thereby making the Hebrew Bible an ongoing focus of attention. Toward the end of the Second Temple period, expertise in the text became a source of authority; that in turn gave rise to the centrality of the scholar in the Jewish hierarchy rather than to the priests and prophets. In the period of Jewish proselytism, the very idea that Bible study could lead to a place of high regard within the community of believers increased its appeal to educated Gentiles. This is a very important aspect of the Jewish missionary period which followed.

Maccabean Revolt

During the period 200-165 BCE, the Jews of Israel were under considerable pressure from their overlords, the Seleucids, who inherited their part of the world upon the death of Alexander. The Seleucids were involved in an ongoing war with the Ptolemies who inherited Egypt and Cyprus. The cost of that war forced the Seleucids to raid various religious institutions in their empire for spending money. Their efforts to raid the Jerusalem Temple treasury were resisted by the Jews. In 167 BCE Antiochus IV Epiphanes of the royal Seleucid line, having failed to clean out the Temple treasury on previous attempts, challenged the precepts of the Jewish religion and desecrated the Temple altar by sacrificing a pig thereon, instigating the Maccabean revolt.

The Maccabean revolt, which was touched off in 165 BCE, named for Judas Maccabee the leader, is of great significance in the history of the Jews not only for its demonstration of Jewish military might, but also for the fact that during this period the Hebrew Bible began to become a familiar document in many communities. We know this from *I Maccabees* which reads as follows:

> *Whatever scrolls of the Torah they found, [the followers of the Seleucid king] they tore up and burned; and whoever was found with a scroll of the Covenant in his possession or showed his love for the Torah, the king's decree put him to death.* (I Macc. 1:56-57)

This is a rather surprising passage which seems to indicate that a fair number of Bible scrolls were in circulation at the start of the revolt. And the importance of the Bible in the daily life of the people is expressed in the battle cry of Mattathias Hashmonay, father of Judas Maccabee and five other sons:

> *All who are zealous for the sake of the Torah, who uphold the covenant, march out after me!* (I Macc 2:27)

When the revolutionary victory was achieved in 152 BCE, a ruling dynasty of descendants from the patriarch gave name to the subsequent

"Hasmonean Period." The Jews reigned in Judea for about ninety years (152-63 BCE). They adopted Greek ways and used the military to terrorize neighboring communities, a violation of the covenant. They also favored Greek society as well as Roman military ways. The Greek manner of calendar management may imply that the Jewish calendar (lunar) was replaced with a Greek calendar (solar). The Essenes had long advocated such a system.

Jewish coins of the mid-Hasmonean period proclaimed the name and title of the king in Greek on one side and in Hebrew on the other. Note that Greek was the international language of the time, and the primary unit of coinage was the Greek drachma. If the coins were to be traded outside Judea, Greek inscriptions would be understood. In fact, Jerusalem became the most Hellenized of all Greek cities in Palestine. When Herod the Great became ruler in Judea (39-4) BCE) his mammoth building projects, including the rebuilding of the Temple, were the wonder of the time, and Jerusalem became the primary tourist center of the eastern Mediterranean world.

Synagogues and Pharisees

At the time of the Hasmoneans, synagogues (from the Greek for "place of assembly") were spreading rapidly in response to a rapidly growing Jewish population. By mid-first century CE, there were 480 in Roman-ruled Jerusalem alone, and synagogues in more than fifty Palestinian cities of which we are aware. No doubt multiple synagogues existed in many of these cities, and surely there were other cities with synagogues as well. The evidence is considerable for the widespread construction of synagogues throughout the diaspora as well in the first century CE From our study of the Maccabean revolt, we also know that scrolls of the Bible were widely available throughout Judea primarily for synagogue use, and, to a limited extent, for use in homes of the well to do.

As synagogue worship became the general practice, disciple circles (or academies) sprung up. These were groups of novices (or apprentices) who studied the Torah with a learned person by listening attentively to all he had to say. Greco-Roman schools were similar. The origin of these Jewish schools goes back to c. 200 BCE and is described in the apocryphal book of Ben Sirach (Ecclesiasticus).

> *Many great teachings have been given to us through the Law and the Prophets and the others [scriptures] that followed them, and for these we should praise Israel for instruction and wisdom. Now, those who read the scriptures must not only themselves understand them, but must also as lovers of learning be able through the spoken and written word to help the outsiders.*

Near its conclusion The Book of Ben Sirach, at 51:23-28, commands:

Draw near to me, you who are uneducated, and lodge in the house of instruction. Why do you say you are lacking in these things, and why do you endure such great thirst? I opened my mouth and said, Acquire wisdom for yourselves without money. Put your neck under her yoke [i.e., wisdom's], and let your souls receive instruction; it is to be found close by. See with your own eyes that I have labored but little and found for myself much serenity. Hear but a little of my instruction, and through me you will acquire silver and gold.

The Ben Sirach Torah instruction method is called *bet midrashi*, which means literally "sit in my house." The disciples would meet at the home of the master or sometimes in a special school building. Often the disciples lived with and traveled with the master as he decided cases of law. This, of course, was the manner in which Jesus instructed his disciples.

Men learned in Torah emerged from the *bet midrashi* movement. They became known as "Pharisees" (Latin derivation means: set apart.) The Pharisaic movement emerged in the early years of the second century BCE as a natural outgrowth of the disciple circles. A key figure in the evolution of the *bet midrashi* schools was the legendary Hillel the Elder (the name means "shining one" or "praised") who taught in the late first century BCE, and is credited by many as being the founder of the school of Pharisaic rabbinic leaders.

Although Hillel likely lived in the first century BCE, his eminence was quite exaggerated by the later rabbis. Hillel or his school is often depicted in debate with the School of Shammai (the word simply means "name".) These debates, written well after Hillel's time, were intended to advance the rabbinic position on chosen issues using Shammai as a straw man.

It was in the first half of the first century CE that this Jewish movement to train men in the Pharisaic ways began to sweep through the Mediterranean world. How many such Pharisaic leaders there were during the high point of this movement in the first half of the first century is not known. But in Jerusalem, it is alleged that each synagogue had a school and presumably a Pharisaic teacher. Josephus reported this movement as follows:

> ... our laws have been such as have always inspired admiration and imitation in all other men ... the earliest Grecian philosophers, though in appearance observed the laws of their own countries, in their actions and their philosophic doctrines follow our legislator, and instructed men to live sparingly, and to have friendly communication with one another. ... the multitude of mankind have had a great inclination for a long time to follow our religious

observances; for there is not any city of the Grecians, nor any
of the barbarians, nor any nation whatsoever, where our
custom of resting on the seventh day has not come, and by
which our fasts and lighting of lamps, and many of our
prohibitions as to our food, are not observed; they also
endeavor to imitate our mutual concord with one another,
and the charitable distribution of our goods, and our diligence
in our trades.

Although Josephus gives an appreciative nod to the Greek
philosophers, he may have understated the effect that their writings had on the
Jewish missionary movement. The most highly respected names in the Greek
school had, in essence, endorsed a form of religion that paid homage to the
one true God. This theology was carried forward by highly regarded Roman
philosophers as well. For example, Cicero (106-43 BCE), the most famous
Roman statesman, philosopher, and orator, had this to say about God's
creation:

Is he worthy to be called a man who attributes to chance, not
to an intelligent cause, the constant motion of the heavens,
the regular concourses of the stars, the agreeable proportion
and connection of all things, conducted with so much reason
that our intellect itself is unable to estimate it rightly? When
we see machines move artificially as a sphere, a clock, or the
like, do we doubt whether they are the productions of reason?
And when we behold the heavens moving with a prodigious
celerity, and causing an annual succession of the different
seasons of the year, which vivify and preserve all things, can
we doubt that this world is directed, I will not say only by
reason, but by reason most excellent and divine?
To this skill of nature and this care of providence, so diligent
and so ingenious, many reflections may be added, which show
what valuable things the Deity has bestowed on man. He has
made us of a stature tall and upright, in order that we may
behold the heavens and so arrive at the knowledge of the
gods; for men are not simply to dwell here as inhabitants of
the earth, but to be, as it were, spectators of the heavens and
the stars, which is a privilege not granted to any other kind of
animated beings ... He who does not perceive the soul and
mind of man, his reason, prudence, and discernment, to be
the work of a divine providence, seems himself to be destitute
of those faculties.

Cicero's view of the universe and humanity's role therein is quite similar to the view expressed in Psalm 8:2-5 of the Hebrew Bible:

> *O Lord, our Lord, how majestic is Your name throughout the earth.*
> *You who have covered the heavens with Your splendor! ...*
> *When I behold Your heavens, the work of Your fingers,*
> *the moon and stars that You set in place,*
> *what is man that You have been mindful of him,*
> *mortal man that You have taken note of him ...*

And in Alexandria Egypt, Hellenistic Judaism was the norm among the large Jewish population. It was variously estimated at this time that 10 percent to 20 percent of the Roman Empire were Jews or "God-fearers," those who did not strictly obey the Law or, in the case of males, were not circumcised. At the turn of the millennium, the philosopher Philo (40 BCE-20 CE) expressed the same general thoughts as Plato and Cicero, but with an unmistakable Hebrew bent.

> Some persons have conceived that the sun, and the moon, and the other stars are independent gods, to whom they have attributed the causes of all things that exist ... But the most sacred lawgiver [Moses] changes their ignorance into knowledge, speaking in the following manner: "[When] you look up to the sky and behold the sun and the moon and the stars, the whole heavenly host, you must not be lured into bowing down or serving them" (Deuteronomy 4:19) ... Transcending all visible essence by means of our reason, let us press forward to the honor of that everlasting and invisible Being who can be comprehended and appreciated by the mind alone; who is not only the God of all gods ... but is also the creator of them all.

From a very practical viewpoint, Judaism at this time was following the rise of the local synagogue, a family religion and one that could be practiced in small groups. It also offered, according to the Pharisees, the promise of a blissful existence after death. And the Pharisees were advocates of personal prayer as a means of expiating sin as well. All of this had great appeal for the masses and to intellectual Greeks who found the newly "discovered" Hebrew Bible, then widely available in Greek translation, fascinating.

Greeks and the Bible

The Greek world became aware of the Hebrew Bible around the time of the Maccabean revolt. It is difficult to overestimate the awe in which the Hebrew Bible was held by Gentiles. They viewed the Bible primarily as a history of the monotheistic God that the great Greek philosophers, and subsequently the Roman philosophers, assumed to be the force that created the universe. When the Septuagint translation of the Bible became public knowledge, it embodied the story of how that God first entered into the lives of those whom God had created. This was a stunning revelation. And, the book held not only the story of God acting in the universe, it was replete with moral *dicta*, historical details, allegorical tales, and songs of divine praise. In other words, the Bible had immediacy and infinite interest.

Many Greek-speaking people became devotees of Judaism, so much so that the world-wide population of Jews rose from about half a million around 200 BCE to between 3 and 4.5 million by the millennium. It is not clear whether this increase included the so-called "God-fearers." Some of the God-fearers may well have been Greek-speaking people of Jewish blood who had social or intellectual problems with the Law. But expansion at this rate also implies Jewish-Gentile intermarriage and conversion.

One of the likely outcomes of such a massive increase in the Jewish population was the desire on the part of Pharisees to found new synagogues and to increase the congregational size of existing synagogues. It appears likely that the proselytizing effort went on wherever Jewish synagogues were already established. However, it does not seem plausible that a Pharisee whose home synagogue was in Jerusalem, for example, would travel to some remote locale to make a convert. Nor does it seem plausible that this loosely-organized group called the Pharisees could agree upon a concerted missionary effort to convert the civilized world to Judaism. Furthermore, it does not seem plausible that such a successful missionary outcome could result from the efforts of a few well-spoken and well-traveled Pharisees over a relatively short period of time. However, this does not mean that proselyting was not going on elsewhere in the dispersed Jewish world.

Jews in the diaspora were particularly well represented in Rome during the first century BCE. They maintained close links with Jerusalem, and contributed to the upkeep of the Temple. Horace, the great Roman poet and satirist of the time, gave us a gentle hint of Jewish proselyting (or perhaps politicking) activities in the head note to this chapter. Cicero said this about the Jews of Rome "You know how large a troop they are, how they stick together, how influential they are in political assemblies ... "

This period of great Jewish religious exuberance reached its high point in the first half of the first century CE. During that time, it was not only a religion to observe at home, but also one that attracted great numbers of believers to Jerusalem to savor the ceremonies at the Temple in Herod's beautifully reconstructed Jerusalem. For the major ceremonial holidays of Passover, Shavuot (The Festival of the First Fruits), and Sukkot (The harvest Festival of the Tabernacles) the crowds assumed awesome proportions. At one time, King Agrippa I of Israel had the priests estimate the number of pilgrims who participated in the Passover service; their count was at least 1.2 million! These splendidly orchestrated ceremonies united the Jews at home with those in the diaspora and strengthened their religious commitment.

Wealthy and Poor

At this point it appeared that the world would be swept up in observance of Judaism and its Bible. Instead, the peak was reached and the exuberance subsided. The main reason was the huge gap between the wealthy and the rest of the people — the overwhelming majority. During this period, it has been suggested that a close relationship existed between literacy and sectarianism. Most sect members (Pharisees, Sadducees, and Essenes) originated from the literate and urban sectors of society. They considered themselves to be the elite distinct from the unlearned people of the land (everyone else).

A society so unbalanced could not long survive, nor could a religion, that permitted such conditions to exist, stand as a bright light to the nations. To illustrate how unjust the situation was at this time, consider the following quotations from the apocryphal Book of Enoch, written between the third and first centuries BCE by a number of authors. It has five chapters proclaiming woe to sinners among its 108 chapters. The fact that it was started perhaps a century before the Maccabean revolt, lends credence to the belief that the societal ills that beset Israel since the time of King Solomon, some eight centuries before, continued and probably worsened. It also provides more reasons to believe that the Maccabean revolt was in many ways a fight not only against the Seleucid kings, but also a means for the proletariat to seize power in Jerusalem from the wealthy and aristocratic. This societal struggle within Judaism reached a peak in the years immediately preceding the revolt against Rome (66 CE). The groups that initially comprised the Israelites at the time of Moses, had now been replaced by the wealthy and the poor.

The following passages from Enoch and from the prophets speak to the belief among the rich that being wealthy meant God was smiling on you; being poor meant you had sinned and were being punished.

BOOK OF ENOCH

> *Woe to you, sinners, for your riches make you appear to be righteous, but your heart convicts you of being sinners; and this word will be a testimony against you, a reminder of your evil deeds.*

COMPARE PSALM 1:5:

> *Therefore the wicked will not survive judgment, nor will sinners in the assembly of the righteous.*

> *Woe to you who devour the finest of the wheat and drink wine from the kraters (mixing bowls) while you tread on the lowly with your might.*

COMPARE AMOS 6:4 AND 6

> *Alas for ... those who drink wine from bowls.*

> *Woe to you who drink water from every fountain for quickly you will be repaid, and cease and dry up, because you have forsaken the fountain of life.*

COMPARE PROVERBS 14:27

> *The fear of the Lord is a fountain of life.*
> *Woe to you who commit iniquity and deceit and blasphemy; it will be a reminder against you for evil.*

COMPARE ISAIAH 1:4

> *Ah, sinful nation people laden with iniquity.*

1 ENOCH 96:4-9

Woe to you, mighty, who with might oppress the righteous ones; for the day of your destruction will come.

COMPARE JEREMIAH 9:6 AND 9

> *Oppression upon oppression, deceit upon deceit! Shall I not punish them for these things? Says the Lord*

In the days of our tribulation, we toiled laboriously; and every tribulation we saw, and many evils we found.

We were consumed and became few, and our spirits, small; and we were destroyed and there was no one to help us with word and deed; we were powerless, we found nothing.

1 ENOCH 103:9-15

We were crushed and destroyed, and we gave up hope any more to know safety from day to day; we had hoped to be the head and became the tail. We toiled and labored and were not masters of our labor; we became the food of the sinners.

The lawless weighed down their yoke upon us; our enemies were our masters, they goaded us on and penned us in, and to our enemies we bowed our necks and they had no mercy on us.

We sought to get away from them, so that we might escape and be refreshed; but we found no place to flee and be safe from them.

We complained to the rulers in our tribulation and cried out against those who struck us down and oppressed us; but our complaints they did not receive, nor did they wish to give a hearing to our voice.

They did not help us, they did not find anything against those who oppressed us and devoured us; but they strengthened against us them who killed us and made us few.

They did not disclose their iniquities, nor did they remove from us the yoke of them who devoured us and dispersed us and murdered us.

COMPARE JEREMIAH 7:9-10

Will you steal, murder, commit adultery, swear falsely, make offerings to Baal, and go after other gods that you have not known, and then come and stand before me in this house which is called by my name and say, "We are safe!" — only to go on doing all these abominations?"

COMPARE EZEKIEL 22:28 AND 22:31

Thus said the Lord God, the people of the land have practiced fraud and committed robbery; they have wronged the poor and needy, have defrauded the stranger without redress ... I will repay them for their conduct — declares the Lord.

The indictment of the powerful and rich is relentless in this passage. Incipient revolt seems to lie in the near background, but apparently any such move was met with murderous retaliation. The situation of most people appears to be about that of slaves. For twenty years prior to the outbreak of rebellion in 66 CE, travel to and temporary residence in Jerusalem became increasingly dangerous.

Group-versus-group is a principal driving force that made us what we are. When we are defamed, threatened, or derided we turn to deadly combat. In this respect a group seeking revenge on the powerful and rich arose known as The Sicarii. They carried *sicae*, or small daggers, concealed in their cloaks, hence their name. At public gatherings, they pulled out these daggers to attack Romans or Roman sympathizers, Herodians, and wealthy Jews comfortable with Roman rule. Lamenting ostentatiously after the deed, they blended into the crowd and escape detection.

Travelers from the diaspora, whether people of Jewish blood or converts to Judaism, were probably not dirt poor. Did they notice the condition of Jerusalem's poor; did it matter to them? Did they make the connection between the manner in which Judaism was practiced in those days and the words of the prophets in their wonderful Bible? Probably not. Poverty was an unfortunate fact throughout the Empire, and well-off Greeks and Hebrews often were candidly contemptuous of most of the human race. But there was one who was concerned in Israel and he spoke out as did Moses to the Israelites:

> *Blessed are you who are poor, for yours is the kingdom of God.*
> *Blessed are you who are hungry now, for you will be filled.*
> *Blessed are you who weep now, for you will laugh.*
> *Blessed are you when people hate you, and when they exclude you, revile you and defame you on account of the Son of Man.*
> *Rejoice in that day and leap for joy, for surely your reward is great in heaven; for that is what their ancestors did to the prophets.*
> *But woe to you who are rich, for you have received your consolation.*
> *Woe to you who are full now, for you will be hungry.*
> *Woe to you who are laughing now, for you will mourn and weep.*
>
> Luke 6:20-25

Notes for Chapter Three

The apex of Greek society was the defeat of the Persians three times as they invaded but failed to conquer the Greeks in the first half of the fifth century BCE. This influenced the growth of Athens and its bearing on the Jewish community. To understand this interaction the best reference is Levine, Lee I. *Judaism and Hellenism in Antiquity*, Hendrickson, 1999.

The link between the aristocratic Greeks and the Jews was the not subtle Greek belief in an all-powerful God. This became general knowledge about 400 BCE when Socrates was tried for subverting the state religion and thereby causing a disastrous defeat by Syracuse. Brought to trial, Socrates spoke feelingly of his belief in God in a speech that Plato reported and which can be read in *The Dialogues of Plato*. My copy was published in1927, no doubt there are many other current sources.

The event that changed everything about the use of the Hebrew Bible was its translation into Greek. The number of translators is uncertain David Noel Freedman, *The Anchor Bible Dictionary*, Doubleday, 1992,V:5, article by Melvin K. H. Peters.

When it became expeditious to translate the Bible into Greek about 270 BCE for the many Jews living in Alexandria, the Greek aristocracy became, openly, believers in God. The Jews then came to be known as People of the Book.

Moshe Halbertal, *People of the Book: Canon, Meaning and Authority*, Harvard
    University Press, 1997

MACCABEAN REVOLT

The revolt ended in 165 BCE as the Jews took over the operation of Israel. That reign lasted for about a century, during which Rome became the dominant nation in the eastern Mediterranean. Internal strife prompted the Hasmoneans to invite the Romans to govern the country.

Richard Strauss *Timelines in Jewish History: 1000 BCE-1925 CE: With Parallel Time
    Lines in Relevant General History*, 2009, self-published.
Nathan Goldstein, *I Maccabees*, The Anchor Bible, Doubleday, 1967

SYNAGOGUES AND PHARISEES

There is a good deal of discussion regarding the number of synagogues in Israelite Palestine when the Hasmoneans had control of the governmental reins. The figure of four to five hundred is disputed as much too high.

David Noel Freedman uses the figure 480 in Vol. 2 of the *Anchor Bible Dictionary*.

Geoffrey Wigoder, editor of the *New Encyclopedia of Judaism*, New York University Press, 2002, claims "some 400."

The evidence for more than fifty cities with synagogues throughout Palestine in the first century BCE is from Steven Fine, *Did the Synagogue Replace the Temple?* Bible Review, 12:02, 1996 and Freedman VI: article by Eric M. Meyers.

The statement re: ubiquitous spread of synagogues is from Lee I. Levine, *The Nature and Origin of the Palestinian Synagogue*, JBL It has also been said that the numbers are exaggerated and unlikely to contain any historical truth. Hezser, 47.

Chapter Four
Paul and the Jews

For now we see in a mirror, dimly, but then we will see face to face. Now I know only in part; then I will know fully, even as I have been fully known. And now faith, hope, and love abide, these three; and the greatest of these is love.

First Letter of Paul to the Corinthians 13:12-13

The heady period when people of the Hellenistic world streamed into the camp of Judaism is starting to be challenged by a Judaism of a different sort: The People of the Way. These are the Jews who saw in the ministry and death of Jesus of Nazareth (ca. 4 BCE-33 CE), a new sense of spiritual and ethical morality that was sympathetic to their desperate needs.

When Jesus (Hebrew name Yehoshua) died on a cross outside the city walls of Jerusalem, he left the witnesses to his life with the memory of a truly remarkable person. But he did not leave a concerted theology that would unite his followers or draw converts to the fold. His followers, under the leadership of the apostle Peter (Hebrew name Shimon), and the family of Jesus (blood relatives) under the leadership of James, the brother of Jesus, (Hebrew name Jacob), stood ready in Jerusalem to provide guidance to the Jews who wished to join the People of the Way.

At this very early stage in the development of what would become a new religion, there was no thought of abandoning Judaism. Rather it was believed that the words of Jesus could provide inspiration in the lives of his followers much as the words of the great prophets in the history of Israel had done. Therefore, the followers of Jesus both Jews and Gentiles envisioned a fellowship tied by their common faith in Jesus (Acts 15:4, 15). This simple plan would soon change with the conversion of Saul.

Saul's Early Life

Saul was born in Tarsus, a city in Cilicia (southeastern Turkey) (Acts 22:3), in the early years of the first century CE. He was, by his own claim, a Pharisee and the son of Pharisees. (Acts 23:6 and 26:5) While still a young man, Saul was commissioned by the Sanhedrin (the Great Assembly of wise men) to persecute the Jewish-Christians of Damascus whom he, in agreement with the authorities at Jerusalem, regarded as apostates. The main reason for this persecution seems to have been that these Jewish-Christians did not require the Gentile proselytes to live by Torah and undergo circumcision, thereby violating the traditions of the forefathers which Saul so zealously enforced.

While approaching Damascus on this mission Saul purportedly experienced a brilliant vision in which Jesus himself commissioned him to proclaim the gospel among the Gentiles (Acts 9:3-8, 22:6-11, 26:12-16). As best as can be estimated, this vision occurred about seven years after the crucifixion of Jesus (c. 40 CE). In his vision, Saul experienced the love of the Nazarene Jew who in his person embodied God's love for the Jewish people. Keep in mind that the Damascus Road stories were written by Luke in his Book of Acts (c. 60). Paul never reported them, but he did write the following in his Second Letter to the Corinthians.

> *I know a person in Christ who fourteen years ago was caught up to the third heaven (that of God) ... And I know that such a person ... was caught up into Paradise and heard things that are not to be told, that no mortal is permitted to speak. On behalf of such a one I will boast, but on my own behalf I will not boast.* (II Corinthians 12:2-5)

Most commentators say that Paul is speaking of himself. The fourteen years tie in with his stay at Ephesus, where the vision probably occurred.

The impact of this feeling of overwhelming love had dramatic consequences which changed Paul's life and turned him from "Saul," a persecutor of Jesus' followers, to "Paul," an evangelist for Jesus. It was through his evangelical missions and his communications with fledgling churches in the Greek-speaking world that the Gentile character and theology of Christianity was formed.

Paul's Ministry

Paul was the prototype of Christian spirituality: uninhibited and fully believing in the redeeming power of love as demonstrated on earth, and for him beyond, by Jesus. The church that Paul founded declares that what matters is not one's corporeal identity as either Jew or Gentile, but one's inward spiritual identity. In this respect and others as well, Paul was set off from the Jewish world of his time, and yet indebted to the Hebrew Bible, which represented to him and to many Christians theologians that followed, the incubation text for the coming of Jesus.

Paul's travels over the years circa 35 to 64 CE carried him from Jerusalem to Rome and throughout Asia Minor and Greece on three major journeys which were indelibly marked by his communications to the churches he started or those he visited.

Our concern here is the impact that Paul's theology had upon Judaism, because of the influence on Christian theologians throughout the period from Paul's time to 200 CE. Paul, throughout his missionary travels, was a conflicted man. He strove to evolve a theology that was basically new while trying to understand how that theology would register with the people he was addressing. He was also under constant attack by James and the family of Jesus, who formed what was called: "the Jerusalem Church," and who held to a simple theology based on the life and sayings of Jesus as a new prophet, in what was then the age-old life of Judaism. The theology of the Jerusalem Church was more by the book than by the spirit, while the theology of Paul, in keeping with his other-world experience, was more by the spirit than the book. But, Paul was also internally conflicted over his concern that the Christology he espoused could be harmful to the Jewish life into which he had been born and trained as a Pharisee, and to which he still held a modicum of allegiance.

Paul deals with a number of very important issues of prime importance to the Jewish people. They can be summed up as follows: Judaism and the Law, Justification by Faith, Election of the Gentiles, and Election of Israel. These theological matters form the basis of what will become a consistent belief structure for Christianity, a structure which entwined the Jews to the Christians and the Christians to the Jews through the venerable Hebrew Bible. Since these issues are discussed in various parts of Paul's letters, we will proceed topically rather than chronologically.

Judaism and the Law

Paul developed a theological concept regarding Judaism and the law which he expressed initially in his Letter to the Galatians (Gal. 3:19).

> *Why then the law? It was added because of transgressions [by the Jews], until the offspring [Jesus] would come to whom the promise had been made; and it was ordained through angels by a mediator [Moses].*

This theology, however, puts Paul in the untenable position of saying that the Law given by God to the Israelites is no longer an agent of salvation. Rather faith in Christ Jesus, whose agency arises from the Hebrew Bible, is now the pathway to God. How could God bring this deception upon the Israelites? How does Paul get around this heresy?

This view of the transmission of the Law was not original with Paul. Apparently, it was well known in the Jewish-Christian community when Luke wrote the Book of Acts. In that New Testament book, he described the death of Stephen, a convert to Pauline Christianity, by stoning (c. 35), who said, speaking to Jews and Jewish-Christians, *You are the ones that received the law as ordained by angels.* (Acts 7:53). In other words, angels, who did not speak for God, conveyed the Law through Moses. This view, which probably has roots in the Greek version of Deuteronomy 33:2, implies that the Law is a construct unknown to God and was certainly not delivered by God!

This, of course, is a very serious charge, since the pathway to God for all Jews is the aw. Obviously, it is clear from a careful reading of the Hebrew Bible that God laid down the Law as His condition of the covenantal agreement.

In Galatians Paul went too far in minimizing the meaning of the Law for Jews, and then later drew back. In Romans 1:16, Paul declares the Law

> ...*the power of God for salvation to everyone who has faith, to the Jews first and also to the Greeks. For in it the righteousness of God is revealed through faith...*

However, all of Paul's letters were preserved, and served as theological compost for future interpreters of Christianity.From whence, then, did the Law arise? If, as the Jews believe, it was given "on the authority of God," does that not mean that putting oneself under the Law is an act of faith in God? If so, then faith does play a part in Judaism as well. To prove this we must go back to the giving of the Law in Exodus:

> *[The Lord called to Moses, saying] Now then, if you will obey me faithfully and keep my covenant, you shall be My treasured possession among all the peoples. Indeed, all the earth is Mine, but you shall be to Me a kingdom of priests and a holy nation.* (Exod. 19:3-6)

It appears then that the Israelites in swearing their allegiance to the covenant with God, did so strictly on faith. It is interesting to note that neither the New Testament nor the Septuagint include the word, "faithfully," in this passage. This is an important difference between the Hebrew Bible and the Christian Old Testament that has echoes going back sixteen hundred years, and, yet, is generally overlooked today.

Paul's harsh line regarding the ungodly gift of the Law upset the Jerusalem Church and many other Jews as well. Softening his concept that the Law was not given by God but by wayward angels, Paul later calls the law "holy" but misleading:

> *What then should we say? That the law is sin? By no means! Yet, if it had not been for the law, I would not have known sin. I would not have known what it is to covet if the law had not said, "You shall not covet." But sin, seizing an opportunity in the commandment, produced in me all kinds of covetousness. Apart from the law sin lies dead. I was once alive*

*apart from the law, but when the commandment came, sin revived and I
died, the very commandment that promised life proved to be death to me.
For sin, seizing an opportunity in the commandment, deceived me and
through it killed me. So the law is holy, and the commandment is holy
and just and good. Did what is good, then, bring death to me? By no
means! It was sin, working death in me through what is good, in order
that sin might be shown to be sin, and through the commandment might
become sinful beyond measure.* (Rom.7:7-13)

However, this leaves one with the feeling that God did not do a
thoughtful job in preparing the law. So, finally to avoid a breakdown between
himself and the Jerusalem Church, Paul says rather emphatically:

*Do we then overthrow the law by this faith? By no means! On the
contrary, we uphold the law.* (Rom. 3:31)

But Paul's emphatic statement about the Law may be intended only as
his assurance to the brothers back in Jerusalem that he had not given up on the
mission to the Jews, nor deserted the Jewish-Christians (and Gentile-Jews) who
remained observers of the Law. He may also have been trying to discourage
any attempt to silence him. Thus, in Romans 7:12, Paul said: *the law is holy, and
the commandment is holy and just and good.* Paul still insists, however, that when this
holy law is overwhelmed by the malignant power of sin, it succumbs to that
force. (Gal. 3:21, Rom. 8:3), and sin has been able to use the Law to kill human
souls (Rom. 7:7-11). This position certainly has merit. However, it is basic to
the human condition.

Paul is in the position of having to debate the demerits of the law to
God-fearers and Gentiles in the face of opposition from the Jerusalem Church.
His point that the law can bring knowledge of sin is an attempt to discourage
those not fully under the Law from assuming that burden, and the
consequences of not fulfilling it. Paul's point may well be an exaggeration, but
Paul is a clever debater who can usually find an alternative means to bolster his
case. Here, Paul is saying that the Law, in enumerating sinful deeds, opens the
mind to sinful acts. Thus,

*... no human being will be justified in his (God's) sight by deeds
prescribed by the law, for through the law comes the knowledge of sin.*
(Rom. 3:20, Gal. 2:16)
*You shall keep my laws and my rules, by the pursuit of it man shall live.
I am the Lord.* (Lev 18:5)
Keep my commandments and live. (Prov. 7:2)

For Paul to say that the law leads to sin and death is a misstatement (or misunderstanding) of how the law is to be applied. Paul implies that failure to keep all the provisions of the law undermines the entire system and permits the intrusion of sin. Can we not take *by the pursuit of it* to mean that keeping the Law is the objective, not necessarily the demand? Alternatively, is it not true that as one matures, one comes gradually to adhere to the fullness of the Law?

Paul expands upon his life-under-the-law argument by introducing the role of conscience:

> *All who have sinned apart from the law will also perish apart from the law, and all who have sinned under the law will be judged by the law. For it is not the hearers of the law who are righteous in God's sight, but the doers of the law who will be justified. When Gentiles who do not possess the law, do instinctively what the law requires, these, though not having the law, are a law to themselves. They show that what the law requires is written on their hearts, to which their own conscience also bears witness; and their conflicting thoughts will accuse or perhaps excuse them on the day when according to my gospel, God, through Jesus Christ will judge the secret thoughts of all...* (Rom. 2:12-16)

Jews who have the Law and are trained in it, are juxtaposed to pagans who do not have the Law and yet live as if they did. Pagan life is unregulated, deriving guidance from a God-given conscience. But unlike the Jewish law, it is not burdened with many other rules that may thwart passage through life. Yet if pagans live in a lawless manner, they will perish. Paul believes Jews, too, will perish for failure to keep the Law. Human beings are judged by how they keep the moral laws, *i.e.*, what they do, rather than how carefully they read the Law.

There is no counterpart in the Hebrew Bible for conscience, but it was a Greek philosophical principle from at least the sixth century BCE, and entered into Jewish tradition in Jeremiah 31:33: about a century earlier. *I will put My Teaching into their inmost being and inscribe it upon their hearts* (a synonym for "minds," see also Isa. 51:7 and Ezek. 36:26-7). In Judaism, it is the Law that should guide all human actions since it is the God-given way. Thus, the Jeremiah passage from the Jewish viewpoint is intended to mean that the written law, which in Jeremiah's time (ca. 600 BCE) was not readily accessible, and could, therefore, be easily overlooked, would be "placed in their heart" (*i.e.*, memorized). Obedience to the Law is still demanded.

The Hebrew Bible walks carefully around passages that may imply a reliance on conscience rather than law. For example, in Job 27:6, as presented in the LXX, reads: *keeping fast to my righteousness I will by no means let it go: for I am not conscious to myself of having done anything amiss.* In essence what is being said here to Jews, is that one's personal conscience is no substitute for God's law.

Justification by Faith

Basic to the theology of Paul is the conviction that those who believe in Jesus will be justified by faith. They will be absolved of sin, a precondition to enter heaven. In Romans, Paul's last and theologically most mature letter, he says:

> But now apart from law, the righteousness of God has been disclosed, and is attested by the law and the prophets, the righteousness of God through faith in Jesus Christ for all who believe... (Rom. 3:21-22)

Paul continues, assuming the favor of God for the Gentiles, that those without the Law must have a means of justification: *For we hold that a person is justified by faith apart from works prescribed by the law.* (Rom. 3:28) In other words, faith alone will suffice to justify one in the eyes of the Lord as it did for Abraham. Faith in God leads to a life of good works, one could say, and be comfortable with Paul. But Paul is not saying that good deeds demonstrate faith or faith prompts good deeds, he is simply saying that faith in God through Christ Jesus who embodies the Spirit of God's love is sufficient reason for justification. In so saying, Paul is relying upon his personal vision of Jesus.

Justification in the eyes of the Lord through faith in Christ Jesus wipes the soul's slate clean, but sinful acts that follow must be expiated. Thus Paul now has to lay down his own law to the faithful. In First Thessalonians, Paul opens the discussion of a pure and holy life upon which he will elaborate in later writings. This life for Paul is the very base of Christian living, the equivalent of the commandments for Jews and a necessity for drawing nearer to God.

> For this is the will of God, your sanctification: that you abstain from fornication; that each one of you know how to control your own body in holiness and honor, not with lustful passion, like the Gentiles [i.e., Greeks] who do not know God; that no one wrong or exploit a brother or sister in this matter, because the Lord is an avenger in all these things; just as we have already told you beforehand and solemnly warned you. For God did not call us to impurity but in holiness. Therefore who ever rejects this, rejects not human authority but God, who also gives his Holy Spirit to you. (I Thess. 4:3-8)

Jewish apologists essentially agree, but hold that the morality of Jews is superior because every aspect of their lives is governed by their belief in God and obedience to God's law. This, too, cannot be taken as an absolute. It is well held that no one can be perfect in the application of the Law, thus all must seek the mercy of God at judgment. And as the people of Israel know, it applies in the corporate sense as well. Later Christian apologists followed in this tradition, saying that the one true God instructs in religion and ethics, and that morality begins with belief in one God, the Creator.

James, the brother of Jesus, burst into open disagreement with Paul's theology of justification by faith. James says in his New Testament letter:

> *What good is it, my brothers and sisters, if you say you have faith but do not have works? Can faith save you? ... Someone will say, "You have faith and I have works." Show me your faith apart from your works, and I by my works will show you my faith ... Do you want to be shown, you senseless person, that faith apart from works is barren?* (Jas. 2:14, 18-20)

The *senseless person* is most likely Paul. James is responding as a person trained in the Jewish faith.

Jews must have wondered what Paul meant. In their belief, you did not seek personal "justification." You were within the bounds of the law or you were not. Good deeds were always rewarding to the giver as well as to the receiver. So far as "faith" is concerned, they turned to Torah to recall God's direction. The most important of God's rules is to *love the Lord your God* (Deut. 6:5). Or, to put it another way: "What would God have done?"

Selection of the Gentiles

The selection of God's new chosen is a critical portion of Paul's theology. Christian preference as proposed by Paul is based upon the progeny of the Israelite patriarch Abraham. God, before He chose Israel, loved Abraham for his uncritical belief in Him. Paul too sees in Abraham the first righteous person because he had faith in God when an invisible, all powerful deity was not conceivable by anyone else (Gen. 12). No argument up to this point.

The next step in Abrahamic theology is his descendants. God promises Abraham progeny because he believed in the Lord, and it was God's plan to form a group of believing people. So it was not Abraham's righteousness that prompted God to give him progeny, but rather God's righteousness. This absolute righteousness of God constituted an absolute covenant between Abraham and God to father the first race of believing people— the Israelites.

Abraham had many children from his wife and concubines, but only two are of theological interest: Isaac, the first male child of the new nation, born of Sarah in her old age in accordance with the promise of God (Gen.18:1-15), and Ishmael, the first born son of the maid Hagar. The descendants of Isaac will form what is conventionally considered the Israelite patriarchal line, while the descendants of Ishmael will become the children of Islam. Paul, in Galatians 3:16, whisks through a fast slight-of-hand by claiming that *"the promises were made to Abraham and to his offspring; it does not say, 'And to his offsprings'* ... *that is to one person who is Christ."* Thus, by Paul's reasoning, the "children of the promise," Sarah's descendants, are the Christians because "the promise" was really embodied in Jesus, an offspring of Abraham.

> *... in Christ Jesus the blessing of Abraham might come to the Gentiles, so that we might receive the promise of the Spirit through faith.* (Gal 3:14)

And, the children of Hagar the slave are the Jews, who are slaves to the Law.

Certainly this contention is nonsense. Aside from the fact that there is no basis in the Hebrew Bible or the New Testament for the assumption that Jesus was an offspring of Abraham, Paul's reasoning does not seem sensible. Whether the word "offspring" in this context means singular or plural can be readily determined from reading Genesis 15:1, 5 in which the Hebrew Bible uses "offspring" in a context that clearly means an infinite number. "The promise" to Sarah, who bore the first son of the Israelite race, does not equate to Paul's claim regarding "the promise of the Spirit." Further, as discussed before, Jews are not slaves to the law, but rather are blessed by the law. But keep in mind that no matter how absurd it may seem on analysis, it is Pauline theology and, therefore, open for interpretation by later, less skilled gospel theologians.

The claim that all believing people descended from Abraham left the God-fearers and other Gentiles with the uneasy feeling that they, too, were of Semitic extraction. This is one of those dilemmas that Paul encountered when propagating a new concept without first discerning how it would be received. To calm those fears, Paul explains in Romans 1:3-4 that:

> *Jesus was descended from David according to the flesh and was declared to be Son of God with power according to the spirit of holiness by resurrection from the dead.*

The living Jesus becomes a scion of the Davidic lineage, the messianic line. The Talmud tells us that the arrival of Messiah could be in a time of turmoil, when a Davidic figure could be counted upon to insure peace. This description did not seem to fit Jesus, and it was one reason the Jews doubted his fitness as Messiah. The claim that he was the son of God caused more doubt. It was not uncommon for Jews to claim to be the children of God, but to see God as having an actual child might suggest that God had despaired of the Jews' ability to live up to the covenant and sent a leader to take charge. This too was hard to believe, since Jesus soon returned to the Father.

However, in the eyes of the God-fearers and Gentiles, the resurrected Christ becomes a universal heavenly figure. This gave new Christians two things: their exclusive racial identity and a resurrected savior whose ethnicity could be whatever believers desired. This reasoning will lead to anti-Semitism.

Paul employs the story of Jacob and Esau to claim dominion of Christianity over Judaism. And the Lord said to her [Rebekah wife of Isaac], "Two nations are in your womb, two separate peoples shall issue from your body; one people shall be mightier than the other, and the older shall serve the younger" (Gen. 25:23). They were fraternal twins; the first born was Esau. This story, which also supported the claim of other contesting communities, was originally intended to show that Jacob would father the line of Israel, while Esau would do the same for the Edomites who were usually under the Israelite sword. Jewish Midrash has gone on to identify Esau (the older) with Rome and Roman Christendom, thus showing that the younger Jacob (i.e., Judaism) would prevail over the older Esau (i.e., Christianity). Paul, of course, is saying that the older religion of Israel (in this case Esau) will serve the younger religion of Christ (now identified with Jacob). Extracting a biblical line out of context, however, hardly proves his case.

Paul is attempting to proclaim the election of the Gentiles by God either as children of God or as the new chosen of God. In Galatians 3:8, he writes:

> *And the scriptures foreseeing that God would justify the Gentiles by faith, declared the gospel beforehand to Abraham, saying: "All the Gentiles shall be blessed in you."*

This is taken from Gen. 12:3 which in the Hebrew Bible reads, *[A]ll of the families of the earth shall bless themselves by you,* which means that Abraham will be the father of the Israelite/Jews who will bring God into the life of all nations.

Taking this a step further, Paul writes in Romans 9:22, 24-26:

> *What if God [has] included us whom he has called, not from the Jews only but also from the Gentiles? As indeed he says through Hosea, "Those who were not my people I will call my people, and her who was not beloved I will call beloved." And in the very place where it was said to them, "You are not my people," there they shall be called children of the living God.* (Hosea 2:1 HB/1:10 NT)

These biblical extracts can be read essentially the same way in both Bibles, but here they are taken out of context by Paul. In their original meaning

God tells the people of the Northern Kingdom (Israel) and of the Southern Kingdom (Judah) to give up their idols and together return to the Lord at which time the Lord will reaffirm, *You are my People* and the people will respond, *You are my God.* (Hos. 2:25 HB/2:23 NT) But however it is read, Paul's intent is clear. He is moving beyond a parallel choice to a new exclusive choice by God and a clearly defined Gentile pathway to God.

This rationalization, tortuously extracted from the Hebrew Bible, has some commentators accusing Paul of inconsistency or even incoherence. In fact, Paul makes one wonder what his intent might be when in Romans 11:26, he says, *all Israel will be saved,* but hedges that statement as well. In any case, this bit of theology will return in more virulent form in the second and third centuries when a new generation of church theologians grapple with Paul's dual exegesis style and come down hard on the side of Christianity.

In Romans Chapter 11, Paul continues his discourse on the election of the Gentiles by introducing a concept that will be interpreted later by the Church as "replacement theology" (also known as "supersessionism") in this passage:

> *But if some of the branches [of an olive tree] were broken off, and you, a wild olive shoot, were grafted in their place to share the rich root of the olive tree, do not boast over the branches. If you do boast, remember that it is not you that support the root, but the root that supports you. You will say, "Branches were broken off so that I might be grafted in." That is true. They were broken off because of their unbelief, but you stand only through faith. So do not become proud, but stand in awe. For if God did not spare the natural branches, perhaps he will not spare you.* (Rom. 11:17-21)

Paul then presents, in Romans 11, his retooled thesis on the fate of Israel. Quoting Isaiah 59:20, which (in the Hebrew Bible) reads, *He shall come as redeemer to Zion to those in Jacob who turn back from sin,* Paul carries his thesis forward, again using balanced verities:

> *[The Israelites] are enemies of God for your sake; but as regards election they are beloved of God, for the sake of their ancestors; for the gifts [of God to the Israelites, i.e., the Bible] and the calling [to the service of God, i.e., the covenant] are irrevocable.* (Rom. 11:28-29)

Why does Paul preach that the Israelites are enemies of God for the sake of the Gentiles? For despite the belief of Israel that it is God's chosen, God's aim is for all people to believe and to uphold God's kingdom on earth. But that does not mean that God has withdrawn his covenant from Israel. The new believers, cleansed of their sins and accepted by the mercy of God, should uphold the Israelites who, Paul claims, stood in the way of God, but are now to be shown mercy as well. God wishes all His people to be of one mind in Him. While it might be argued that Paul was not a supersessionist, his writings on this matter leave wide openings for less compromising theologians to exploit.

Supersessionism is the Christian belief that Jews have not upheld the terms of the covenant, therefore they have replaced them in God's eyes. Supersessionism also places God in a curious role, that of the covenant bestower who had lost interest in His chosen. We know from our biblical readings that the only reason He would abandon His role is if Judaism ceased to exist as a religious group. Aside from that fact, the culture of much of the world is based upon the covenant. Yes, the Christians could pick up that role, but the discord that would result would cause conflict among religions and leave all parties concerned that we are no longer of interest to Him. Finally, without God's continual concern for our well-being, can this earthly home survive?

Choosing of Israel

Paul affirms the choosing of Israel in Romans:

> I am speaking the truth in Christ — I am not lying; my conscience confirms it by the Holy Spirit — I have great sorrow and unceasing anguish in my heart. For I could wish that I myself were accursed and cut off from Christ for the sake of my own people, my kindred according to the flesh. They are Israelites, and to them belong the adoption, the glory, the covenants, the giving of the law, the worship and the promises; to them belong the patriarchs, and from them, according to the flesh, comes Messiah, who is over all, God blessed forever. Amen. (9:1-5)

But Paul's apparent endorsement of God's choice of the Jewish people is complicated by his assertion that God has the right to elect a new chosen people in each generation. This aspect of supersessionism leaves the world to ponder our relationship with Him.

This, of course, is not what the Jewish people believe. They consider God's choice at Mt. Sinai, endorsed by all present, a singular moment not subject to change.

> I make this covenant, with its sanctions, not with you alone, but with both those who are standing here with us this day before the Lord our God and with those who are not with us here this day. (Deut. 29:13-14)
> But hear now O Jacob my servant, Israel whom I have chosen! Thus said the Lord, your Maker, Your Creator who has helped you since birth:

Fear not, My servant Jacob, Jeshurun whom I have chosen, even as I
pour water on thirsty soil and rain upon dry ground, so will I pour My
spirit on your offspring, My blessing upon your posterity. (Isa. 44:1-3)
Thus said the Lord, who established the sun for light by day, the laws of
moon and stars for light by night, who stirs up the sea into roaring
waves, whose name is Lord of Hosts; if these laws should ever be
annulled by Me — declares the Lord — only then would the offspring of
Israel cease to be a nation before Me for all time. (Jer. 31:35-6)

Paul was thoroughly familiar with the Hebrew Bible and could well
have been questioning the Jewish charge under the covenant. But we must
keep in mind that in pondering Paul's suggestion that God might reconsider
the covenant with Israel. we must seriously consider our relationship to God
and its future trustworthiness to this world. Should God elect to change the
covenantal relationship with the Jews, the social implications to the world
would be incomprehensible.

Even if one takes the position that Paul has made a reasonable case,
and the distinction between Jew and Gentile is no longer meaningful, it still
endures based on God's irrevocable love for the people Israel, and in
connection with Israel, for the world as a whole.

In Romans 3:29, Paul plaintively poses and answers the primary
question of monotheistic theology: *Is God the God of Jews only?* He answers that
God is the God of Gentiles as well. This is the fundamental point that the Jews
are charged to teach under their covenant. This is the Pauline statement that
should have aroused the missionary spirit of Judaism. After all, God did not
want the Israelites to sell themselves; God chose them to sell God. When a
new form of monotheism arises, the first consideration should always be
whether God's purpose is being served.

Chosen to be the representative of Jesus in bringing the knowledge of
God to the pagan world, Paul carried out his directed assignment employing
the full capabilities of his mind, body, and spirit. Paul was an intelligent,
educated, literate, and expressive person which in Jewish society of the time
was very unusual. In addition he had the strength of body, and the will to
sustain himself throughout his extraordinary mission. Viewed in this
perspective, it is not surprising that it was he who was called.

Notes for Chapter Four

The discussion of Paul, his heaven directed conversion, his trips to
spread the word, and most importantly, his letters which give us today nearly
two thousand years later, a clear picture of the beginning of Christianity. There

have been many books written about Paul. Contemporary biographies, well received are: *The Life of St, Paul* by James Stalker, *Saint Paul* by Pope Benedict XVI, *The Apostle: A Life of Paul* by John Pollock, *Paul and Jesus: How the Apostle Transformed Christianity* by James D. Tabor. biblical commentary on each of Paul's letters is also readily available There have been many books written about Paul. biblical commentary on each of Paul's letters is also readily available.

Well-received biographies include *The Life of St, Paul* by James Stalker, *Saint Paul* by Pope Benedict XVI, *The Apostle: A Life of Paul* by John Pollock, *Paul and Jesus: How the Apostle Transformed Christianity* by James D. Tabor. biblical commentary on each of Paul's letters is also readily available There have been many books written about Paul. biblical commentary on each of Paul's letters is also readily available.

Judaism and the Law

Deuteronomy 33:2 in LXX — *And he (Moses) said the Lord is coming from Sinai and has appeared from Seir to us, and has hasted out of the mount of Paran with the ten thousands of saints; on this right hand were his angels with him.*

Deuteronomy 33:2 in DSS — *And he (Moses) said: [The Lord] came from Sinai, [and rose from Seir upon them; he shone forth from Mount Paran, and came] from the ten thousand[s of holy ones; at his right hand was a fiery law for them].*

Deuteronomy 33:2 NRSV — *And he (Moses) said: The Lord came from Sinai, and dawned from Seir upon us; he shone forth from Mount Paran. With him were myriads of holy ones; at his right, a host of his own.*

The ideological difference that lies behind this passage points out the "spin" which Bible writers use to enforce their position.

Analysis of Genesis 19:4

The English translation of Tanakh, from the Jewish Publication Society (1985, revised 1999), holds that the word "faithfully" is implied in the Hebrew infinitive absolute construction. No other English translation uses this interpretation. However, this translation is modeled on the following typical passages: Lev. 25:18 and 26:3, and I Sam. 12:24. Most English translations do show the word "faithfully" in these passages which is implied in their construction. It is not possible to determine today whether the word "faithfully" was always implied in Exodus 19:5 because that portion did not survive in the Dead Sea Scrolls. Ulrich, Eugene; Cross, Frank Moore; Davila, James R; Jastram, Nathan; Sanderson, Judith E. *Discoveries in the Judean Desert - XIII; Qumran Cave 4-VII, Genesis to Numbers.* Research for this note by William Fontaine Bibliographer for Hebrew works, Dartmouth College Library. Note: These verses are missing from the *Dead Seas Scroll Bible* (see page 54).

Chapter Five
The Rabbinic Period

Rabbi Moses received the Torah at Sinai and transmitted it to Joshua, and Joshua to the Elders, and the Elders to the Prophets, and the Prophets handed it down to the Members of the Great Assembly. The Members of the Great Assembly stated three principles: Be deliberate in judgment; educate many disciples; and set protective bounds for the Torah.

Pirkei Avos 1:1

At the end of the great revolt in 66-70 CE, the Romans destroyed the Second Temple down to the underlying mount and carted the intact artifacts and trimmings to Rome. This stunning defeat spelled the end of sacrificial rites and disrupted the authority of the Great Assembly (also known as the Great Synagogue). The Great Assembly composed originally of scribes (later rabbis), sages, and prophets held a very important position in the life of Judaism. It sat as a Supreme Court in deciding doubtful points of religion and law, it was the court of last resort for all civil and criminal matters, it was responsible for maintaining the calendar and imposing religious discipline, it codified the Bible, and it represented the state in dealings with occupying authorities. As a quasi-civil body, it regulated all aspects of corporate Judaism.

The major question at this time was how Judaism could survive without the Temple and a centralized authority. The Second Temple had been the center of the corporate religious experience since its dedication in 516/515 BCE almost six centuries before. It was here that the great religious events of the year were celebrated with proper ceremony, and the place to which all Jews made pilgrimage at least once in their lifetime. The Temple also served an extremely important function for individual Jews, since sacrifice at the Temple altar was the only official way of expiating sin. In total, the loss of the Temple struck at the very center of Jewish life— at the city and institution that held world Judaism together. Although it is sometimes assumed that the community synagogue simply replaced the Temple in the life of Judaism, such an assumption fails to consider the great void that opened in corporate religious and judicial life with the loss of the Temple. In fact, certain corners of Orthodox Judaism are still planning the Third Temple today.

The rabbis facing the task of restructuring Jewish life, could not turn their backs on the Temple and all it meant. In the first instance, this would have signaled the abandonment of the Temple, a potentially crushing blow to the people. More than half the early writings of the rabbis is devoted to one aspect or another of the Temple and its cult. In addition to the ideal of a Third Temple, this emphasis could have been due to a sense that the word of God could also be discerned through the Temple rites. Therefore, in later writings, the rabbis discussed the intricacies of Temple rituals with the same intensity, as for example, their discussion of Sabbath rules.During the second century, Judaism came under increasing and unrelenting pressure from both Rome and the burgeoning Christian religion. A period of multiple sects with differing theological viewpoints could no longer be tolerated neither in Judaism nor in Christianity. To preserve core beliefs and insure a corporate basis to religious observance, the leaders of both religions found it necessary to codify their doctrine. The first step in Judaism was codification of the Oral Law, *i.e.*, traditional societal rules. The purpose was to instruct adherents in holiness by faithfully keeping the Scripture.

In the Christian world, the need was to pare down not only the extensive gospel accounts, which to our present knowledge totaled at least thirty four different viewpoints, but to choose among the versions of the canonical gospels as well, so that a unified doctrine of Jesus' message could be set before the Christian world. Not so well known as the Dead Sea Scrolls is the Nag Hammadi find of early Christian texts. In 1945, about two years before the discovery of the Dead Sea Scrolls, a library of fourth-century papyrus manuscripts consisting of twelve codices plus eight leaves from a thirteenth, containing fifty-two separate tracts covering forty-five separate titles, was found in a large sealed earthenware jar buried at the base of a cliff near Egypt.

Nag Hammadi Manuscripts

The manuscripts, written in Coptic, the language of Egyptian Christians, would have been considered heretical at that time. They are known today as Gnostic Gospels. Among them are such titles as: the Gospel of Truth, the Gospel of Thomas, the Gospel of Philip, the Gospel of James, the Gospel of the Egyptians, and the Gospel of Mary. The composition of some can be traced back to as early as the second century. A subsequent find entitled The Gospel of Judas was widely circulated in 2006. Many other non-canonical documents are also in the collection.

Of particular interest to scholars is the Gospel of Thomas. This document is not a narrative, but rather a collection of 114 sayings of Jesus. Eight of these sayings can be found in the synoptic gospels, and six can be found in the Gospel of John. Some are nearly identical to the canonical gospels and some are decidedly different. In a sense, these latter sayings throw a light upon the conflicts within the early church. Let me give you one example from the contemporary NRSV and the Gospel of Thomas respectively.

> He (Jesus) asked his disciples, "Who do people say that the Son of Man is?" And they said, "Some say John the Baptist, but others Elijah and still others Jeremiah or one of the prophets." He said to them, "But who do you say that I am?"
> Simon Peter answered, "You are the Messiah, the Son of the living God."
> And Jesus answered him, "Blessed are you, Simon son of Jonah! For flesh and blood has not revealed this to you, but my Father in heaven ... and on this rock I will build my church. (Matt. 16:14-18)

> Jesus said, "Compare me to someone and tell me whom I am like."
> Simon Peter said to him, "You are like a righteous angel."
> Matthew said to him: "You are like a wise philosopher."
> Thomas said to him, "Master my mouth is wholly incapable of saying whom you are like ... "
> And he (Jesus) took him (Thomas) and withdrew and told him three things. When Thomas returned to his companions, they asked him, "What did Jesus say to you?"
> Thomas said to them, "If I tell you one of the things which he told me, you will pick up stones and throw them at me; a fire will come out of the stones and burn you up. (G. Thom. 13)

The Rabbis

Once community life had been reestablished in Judea, scholars, rich and poor, lay and priestly, rural and urban came to rabbinic meetings.

True believers today look back on the history of Judaism as guided by rabbinic influence from the time of Moses, whom they call "Moses our rabbi (teacher)." It appears, however, that at the time when the rabbis began the process of codifying the oral tradition, their authority to do so had to be defined. Therefore, they too reached back to Moses as their authority, citing a transmission of that authority through a string of elders and prophets and eventually intact to them. This transmission is defined in the head note to this chapter as quoted from the tractate *Pirkei Avos* which means "wisdom of the fathers."

For the historian, the rabbis" and "the rabbinic period" "become meaningful only after 70 CE." Since it is difficult to define clearly just what "rabbinic influence" might be, it is also difficult to trace that influence before the time of the rabbis in the second century CE. What is known is that the rabbis were related to the Pharisees whose period of greatest influence was about 150 BCE to 70 CE. A century prior to that period, there is little evidence for widespread societal reading of Torah.

Historically, the rabbinic period may be broken down into three stages. The first stage, the Age of the Tannaim (*tah-nah-EEM*, meaning "teachers") lasted approximately from the destruction of the Temple in 70 CE to the death of Patriarch Judah I in 235 CE and comprised the completion of the Mishnah. The second stage, the Age of the Amoraim (*ah-MOE-rah-eem*, "explainers"), extended from 235 to the abolition of the patriarchate in 420, and saw the completion of the Tosefta. The third stage, the Age of the Geonim (*geh-OWN-eem*, "experts"), was the period from 420 to 640 CE, and accomplished the completion of Gemara and two Talmuds: that of the Land of Israel, the *Yerushalmi* (400) and that of Babylonia, the *Bavli* (600). The period also generated a considerable body of additional material, the Midrash (meaning "interpretation"), books of investigation and commentary into the deeper meaning of the biblical books and the liturgical calendar.

The Mishnah

The age of the Tannaim began with the siege of Jerusalem in 70 CE. Rabbi Yohanan ben Zakkai escaped from the radical defenders of Jerusalem and surrendered to the Romans. With his associates, he began Torah study in the city of Yavneh or Jabneh (present-day Jamnia, about twenty miles west of Jerusalem), leading to a system of Judaism without the Temple. Rabbi Yohanan, founder of the rabbinic movement, was a spiritual, if not an actual, disciple of Hillel the Elder, the legendary sage of the late first century BCE. With his associates, some of whom were also former members of the Great Assembly, R. Yohanan removed from the priests the monopoly on the sacred calendar, festivals, and rites. He also made the priests subject to the rabbis, a major step in restructuring corporate Judaism. In addition he established a High Court (*Beth Din*) which would take over some of the functions of the Great Assembly, and a High Academy (*Beth Midrash*). Rabbi Yohanan was a leader in the effort to keep the Temple ceremonies alive by transferring corporate aspects of the high holy days to community synagogues and homes. These were the steps necessary to place Judaism on a sound footing so that it was able to survive and grow.

Most importantly, under R. Johanan's leadership the rabbis began the process of compiling the oral traditions which would constitute the Mishnah (c. 90 CE). The Mishnah is an extensive study which led to interpretation of scriptural and non-scriptural ordinances. The intent of the study was the regulation of all aspects of Jewish life previously controlled by the Temple authorities and local traditions. The quest was two-fold: to delineate in precise detail the manner of carrying out the Law (*halakhah*), and to expand on moral ideas and religious history in order to insure a society of godly mores and ancestral respect (*aggadah*, non-legalistic exegetical texts).

After about a twenty year period of leadership, R. Yohanan retired and R. Gamaliel II headed the working group as patriarch (*nasi*). During Gamaliel's stewardship (c. 90 -110), the authority of the *Beth Din* was greatly strengthened as was the authority of the office of patriarch, and ties with the diaspora. But it was also during this period that R. Gamaliel took a step that was to have far reaching religious consequences. His *Beth Din* (biblical court decision), circa 90-95 CE, declared in unequivocal terms that those who declared Jesus to be the Messiah could no longer be considered part of the Jewish community, nor the Jewish people. This portentous decision was not a major issue at the time since Judaism was approaching 3.5 million while Christianity was only a few thousand.

Second Revolt

About the end of the first century, the people again became restive. After a period of relative calm in the land of Israel, the Emperor Hadrian (117-138) imposed a ban on circumcision, declaring it a barbaric practice. Shortly after, in 131, when it was rumored that Hadrian intended to build a Roman city on the ruins of Jerusalem, the second revolt broke out under the leadership of one "Bar Kokhba," or "Son of the Star," a reference to Num. 24:17: *A star rises from Jacob, a scepter comes forth from Israel ... "*

Bar Kokhba was believed by the people to be the Messiah who would lead Israel to freedom. The rabbis were opposed to this uprising and titled the leader "Bar Koziba" or "Son of the Lie." Rabbi Akiba (c.45-135), however, one of the most respected men of the early rabbinic period, supported the revolt whole heartedly, and hailed Bar Kokhba as the long-awaited Messiah. When the uprising finally was over with the capture and execution of Bar Kokhba in 135, the whole of Judea was a desert. For his part, R. Akiba, at the age of about **ninety,** was tortured to death. He is remembered today as one of the martyrs of that revolt. During the second century, the Christian population had risen to about fifty thousand, while the Jewish population, following now two failed revolts, had declined to about 2.5 million.

The failure of the Bar Kokhba revolt resulted in the expulsion of the Jews from Jerusalem and the Roman reconstruction of the city. The land of Judea became Palestine, a separate province, although the name Judea continued in general use for many years thereafter. The surviving rabbis migrated to Usha, about ten miles southeast of contemporary Haifa, where Rabban Shimon ben Gamliel II lived. They would later move several more times ending in the Galilee city of Tiberius. In effect, Judea was now no longer a (subject) state, but "could exist only as ... a socially and nationally distinct group with certain rights to administer its own internal affairs." It then became manifest to the Jews that the Temple would not be rebuilt, and the break with past tradition was irreparable.

Mishnah Completion

In defining a workable form of Judaism, the rabbis themselves believed they became more like God by enunciating God's will, promulgating a moral code for all Jews to live by. The rabbinic act of teaching is a kind of divine revelation which produced in the Tannaim a heady mixture of extreme self-confidence and equally extreme deference toward the ancestral tradition. To avoid the belief that they were personally responsible for the resulting Mishnah, many rabbis claimed that they taught nothing new or original; they simply restated both written and oral laws which had been handed down through the generations.

The importance of the Mishnah in the life of Judaism cannot be overstated. In the age immediately following the great revolt, the people placed their greatest hope on an understanding and observance of Torah. The Torah was the only aspect of Judaism that survived the great revolt intact, and its importance in the life of the people prior to the revolts constituted their main hope for the future. To avoid criticism, the work of the Tannaim was directed to augmentation of Torah presumably written by God. The Mishnah was the first document to draw together the Torah and the Oral Law. It is considered incontrovertible fact by the rabbis.

The completed Mishnah is arranged according to subject matter into six "Orders" (*Sedarim*, from *Seder* singular). It is also traditionally referred to as *Shas*, a Hebrew abbreviation of *shisha sedarim*, the "six orders" of the Oral Law of Judaism. Each order is divided into tractates (*massichtoth*, from *masechet*, *m*eaning "webbing") of which there are sixty-three in total. Each tractate is divided further into chapters and paragraphs. There are 523 chapters in the Mishnah dealing with the following topics:

- *First Order*. Agriculture (Hebrew name *Zera'im* meaning "Seeds") — planting, harvesting, grafting, food preparation and blessing, tithing of food, food, sacrifice.
- *Second Order*. Festivals (Hebrew name *Mo'ed* meaning "Festival") — identification, Sabbath rules, Passover rules, Temple fees, Yom Kippur rules, Rosh HaShanah rules, fast days, holiday readings, Temple attendance.
- *Third Order*. Women (Hebrew name *Nashim* meaning "Women") — marriage, levirate obligations, marriage deeds, vows, adultery, divorce, betrothals, also includes law of the Nazirites (orders of holy men).

Fourth Order: Crime and Punishment (Hebrew name *Nezikin* meaning "Damages") — damages, civil acts, financial matters, partnerships, criminal acts, criminal punishment, court oaths, testimonies, idolatry, ethical duties and conduct, court decisions.

- *Fifth Order*: Temple (Hebrew name *Kodashim* meaning "Holy Things") — rules of slaughter, meal offerings, non-sacrificial slaughter, firstlings, value of dedications, substitution of sacrifices, guilt offerings, sacrilege, daily sacrifices, Temple layout, bird sacrifices.

- *Sixth Order*: Purities (Hebrew name *Tohoroth* meaning "Purities") — vessels, tents, leprosy, red heifer cleansing, purification, ritual baths, menses, food preparation, secretions, washing of hands, inedible part of fruits.

Although the people believed that the Mishnah was based on age old oral tradition, the final discussions of the Tannaim showed that their outline was based only on what was then known, particularly regarding agriculture practice. The resulting document had a decided economic impact.

In the past, court monetary awards had been based on scripture. Now, the finely detailed Mishnah was consulted, and litigants were assessed damages for violating previously unknown rules. In effect, it was the modernization of the old Israelite economic system to accommodate a larger population and standardization of the rules. In the process, the elite were enriched by the more active courts.

The Wisdom of the Fathers circulated approximately a generation after the promulgation of the Mishnah itself and contained two provisions to insure the principle role of Torah. It treated *torah* as a common noun; any document that stood in the line of tradition from Sinai fell into the classification of Torah. And it treated Mishnah as subordinate to, and dependent upon, Scripture.

Religious persecution of Jews in Palestine became more intense in the third century. The non-Jewish population of Palestine was growing and displacing Jews, many of whom chose to immigrate to Babylonia. There had been a strong Jewish community in Babylonia since the time of the exile in the sixth century BCE. But the community flourished during the great revolt because it was not under Roman domination. In fact, it was the only large Jewish community still outside of the Roman Empire. And because of its remote location, it was not markedly affected by Greco-Roman culture. By the third century CE, Jews in Mesopotamia considered themselves the aristocracy of the Jewish world, and their land second only to the land of Israel in holiness. Starting at this time the sages in Babylonian academies, a number of whom had come from Jerusalem, developed a method of biblical commentary that was to become the basis for the Babylonian Talmud.

Tosefta and Gemara

At the same time that *Wisdom of the Fathers* was circulating, other rabbis decided that the Mishnah did not cover every case that was required for a full understanding of Torah, nor did it tie the law expounded therein to Scripture in all cases. A careful review of these aspects resulted in the book called *Tosefta* (Supplement). The intent of Tosefta was to fill the gap and link statements of the Mishnah to statements of Scripture, and to contribute additional rules as necessary. This work is reputed to have been prepared during the third or fourth century by two prominent Palestinian rabbis. It quotes liberally from the Mishnah, giving brief explanations of difficult passages and referring to principles which it does not repeat verbatim. Thus, in total, Tosefta is about four times longer than Mishnah.

Overall, it provides an extended form of commentary that may be abbreviated or treated only indirectly (if at all) in the Mishnah (so called *baraita*). Talmudic *halakhah* rulings are sometimes based on Tosefta when they are not in conflict with other primary sources. It is not unusual for Tosefta to inform discussions in both Palestinian and Babylonian Talmuds. Three copies of Tosefta manuscripts are known to exist today: one in Vienna (late 13th century, Oesterreichische Nationalbibliothek), one in Erfurt (c. 14th century, Staatsbibliothek, Berlin), and the third in London (15th century: British Library, London).

Immediately upon completion of the Mishnah, discussions concerning its teachings sprung up primarily in the academies of both Palestine and Babylonia. These discussions were collected in anthologies which are known as *Gemara*. The meaning of that word varies from one interpreter to another, but is best described as "study or learning." Gemara consists of rabbinic discussions on laws in Mishnah and, in some cases, areas not covered in Mishnah. Gemara served the subsequent writers of Talmud by preserving the commentary on Mishnah when it was first prepared. In contemporary publications of Talmud, the Gemara usually follows the mishnahic statement. The Gemara text, which is intended to clarify or amplify the Mishnah (disagreement is not permitted), is presented in units each known as a *suyga* or "topic."

The Talmuds

The rabbis, studying and discussing the rules of the Mishnah in the academies of Israel and Babylonia, produced two different Talmuds. The Talmud of the Land of Israel (the *Yerushalmi),* was completed about the year 400, several centuries before the Babylonian Talmud (the *Bavli).* During the time following completion of the Mishnah, when the discussions were in progress leading to the Talmud of the Land of Israel, the central Roman government disintegrated giving rise to anarchy and wars between rival claimants to the throne and bringing about economic collapse. In the sixteen years from 238 through 253 CE twelve different men occupied the imperial throne, and a period of plague decimated the population of the empire between 250 and 268 CE. This period also witnessed the start of barbarian invasions. At the beginning of the fourth century, Christianity became the official religion of the empire. The empire divided permanently in 395 CE into Eastern and Western Empires, and Rome fell in 410.

These factors greatly increased pressure on the Jewish population of Palestine, forcing the rabbis still remaining to cut short their deliberations. The efforts of the remaining Palestinian Amoraim then turned to interpretation and explanation (*aggadah*) which is not subject to definitive ruling, such as moral issues and liturgical poetry. Talmud Yerushalmi is known to have been informed frequently by midrashic books of deeper material, all of which was written in Palestine, and on occasion by material from the Babylonian Talmud (*Bavli*). The scholars of both Talmuds were in continuous contact.

When it became apparent that the Babylonian Talmud would be the predominant publication, the Yerushalmi was neglected, although it continued to be used for study by some in Palestine as late as the 11th century. Very few copies of the early text remain; of these, many are influenced by passages from the Babylonian Talmud. Later translators were unable to cope with some of the wording in the Yerushalmi manuscript and corrupted the text. There is only one reliable complete manuscript today. It was prepared in 1289, and is housed in the University Library at Leiden in the Netherlands.

The Bavli is not directly informed by midrashic material nor does it quote any passages from Yerushalmi. However, it seems clear that the Bavli Geonim were quite familiar with the Palestinian Midrash, and were informed of Yerushalmi concepts and approaches in cross-cultural discussions, but the Bavli acknowledges only the ancient Israelite Scriptures. The fifth century saw talmudic progress solely in Babylonia with the final redaction of that document occurring around the end of the sixth century. The exact date is not clear because for a century or more thereafter, trimming insertions were made into the text, and after that some marginal glosses were added as well. However, Rabbinic Judaism was finally consolidated under Muslim rule in Baghdad in the eighth century.

Neusner comments that Rabbinic (or Classical Judaism) "appeals for its ultimate authority to the Talmud of Babylonia, and, therefore, it is also called 'Talmudic Judaism.' Talmudic Judaism enjoys the status of orthodoxy to this day. It forms the court of final appeal for all Jews from Orthodox to Reform, Conservative, Reconstructionist, and any other known Judaic system of a religious character. Each branch invokes in its own way and for its own purposes the received writings of the dual Torah, *i.e.*, the Scripture and the Oral Law."

In order to understand the dynamics of Talmud, a review of one Mishnahic rule is instructive. What follows is intricate and can be skipped. Those who choose to continue will be rewarded with a peek into the immensity of Talmud.

This illustrative rule (presented in small caps, as is the custom) concerns that which is prohibited on the Sabbath.

THE PRIMARY LABORS ARE FORTY LESS ONE: SOWING, PLOWING, REAPING, BINDING SHEAVES, THRESHING, WINNOWING, SELECTING, GRINDING, SIFTING, KNEADING, BAKING, SHEARING WOOL, BLEACHING, HACKLING, DYEING, SPINNING, STRETCHING THE THREADS, THE MAKING OF TWO MESHES, WEAVING TWO THREADS, DIVIDING TWO THREADS, TYING AND UNTYING, SEWING TWO STITCHES, TEARING IN ORDER TO SEW TWO STITCHES, CAPTURING A DEER, SLAUGHTERING OR FLAYING OR SALTING IT, CURING ITS HIDE, SCRAPING IT, CUTTING IT UP, WRITING TWO LETTERS, ERASING IN ORDER TO WRITE TWO LETTERS, BUILDING, PULLING DOWN, EXTINGUISHING, KINDLING, STRIKING WITH A HAMMER, AND CARRYING OUT FROM ONE DOMAIN TO ANOTHER. THESE ARE THE FORTY PRIMARY LABORS LESS ONE. (M. ŠABB.73A)

"Forty less one" is the number of activities described in making the Tabernacle and the priestly vestments during the Exodus (Exod. 25:10-28:42). The rabbis noted that God used a unique Hebrew word for "work" in those forty activities and used the same word only once again, this time in Exod. 31:15: *"Six days may work be done, but on the seventh day there shall be a Sabbath of complete rest, holy to the Lord."* They reasoned that the activities related to the construction of the Tabernacle must be the activities prohibited on the Sabbath. This illustrates the manner in which the sages looked behind the literal meaning of a biblical passage to find the key to its origin.

The TOSEFTA *(t)* now speaks to the problems involved should a violation of the basic Mishnaic statement occur. Note: [ ] indicates the additions of the translator.

A general principle did R. Ishmael ben R. Yohanan ben state, "In the case of something on account of the deliberate doing of which one is liable to extirpation (uprooting of a planting), and on account of the inadvertent doing of which one is liable for a sin-offering, which one did on the Sabbath, whether one did so inadvertently or deliberately — it is prohibited both for him and for others.

But in the case of something on account of which people are not liable for the deliberate doing of which to extirpation, and on account of the inadvertent doing of which to a sin-offering, which one did on the Sabbath inadvertently — it may be eaten at the end of the Sabbath by others, but not by him. [If] he did so deliberately, it may not be eaten [at all]." (t. Šabb. 2:16)

There is a difference between inadvertent and deliberate violations of the Sabbath, and they have different consequences.

He who plants [seed] on the Sabbath — [If he did so] inadvertently, he may preserve [the plants which come up from the seed.] [If he did so] deliberately, he must uproot [the plants which came up from the seed.] On what account did they rule, "He who plants [seed] on the Sabbath — [If he did so] inadvertently, may preserve [the plants which come up from the seed.] But [If he did so] deliberately, he must uproot [the plants which came up from the seed.] But in the case of [seed planted in] the Seventh Year, whether this is done inadvertently or deliberately, he must uproot [the plants which come up]"? ... R. Judah says, "Matters are precisely the opposite. In the case of the Sabbath, whether one has done the deed inadvertently or deliberately, one must uproot [the plants which come up later on]. In the case of the Seventh Year, [if he sowed the seed] inadvertently, he may allow the plants to grow. If he did so deliberately, he must uproot them." (t. Šabb. 2:21)

He who digs, plows, or cuts a trench — these are deemed a single type of forbidden labor. He who threshes, beats flax, or gins cotton — these are deemed a single type of forbidden labor. He who pulls up, reaps, cuts grapes, harvests olives, cuts dates or hoes — these are deemed a single type of forbidden labor. He who selects, grinds, sifts, kneads, bakes for food [is liable if what is produced is] of the volume of a dried fig; [if this is] for a beast, a lamb's mouthful; [if this is] for dyeing, enough to dye a small garment. He who pulls a wing from a bird, trims it, and plucks the down, is liable for three sin-offerings. (t. Šabb. 9:17, 9:19, 9:20.)

We now turn to the discussion that resulted in the BABYLONIAN TALMUD (*b*) statement on the matter of prohibited Sabbath activities. These discussions make up the Gemara.

The exemplary rule we'll read deals only with sowing and plowing, two of the thirty-nine primary labors. The rabbis followed the form of the Mishnah in commenting on all aspects of the rule. Where Gemara makes reference to Tosefta in this text, the citation is in **bold**. Editorial notations to the text (parenthetical small type) are the product of the translator. [Bracketed material] is from the translation and indicates words added to clarify meaning. *Italicized type displays the comparable Yerushalami passage.* "The Tanna" means a farmer or farmers of the Tannaim period.

This illustration deals s. It does not deal with related talmudic matters.

Why state the number (*i.e.*, 40 less one)? — Said R. Johanan: [To teach] that if one performs them all in one state of unawareness, he is liable on account of each separately. SOWING AND PLOWING. Let us see: plowing is done first, then let him [the Tanna] state PLOWING first and then SOWING? The Tanna treats of Palestine, where they first sow and then plow.

A Tanna taught: Sowing, pruning, planting, bending (bending a vine to draw it into the ground to make it grow as an independent plant), and grafting are all one labor. (y Sabb. 7:2, VIII:B *"sowing, bending, grafting, trimming, nipping shoots, cutting, tying up wounds on a tree, stripping, covering with powder, fumigating, removing wormy parts, cutting, anointing, watering, perforating, preparing a covering, and doing any sort of deed which improves the product ... one is liable on the count of sowing.*)

How does this inform us? — that if one performs many labors of the same nature, he is liable only to one [sacrifice]. R. Abba said in the name of R. Hiyya b. Ashi in R. Ammi's name: He who prunes is culpable on account of planting, while he who plants, bends [the vine], or grafts is culpable on account of sowing. On account of sowing only but not on account of planting? Say: on account of planting too. (Planting and sowing are identical, the former applying to trees and the latter to cereals.) R. Kahana said: If one prunes and needs the wood [too], he is liable to two [penalties], one on account of reaping and one on account of planting. (Cutting wood from a tree is a derivative of reaping. Pruning is done to enable what is left to grow more freely, so it can be

considered a derivative of planting.) R. Joseph said: He who
cuts hay is liable to two [penalties], one on account of reaping
and the other on account of planting. (The hay is cut so that
new grass can grow, a derivative of planting.) Abaye said: He
who trims beets [in the ground] is liable to two [penalties],
one on account of reaping and one on account of planting.
PLOWING. A Tanna taught: Plowing, digging, and trenching
are all one [form] of work. (t. Šabb 9:17A) R. Shesheth said: If
one has a mound [of earth] and removes it, in the house, he is
liable on the score of building; if in the field, he is liable on
the score of plowing. Raba said: If one has a depression and
fills it up; if in the house, he is liable on account of building; if
in the field, he is liable on account of plowing. R. Abba said:
If one digs a pit on the Sabbath, needing only the earth
thereof (but not the pit), he is not culpable on its account.
And even according to R. Judah who ruled: One is liable on
account of a labor which is not required on its own account;
that is only when he effects an improvement, but this man
causes damage (*i.e.*, he spoils the ground by the pit.) (b.
Sabb.73b-75)

The Bavli rabbis seemed to have been informed by Tosefta and,
perhaps, by the Yerushalmi as well. Their main concern is a complete
identification of the aspects of each prohibition. They do have in mind the
concern brought up in Tosefta regarding intentional and inadvertent actions.

In the event of a Sabbath rule violation in a local setting, for example,
the rabbi(s) responsible for rendering a decision will make himself fully
cognizant of the foregoing Gemara in order to render a decision that is in
keeping with the Talmud. Obviously, the concerns here deal with an
agricultural society. As Jews moved from agricultural to urban life during the
diaspora, questions arose that were not specifically addressed in Gemara. In
such instances, the questions were taken to a highly respected rabbi or a board
of sages in one of the diaspora locations who issued a *Responsa*. These
deliberations are comparable to a decision by, let us say, a Court of Appeals in
our country. They may set local or overall precedent. *Responsa* are collected and
serve as a valuable resource today. Compendia of contemporary *Responsa* are
published annually.

Even a brief excursion into the Mishnah, Tosefta, and Talmud leaves
one with a sense of amazement that the rabbis could structure and implement
an entire legal system based upon Torah and oral laws. And, were able to
preserve detailed minutes of their discussions, record the name of the rabbis
who solved individual problems, and those who provided direction to later
scholars. According to Neusner:

The Talmud of Babylonia is the single most important document of ... Judaism. Few documents in the entire history of the west ... have so informed and shaped society in the way in which the Bavli did. This is a document remarkable for its power to define the social order of an entire people living under diverse rules of politics, culture, economy, and society. Wherever Jews lived from the seventh century to our own time, they found in the Talmud of Babylonia the rules that would govern their social order.

The Talmud was carefully worked out over a five-hundred-year period by the most learned Jewish men using their analyses and that of their predecessors. It was an amazing feat which was only possible because accurate records of past sessions were kept on hand, and their work place in Babylonia was not disturbed during that entire period. Although the originators of Talmud were intent on codifying the practices of carrying out their religious precepts, they were also passing on their analytical methods.

As a result, the outcome of talmudic study was the training of the scholarly mind to consider each passage with great care. Study would ensure understanding of the passage's original intent, recognize patterns and identify unexplored issues. Talmudic scholars could resolve such issues and open new questions for exploration. The mental exercise involved in reading, understanding, categorizing and commenting upon talmudic passages prepares one for the methodology used in scientific research, legal analysis, medical diagnoses, financial matters, diplomatic affairs, etc. all applications that contributed to the success of Jews who were permitted to participate in world society and commerce.

This type of analysis when passed on from one generation to the next became the basis for the Jewish mind. Talmud and its content of social issues was of great interest not only to Jews but to Christian scholars as well. It also seems that this work was of some satisfaction to God, as the number of scolding prophetic visits eased off. Thus Talmud, and the *yeshiva* classes it fostered became the pivot point upon which the relationship between God and his chosen people changed. In all of these respects Talmud was a gift to God by His chosen people.

> *His people shall prosper in peace and security so that all the nations know that the Lord sanctifies Israel.* (Eze. 37:25-8, 39:26)

This period of undisturbed study that was primary to the production of the *Bavli* was not the same in the holy land. Here the Jews remaining were forced to leave by the Christians who took over that area. This was the beginning of the diaspora.

Notes for Chapter Five

The analytical work that started about 150 BCE became, over the next five centuries, the saving of the Jewish traditions and religious rules. The citations listed below present the beginning of that time. The Christians were going through a similar organization study trying to describe what the life and teaching of Jesus meant to them.

A complete translation of the Nag Hammadi manuscripts is available in James M. Robinson's *Nag Hammadi Library*, Harper and Row, 1988.

The tumultuous period from the triumph of the Maccabees in150 BCE to the destruction of the Temple in 66 CE is covered by Shaye J.D. Cohen in his book *From the Maccabees to the Mishnah*, The Westminster Press, 1989.

The rise of the Mishnah in Jewish life occurred about 200 CE and is detailed in Jacob Neusner's *Introductions to Rabbinic Literature*. Henderson, 2002, 126.

Following the destruction of the Temple, a group of rabbis worked on the reconstruction of Judaism from their meeting room near Jerusalem as they fashioned a workable religion without the Temple. Neusner, Jacob *Formative Judaism: Religious Historical and Literary Studies*, Scholars Press, 1982.

The Palestine Jews came under considerable pressure in the third century from a breakdown of Roman authority, communicable diseases, and barbarian invasions. Since Babylonia was not under Roman control, the work on the Talmud continued there; the finished product was later known as the Bavli. Steinsaltz, R. Adin *The Talmud Steinsaltz Edition*, Random House, 1989, 25. Illustrates and gives explanation of notations on a typical page in a large size book.

The construction of the Talmud continued for about five hundred years in Babylonia where the rabbis, a number from Palestine joined the working group, were undisturbed. Periodic meetings continued to expand upon all aspects of Jewish life following the Mishnah through continuous commentary and reference to famous past rabbinic statements. The extent and depth of the Bavli is best sampled by reviewing volumes in a religious library. For general information see Strack H.L. and Stemberger G. *Introduction to the Talmud and Midrash*, T and T Clark, 1991 and Steinsaltz previously noted.

Meanwhile, in Jerusalem, the remaining rabbis conceded that the completed Talmud would come from Babylonia. They concentrated on *aggadah* matters not subject to definitive ruling. Before departing Palestine, the rabbis wrapped up their Talmud known as the *Yerushalmi* about 400 CE. Because of the pressures they were under, very few copies were prepared and only three remain today. Never-the-less Professor Neusner managed to translate the *Yerushalmi: The Talmud of the Land of Israel, A Preliminary Translation and Explanation*, University of Chicago Press, 1991.

Chapter Six
European Diaspora

Even though I am about to exile you from the Land [of Israel] to a foreign land, you must continue to be marked there by the commandments, so that when you return they will not be new to you ... Take care, lest the inclination to evil should lead you astray, and you separate yourselves from the Torah, for when a person separates himself from the Torah, he goes and clings to idolatry ... The Holy One, Blessed be He, said to Israel, "Consider the ways which you had followed, and repent, whereupon you will forthwith return to your cities.."

Sifré Deuteronomy Tannaitic Midrash

The Diaspora (Greek for "dispersion"; the Hebrew word is *galut*) has a long history in Judaism. The "ten lost tribes" were exiled from northern Israel to the eastern provinces by the Assyrians in 722 BCE. There they merged into the local populace without establishing a major permanent Israelite community. When the Babylonians conquered southern Israel in 586 BCE the survivors were deported to Babylonia, and formed a community in exile which endured, grew, and became a major center for Judaism. At the same time some Jews escaped the Babylonian destruction of Jerusalem and joined a community in Cairo which also had a long and venerable history.

During the Hellenistic period (301-63 BCE), Jews on their own initiative emigrated to what is now Turkey and Greece, gradually spreading westward into the Balkans. In the second decade of the second century BCE, during the war between remnants of Alexander's Empire, an attack on Jerusalem by Ptolemy I of Egypt sent more Jews scattering to Babylonia, while others were taken prisoner back to Egypt. When the Romans took control of the land of Judah in 63 BCE many Jews left for Italy, while others fled to Cyrene on the northern coast of today's Libya. By the second century, other Jews had settled in Spain.

When one speaks of the Diaspora from Palestine, the actual point of departure was the fifth century CE, when autonomous Jewish rule in Palestine came to a close, and Jews were replaced by Christians urged to settle there by the Church. The tipping point was Constantine's Edict of Milan in 313 CE, declaring that Christianity would be the preferred religion of the Roman Empire. Rabbinical *Midrash* had much to say about the descent into *galut* including the header of this chapter, a quotation from Sifré (Aramaic for Book) Deuteronomy. It is now obvious that the destruction of the Temple was the event that permitted the Jews to expand their presence in the civilized world.

Anti-Judaism

Were the Jews intimidated by their conflicts with the Christians? It appears for the most part, that Jews at the start of the Christian period considered the Christian apologists upstarts not to be taken seriously by the adherents to a religion already one thousand years old. But, as friendly discussions, debates, and polemics continued for a century or more, the Jewish concern grew, and the rabbis took more actively to the debate. Medieval Jewish Bible commentary is filled with anti-Christian polemic to the point where it became an integral part of the work. By the mid-Medieval period (11th to 14th centuries), books had been prepared to provide Jews with answers to Christian polemics. The most thorough of these was The Old Book of Polemic (*Nizzahon Vetus*) which has an encyclopedic array of anti-Christian arguments.

Anti-Judaism had roots extending back into the time of the Hasmonean wars, when Jewish expansion and forced conversion of pagans occurred (c. 100 BCE). In the larger Mediterranean community, the dispersion of Jews with separate and aloof "ritually pure" communities in Turkey, Greece, and Italy, extended these anti-Judaic feelings. The Jewish proselytism prominent prior to the two revolts also was a reason for these feelings. Although Jewish proselytism did taper off during and after the two revolts, it continued after the Bar-Kochba rebellion until legally forbidden in the 330s. In an odd way, the growth of Christianity not only turned the attention of Rome away from the Jews, but it also helped the Jews since the Romans could point to them as an accredited religion and condemn the Christians as deviants.

An often neglected but important reason for the growth of Christianity was the plagues of 165-180 (possibly smallpox) and 250-268 (possibly measles). The classical pagan religions of the time and the philosophy of the Greeks could neither explain nor respond satisfactorily to these extreme conditions. Note, however, that the Christians for the past two centuries had not assumed civic responsibility for the appeasement of the gods. Romans believed that worship of their gods was essential for, among other things, relief from disease. They felt that Christians' refusal to recognize the needs of the gods was a reckless choice that endangered the community.

By this time, the Christians had lived many generations in caring communities, where they protected themselves from Roman persecution. They were in a much better position to cope with a public health emergency. Their adherents had substantially higher survival rates. The plague disasters and the Christian response thereto resulted in substantial growth of the new religion for three reasons: the higher survival rate of Christians, the perceived "miracle" of Christian healing and isolated pagan survivors' need to find a new community.

Christianity was baptizing many new adherents, while Judaism was losing former converts and suffering great losses from the plagues. As the sheer number of Christians became an issue within the Roman Empire, the government found it most expeditious to authorize that religion. This was due not only to the rapid growth of Christianity, but also to the alarming decline in the pagan population of the Roman community. At the time of Constantine and the official adoption of Christianity throughout the Empire (392 CE), there were more than six million Christians and about 1.25 million Jews. Within fifty years of the validation of Christianity as the religion of Rome, there were about 34 million Christians in the Empire.

St. Augustine

Augustine Aurelius, St. Augustine (354-430 CE), whom some call the true founder of Western Christian thought, posited two distinct approaches toward Judaism. The first is the classic Pauline doctrine of Romans, balancing disappointment with the hope that the Jews would accept the "true" religion. This became the basis of normative Church policy. The second is a doctrine of anxiety in which the persistence of the Jews challenged the Christian claim to the right to be Gods people. The longer the Jews persisted, the stronger the challenge. Radicals soon arose, and their practice of demonizing the Jews would grow more disturbing throughout the Middle Ages. Relations between Christians and Jews during the European Diaspora reached a paradoxical point. On the one hand is the grim picture of persecution and humiliation, intolerance, and fanaticism; on the other, the real concern of the Church to protect and preserve the Jews.

Fortunately, there were several reasons why equating Jews with demons did not become universal. First, as Augustine elaborated on other occasions, should the Jews and, along with them, Judaism cease to exist, then Christians too might neglect God's revelation and desert the faith. This is best expressed in Pauline theology: if the root of the olive tree dies, how can the branches survive? Second, continuity of the Jews furnished a permanent counter-example to Christianity's virtues, since the Jews (in the eyes of Augustine) personified the absence of grace (freely given love) and its effects. Third, the Church feared Jewish conversion *en masse*, because the Second Coming was contingent on such an event. (Church doctrine from Paul's day had explicitly linked the two events.) Thus, they were concerned about the consequences should the Second Coming not occur. And finally, the Church was well aware of humanity's inability to nullify God's purpose: the free yet irrevocable love for the people Israel.

Do not slay them (the Jews), lest at some time they (the
Christians) forget your (God's) law; scatter them by your
might ... for if they (the Jews) lived with that testimony of the
Scriptures only in their own land, and not everywhere, the
obvious result would be that the Church, which is
everywhere, would not have them available among all nations
as witnesses to the prophecies which were given beforehand
concerning Christ. (Augustine, *City of God* VIII:46)

While employing this passage to hold that the Jews must remain as an
example to Christians, Augustine also proposed that Jews must bow down to
the superiority of Christianity, to recognize that God had a new covenant
people. This "new covenant" view, which is an inaccurate distillation of Pauline
theology, was not tempered by the Church until the 20th century.

Middle Ages

What principally governed Jewish life in the European Middle Ages
was their legal and constitutional status. Once the Church had been authorized
as the imperial religion, it pressed the government to embody Christian beliefs
in its civil code. The first legal document to attempt to balance the Roman
legacy of tolerance toward the Jews with the intolerance of Christianity was the
Theodosian Code compiled by the Emperor Theodosius II between 429 and
438. The Code incorporates Roman imperial protective legislation dating from
the beginning of the Christian period, and includes as well the restructuring of
the public holidays to specify Sunday as the Sabbath, and insert Easter as a
public festival. Because the Code had considerable influence in the Latin West
during the early Middle Ages, both in its own right and in what it epitomizes, it
is the foundation of Jewry law in Latin Christendom. Titles 8 and 9 of the
Theodosian Code deal exclusively with the Jews. Although Title 8 perpetuates
the features of the old pagan-Roman tolerance, at the same time some of its
phraseology reflects the new concerns of the Church.

Carried over from the pre-Christian period is the all-
important recognition of the legitimacy of Judaism and the
resulting guarantee of Jewish assembly for worship. The first
law on this matter, dated 393, begins with the affirmation: "It
is sufficiently established that the sect of the Jews is forbidden
by no law." Although this may seem a rather negative way of
expressing toleration, the formulation could simply reflect an
attempt by codifiers to anticipate and preempt clerical
objections to the continuation of an indulgent policy...
(Cohen 33)

Reaffirming Jewish citizenship, the Code also confirms that Jews have the right to regulate their own markets and to seek arbitration in disputes concerning civil law.

The statute closes with a statement characteristic of Christian stringency to the effect that "the Jews also shall be admonished that they perchance shall not become insolent, and elated by their own security, commit any rash act in disrespect of the Christian religion." (Cohen 33)

Book 16 of the Theodosian Code is unabashedly hostile toward the Jews, revoking or restricting many of their traditional rights. Notably, Jewish-Christian intermarriage was equated with adultery. Book 16 was accepted by the church as an authoritative source of canon law.

The stated goal of Church policy toward Jews was to achieve stability and to preserve Judaism as a "witness" to Christianity while limiting, to the extent possible, Jewish-Christian intercourse by such means as exclusion of Jews from positions in which they might wield authority over Christians. During the Middle Ages, edicts of ecclesiastical councils and pontifical opinions expanded the corpus of canon law. The resulting regulations were harsh and uniformly repressive. These regulations changed little throughout the Middle Ages, at least until the mid-16th century. But the realization of the ecclesiastical ideal was forever impeded by radical clerical behavior. The result was severe Jewish trauma.

At the same time, the Empire, and even its now Christianized Roman law, had not entirely abandoned tradition. There were limits which the law preserved and to which Christians had to defer. The Jews remained Roman citizens, and their right to practice Judaism and observe its rituals was restated. Pope Gregory the Great (590-604) adhered to the Theodosian Code and the assumption of Jewish subservience in setting Church policy compatible with both Paul and Augustine. His most important pronouncement, which was to become the emblem of papal policy toward the Jews, was: "Just as it should not be permitted the Jews to presume to do in their synagogues anything other than what is permitted them by law, so with regard to those things which have been conceded them they ought suffer no injury." Gregory set a standard that guided the papacy on Jewish matters for centuries. However, not all ranks of medieval society accepted the pope's interpretation of the Code. Therefore, activity vis-a-vis the Jews was ambivalent, but the gap between Pauline dichotomy and political authoritarianism was constantly narrowing.

In the early seventh century, the desire of the Church leadership was to make their religion accepted universally throughout Europe, and this initiative was to include the Jews. This objective was to continue throughout most of the Middle Ages. Its general failure to bring Jews into the fold caused anxiety in the Church because it signified that the Chosen People continued to survive, and, therefore, were still under God's protection. The Jews stayed within their enclaves maintaining a "pure environment" as best they could. As time passed and the Jews continued to persist without changing, the Church became more onerous and militant towards them. France, Spain, and Portugal imposed forced conversion at one time or another. Their efforts were particularly misguided and demonstrated no understanding of Israel's role to be God's servant people. One factor that lay behind these oppressions was the very basic Christian fear of the Jews.

If Christians could come to believe in their heart that they were the inheritors of the great tradition of Judaism, they would also have to be concerned with the possibility that the Jews would be vengeful. In this respect, the Gospel of John should have given them pause. The expression *for fear of the Jews* is twice used in John without explanation (John 7:13, 20:19). These quotations probably do not refer to excommunication from Judaism but rather to simple physical danger. Of course, since the writer of John knew that Paul's life was seriously threatened several times, as written in the Book of Acts (cf. 13:50, 14:19, 21:17ff), it is probable that such a danger did exist at the time of John.

However, the expression for fear of the Jews took on a further meaning when John wrote of the crucifixion that the Jewish high priests shouted, Crucify him! Crucify him! ... We have a law, and according to that law he ought to die because he has claimed to be the Son of God. (John 19:6-7). By indicting the Jews for the death of Jesus (the act of deicide), John instilled in the Christian pagan converts to come that the Jews are to be feared, for they had the power to kill the Son of God. It is but a simple extrapolation to attribute to the Jews such magical torments as torturing the Host, sacrificing Christian children, calling on God to bring a plague upon the Christians, poisoning the wells, etc. This also justified, in the minds of some Christians, the right to kill Jews.

On the domestic front, the European Christian world of the Middle Ages settled down to tolerance and dominance of the Jews. During this period (circa 600-1400), the majority of Jewish men (and many Jewish women) were literate and participated in commerce, finance and various trades (as goldsmiths, leather workers, tanners, glassblowers, weavers, dyers, etc.). With the exception of the French attempt at forced conversion, tolerance was the norm for about five hundred years. German kings induced long range Jewish traders to settle in their land for economic reasons. These people had established trading posts from the Middle East to the Far East often dependent on the good faith of co-religionists who had populated these areas for many centuries as a result of the Assyrian dispersion in 722 BCE and the Babylonian exile in 586 BCE. The earliest Jewish communities in Germany based on long range trading can be traced to 850 CE.

Jewish traders, because of their friendly contacts in the east and their ability to converse in any number of languages, could be counted on to carry goods and money safely in the form of promissory notes, across continents.

Commercial trading provided an outlet for locally made goods and a source of exotic products for home consumption. This trade formed the basis of a productive economy, and thereby a healthier and happier society. Enlightened kings of the multiple German city-states were eager to promote this activity by issuing standard charters of privileges to Jews, including the all-important right to live by their own laws, plus generous dispensations to facilitate their commercial activities. By the 11th century, there were about twenty thousand Jews in Germany.

Lending Practices

Money-lending proved a constant irritant to relations between Jews and Christians, in part because the need for loans was a constant in medieval society. Money was often required to buy seeds for next year's crop. Well-to-do landowners were often in need of protection, and the cost to hire and maintain soldiers was high.

Charging interest for the use of money was deemed "usury," a practice forbidden to Christians. Since lending was deemed to be a Jewish act, anyone who lent money was considered to be a "Jew." Lending had become a primary activity of Jews in the tenth century because they were effectively excluded from farming and from the craft guilds. Jews turned to international commerce and lending.

The medieval concept of time did not include immutable artificial increments. Church moralists and debtors were upset that money, almost mysteriously, increased in value as a function of time. It was as if the lenders were selling time itself, a commodity assumed to be God's alone. From our contemporary perspective the concept of time as a commodity may seem quaint, but when the great Gothic churches were being built in Europe during the period 1150-1400, time seemed mutable. The construction of a cathedral might take hundreds of years. As Judith Dupré writes in *Churches*,

> Although daylight was commonly divided into twelve hours,
> there was no sense that these divisions ought to be of
> uniform length — an "hour" might mean a day or a season.
> Time was not a commodity to possess, not possess, or save. It
> was measured by the larger rhythms of nature — sun rises,
> moon phases, a life...

The concept of money gaining value over time was nothing new for the Jews, who had balanced financial risk by practicing floating interest rates since Second Temple times. For Jews in the lending business, time was not an abstract. For them, time *was* money. That imperative eventually acted as a prod to bring European commerce into "real time."

An important part of the commercial world in Christian Europe during the Middle Ages were the annual fairs, of which there were many. In the Champagne region of France, for example, ten fairs were held annually, the fair at Troyes being the most important. One of the busiest sections of the fair was the money changers. Since fairs attracted clients from outside the sponsoring community, money changing was a pressing need. These services were rendered in the mid-medieval by Italians, local Jews, and Frenchmen with the Italians most prominently represented. Since the Italians and French were identifiable only by nationality, it is quite possible that a number of them were Jewish as well. In addition to money changing, letters of credit could be purchased at the fairs.

The Jews started to lose their competitive trading advantage in the tenth and 11th centuries when a European commercial and monetary reawakening was fueled by the revival of urban centers. Many Jews then immigrated to Italy in order to continue as traders, a profession which they exploited successfully through the end of the Middle Ages. Some invested acquired capital in banking and long-distance commerce. Toward the end of the Middle Ages, banks in German and Italian cities were typically Jewish institutions. Jewish bankers had the satisfaction of knowing that the cities needed them as much as they needed the cities. They also performed a vital service by linking their community to communities they visited while serving as liaison to distant civil authorities. This mutual need did much to weaken the force of Franciscan opposition.

Christians seeking small loans to tide them over from one harvest to the next usually borrowed from Jewish women. Often, the mother of the Christian household would come to the lender's home, children in tow, to seek a loan. Shame fueled rage against Jews. But when Jews were expelled from France after farmers clamored for relief from Jewish lenders, they soon found that the Christian lenders (including Church officials) were charging higher interest rates than the Jews.

During the period when Jews and Christians both were lending, the Jews were forced to charge higher rates because their clients were those of higher risk whose loan application had been denied by Christian lenders. Given all the prejudice that was tied up in the Jewish-Christian transactions, one wonders if French nobles and people ever appreciated the readily available loans at fair rates provided by the Jewish bankers and small lenders.

More than one Christian invested goodly sums with Jews, thereby helping to finance — for a healthy return — Jewish lending operations. Also, the popes seemed to understand that it was preferable to limit sin by dominating and regulating lending, rather than waging an unwinnable war. Jurisdiction over Jewish "usury" was turned over to ecclesiastical courts beginning in the 12th century, most likely because the secular courts did not wish to interfere with an essential element in the growing economy. It was the awareness that credit was a necessity that led the popes to seek the middle course of licensing and controlling Jewish lending, the life blood of the economy, which they pursued until 1682.

Through it all, Northern European Jews remained insistently loyal to their Jewish identity and maintained their own cultural by resisting attempts to convert and by enforcing Judaism's ancient taboo against marriage outside the Jewish community. Although medieval people constructed an image of Jews as the mystical enemy of the Christian society, there was still considerable social interchange between Jews and Christians during the five centuries before the Crusades which began in the last years of the 11th century. Even though Jews clung fiercely to their Law, they were not excluded from society. They lived relatively close to and peacefully with their Christian neighbors. All this was to change shortly.

Crusades

The Islamic religion was founded in 622 CE. The Crusades were undertaken by Rome when the "Golden Age" of Islamic expansion threatened to overrun Europe. Muslim tribes conquered Palestine in 638, Spain in 711, and Sicily in 917. When the Muslims began raiding Southern Italy about 950, the pope became concerned that Christian Europe would be reduced to "an angle of the world." As Europe finally united and began to fight back, the popes took up the call to protect the spiritual health of all Christendom and Christians from their mortal enemies by going on the offense to reclaim Christian holy sites then held by Muslims. It was Pope Urban II who delivered the kickoff speech in 1095.

> With what reproaches will the Lord overwhelm us if you do not aid those who, with us, profess the Christian religion! Let those who have been accustomed unjustly to wage private warfare against the faithful now go against the infidels and end with victory this war which should have been begun long ago. Let those who for a long time have been robbers now become knights. Let those who have been fighting against their brothers and relatives now fight in a proper way against the barbarians. Let those who have been serving as mercenaries for small pay, now obtain the eternal reward. (Tyerman)

As an inducement to join the Crusades, the Church offered remission of penalties for sin, church protection of property and family, and immunity from litigation and debt repayment. Born and conducted in controversy, crusading provoked criticism as an overt embrace of physical war as an act of penance. The conduct of certain Crusades and crusaders was regarded as beneath respect: selfish, not selfless. Still the Crusades continued to find participants because of the lure of riches in the east.

In the spring of 1096, bands of wandering vagrants (more correctly described as "armed pilgrims") followed by an armed contingent destroyed the Jewish communities of Mainz, Worms, and Cologne. Communities also were decimated in Treves and as far away as Prague. Jews in small towns were murdered or forcibly baptized. Thousands of Jews in Germany died, and probably not more than 30 to 40 percent of the Jewish population escaped unharmed. These deaths are remembered on the 23rd of Iyar in the Jewish calendar (May 18). The names of the martyrs are still read in some European synagogues.

The first crusaders disembarked at Christian Constantinople, then fought their way through Islamic Anatolia. The Muslims, not unaccustomed to fighting, were stunned by the sudden appearance of Western European knights in their backyard, with what, to them, were completely incomprehensible motives for being there. Undeterred, the crusaders continued on to Jerusalem, capturing the city in 1099. Although this was an astounding logistical and military success (albeit against a scattered and ineffective defense), the ensuing massacre of the Jews, Eastern Rite Christians, and Muslims of Jerusalem shocked both the Muslim and European worlds (and likely Christ as well). This, however, was common practice at the time. Having made that bellicose statement, the crusaders withdrew, leaving about three hundred knights in southern Palestine.

In the mid-12th century, a Turkish warlord captured the stronghold of Edessa (in contemporary Lebanon), sparking the Second Crusade. German and French forces transported to Anatolia were thoroughly defeated by the Turks in Asia Minor. It took Muslin forces in Egypt and Palestine several more decades to put their internecine ways aside and get their act together. Finally, under the leadership of the legendary Saladin the Great (*Salah ad-Din*), Muslims recaptured Jerusalem in 1187. This action aroused Europe again which then sent the Third Crusader army, an elite force of about 100,000 under Richard the Lionheart of England, Philip Augustus of France, and Frederick Barbarossa of Germany, to recapture the Holy City.

Barbarossa drowned trying to cross a river in Anatolia, and his army was demoralized. Philip became ill and withdrew. Richard and the remaining forces went on to fight Saladin to a draw. Diplomacy then became the order of the day. Saladin and Richard attempted to partition Palestine, but the effort became stuck on the question of jurisdiction within the city of Jerusalem. Saladin pointed out that Jerusalem was Muslim as much as it was Christian. (Jews were not represented in this negotiation.) In the end, an agreement was reached that insured Christians the right to make the pilgrimage to the holy shrines in Jerusalem without interference (as had been the case since the

Muslim occupation). Richard then withdrew his forces, and soon thereafter Saladin died.

The Fourth Crusade, aimed this time at Egypt, which then controlled Palestine, beginning in 1202. It ran into financial trouble early on. In order to repay the Venetian navy for their transport, the crusaders made a deal to assist the young Byzantine king in Constantinople to protect his throne. Although they accomplished this assignment, the financial reward was not forthcoming. As a result, Western Christian crusaders attack and looted the Eastern Christian city of Constantinople, possibly the wealthiest city in Christendom, in April 1204. This event drove a wedge between the already divided Eastern and Western Churches which has never been healed. Back in Palestine, a brief fifteen year period of French control prevailed until the Muslims reclaimed Jerusalem in 1244 and held it until 1917, almost seven hundred years. The crusaders did not again return to Jerusalem.

In 1215 CE, the Fourth Lateran Council of the Catholic Church promulgated the most infamous piece of ecclesiastical Jewry law during the Middle Ages. This law required Jews and Muslims to be distinguished from Christians by their dress in order to prevent accidental commingling, particularly sexual contact. These rules entered canon law during the reign of Pope Gregory IX (1227-1241). In the 15th century, this law was enforced by requiring Jews to wear a yellow wheel on the outer garment, a forerunner of the infamous Nazi "Jewish badge." The same laws forbade Jews from appearing in public during Eastertide, or to blaspheme Christ. Jewish moneylenders were prohibited from oppressing Christians with heavy and immoderate usury.

The German Christian world rise periodically against the Jews when climactic events or plagues threatened the security of society. Jews, who were legally unable to defend themselves, were massacred in various German cities in the 1240s and again in 1298 and 1336 (food shortage due to overpopulation). Three hundred Jewish communities were destroyed by rioters in the German Empire between 1348 and 1349 (the Black Plague). All of these matters started to make life in Germany intolerable for most Jews.

Emerging Talmud

In matters religious, the Talmud reached European Jewry in the ninth century. The text developed by an agrarian society some four centuries before had to be elucidated and rendered into a flexible instrument to serve as the basis for ongoing legislation and communal direction in a society of tradesmen and financial lenders. Due to the efforts of Rabbi Gershom ben Judah of Mainz, Germany, the Talmud was to become well known in Europe by the late tenth century. Gershom's greatest legacy is his contribution to the development of methodology. Talmudic learning in his schools took place in an atmosphere of intense dialogue between master and pupils regarding the interpretation of words and phrases. Gershom's goal was to familiarize youngsters with the basic text, and to stimulate them to ask questions. By doing so, it was hoped that a select few would be ready for the rigors of *yeshiva*, where the primary activity was to absorb and ponder the masters' glosses on individual words and phrases of the text. The glosses were always open to challenge and frequent modifications following vigorous debates, after which they were written down in notebooks (*quntres*).

Rabbi Shlomo (Solomon) ben Isaac, known universally by the acronym "Rashi" (1040-1105), had a rare ability to unify succinctly vast amounts of material without sacrificing clarity. Many of his glosses, displayed prominently today on each page of Talmud, consist of not more than a brief phrase. Moreover, once Rashi had established the meaning of a word or phrase in one location of the Talmud, that meaning usually could be applied to the same word elsewhere, or Rashi would indicate otherwise. Within fifty years of his death, Rashi's glosses had penetrated every Jewish community in Europe; within one hundred years, they were known and used universally by Jews and Christian Hebraists. As a result of Rashi's work and his extant responsa, Jewish learning within Europe acquired an international flavor.

Because of the Crusades, the center of Jewish learning moved from the German Rhineland to the French Champagne and northern regions in the 12th century. There, on the basis of Rashi's finely edited *quntresim*, his son-in-law Judah ben Natan, followed by Rashi's three grandchildren (Samuel, Isaac and especially Jacob ben Meir) reinitiated new schools and a new epoch of Jewish learning, that of the: Commentators (*Ba'alei ha-Tosafot*, literally "the supplementers"). Between the 12th and 14th centuries, the Tosafists turned Talmud into a living work by interpreting thousand-year-old dicta and juristic principles and applying them to contemporary northern European Jewish realities. A 15th-century version of the *tosafot* commentaries was included in the 1484 Soncino printing of the Talmud and remains today in the standard Talmud version.

The most significant codifying achievement to result from the Tosafists' work is the mid-14th century *Arba'ah Turim*, meaning "Four Columns," and known simply as *Tur*, written by Jacob ben Asher (1270-1340) while in Germany. It is a summary of Jewish law from Geonim times including commentary thereon by the Tosafists and Maimonides. The four divisions ("columns" is an allusion to the jewels on the breastplate of the high priest) were the laws of prayer and synagogue, Sabbath, and holidays, laws of marriage and divorce, laws of finance, financial responsibility, damages and legal procedure, and miscellaneous ritualistic laws. The *Tur* eventually became the basis of normative Jewish religious observance. With commentary and abridgement, it was accepted by both Sephardic (basically Iberian) and Ashkenazim (basically German and Slavic cultural areas).

Expulsion of Jews

In the early Middle Ages, Jews lived mainly in communities on the Mediterranean coast, many of which persisted into the 15th century and beyond. Their population never exceeded fifteen hundred in any medieval city, and never more than 1 percent of the population in any kingdom except Spain, where they were about 3 percent). By the 11th century, when Jewish population worldwide was only about two million, or 0.3 percent of the world population, ethnic diversity had receded as a significant factor in Christian-Jewish relations. As the Church universal moved to complete its evangelical mission to the pagans in western and central Europe, the Jews in contrast stood out even more as unrepentant outsiders. As it became apparent that the Church had failed to convert God's chosen, a movement to remove them from Christian Europe began to grow.

Jews were expelled from England and Southern Italy in the 1290s, France in 1306 (and again in 1322 and 1394), and then from numerous German cities and territories beginning in the early 15th century to Poland and the Ottoman Empire. Some Jews managed to remain in Germany by moving their operations from one city state to another. Expulsions from other countries followed: Crete in 1453, Spain in 1492, Portugal in 1497 to the Netherlands and Constantinople and Sicily and southern Italy by 1541 to Rome and North Africa. Rome's Jews were the only community to survived the Middle Ages without dislocation. By about 1550, Western Europe contained very few openly professing Jews. The number of those expelled was: possibly five thousand in England, fifty thousand in Italy, and 100,000 in France. The number from Spain cannot be determined accurately.

Treatment of Jews by Christians during the medieval period was dominated by an attitude of triumphalism. The Jews, scattered and for the most part powerless, were in no position to offer resistance. On the other hand, Christians were unable to impose their will on Muslims. That latter struggle was not one of wills but of arms. No concerted effort was made by Christians to convert Muslims. The armed struggle would not go well in the longer run for Christianity. As the Muslims came into power, they were much less tolerant of Christians because of past battles, including the Crusades, and much more tolerant of Jews.

Notes for Chapter Six

With the Temple gone, Palestine invaded by Christians, Roman occupation of Judea, and Christianity the chosen religion, the Jews for the most part sought refuge elsewhere. This was the beginning of the diaspora about 400 CE. It would last until 1947 CE when the Promised Land would once again be Jewish.

Wistrich, Robert S. *Demonizing the Other: Antisemitism, Racism, and Xenophobia*, Harwood Academic Publishers, 1999.

GROWTH OF CHRISTIANITY

As the Christian religion claimed an increasing number of believers, St. Augustine wrote in his *City of God* that the Jews should accept the true religion, but the longer that did not occur, the stronger the Jewish continuing claim to be God's Chosen People.

Knowles, David, *Augustine: Concerning the City of God*, Against Pagans, Penguin Books, 1972. This book is based on Psalms 59:12a, "[Do] not kill them lest my people be unmindful, with Your power make wanderers of them," and Psalms 59:11 which reads: "Do not kill them, or my people may forget; make them totter by your power and bring them down O Lord our shield." This is originally a prayer of King David seeking protection against the agents of King Saul who were out to kill him.

Stow, Kenneth R. *Alienated Minority. The Jews of Medieval Europe*, Harvard University Press, 1992. Concerning Jewish life under Christian rule, see Mark R. Cohen, *Under Crescent and Cross: The Jews in the Middle Ages*, Princeton University Press, 1994.

Berger, David, *The Jewish-Christian Debates in the High Middle Ages*, The Jewish Publication Society, 5739-1979

LENDING PRACTICES

While living in what they considered foreign lands, Jewish access to employment was nil. Therefore, many took up moneylending. Although this was necessary, for example, to raise seed money for farming, it was very unpopular with the church. Inevitably, bad feelings arose. For more insight, see Stark, Rodney, *The Rise of Christianity*, Princeton University Press, 1996. See also Harries, Jill and Wood, Ians, *The Theodosian Code*, Cornell University Press, 1993

Geis, Francis and Joseph, *Daily Life in the Medieval Times*, Black Dog and Leventhal, 1990

THE CRUSADES

The Crusades' focus was Palestine, the home of Jesus and the site of many Christian shrines. The Catholic Church raised the warning that the rampaging Muslims had to be expelled to save the Christian religious sites. See Tyerman, Christopher, *Fighting for Christendom: Holy War and the Crusades*, Oxford University Press, 2004.

Chapter Seven

The Arab-Jewish Diaspora

Now the New Year reviving old Desires,
The thoughtful soul to solitude retires,
Where the white hand of Moses on the Bough,
Puts out, and Jesus from the ground suspires.

Omar Khayyám (1048-1131)

We left the diaspora Jewish families following God's wishes that they spread His name in European countries where their presence was, initially, not welcome. Another group of Jewish families moved into traditional Arab countries about the eighth century. Here the impact of the Muslim world on the resident Jewish population, then the largest in the world, was quite different than Christian-Jewish relations in the West.

Islam the monotheistic religion of the Arabic world was founded early in the seventh century. At that time Jews in Muslim dominated countries were only one of many diverse minorities and were rarely singled out for special treatment. Secondly, Judeo-Muslim conflict, where it did exist, was not theological. Also, the indigenous Jewish population was very similar in physical appearance, commercial endeavors, religious practices, and societal mores to their Muslim neighbors. As a result, the prejudice of the demonic "other," which was ever-present in European medieval society, was not a factor in the Arab-Jewish world. Generally speaking, the Jews in Arab countries at this time dwelt in prosperity, peace, and security with their Arab "cousins."

History of Islam

The history of Islam began with Muhammad ibn Abdallah, born of humble parentage in the city of Mecca about the year 570 CE. Orphaned while an infant, he was brought up by his uncle and married to a wealthy widow. In those years, he lived the life of a successful trader. When Muhammad was forty and meditating in a cave, he felt called by God to be a prophet to the Arabs. Assuming the prophetic biblical mantle, he started preaching about the year 610 by denouncing tribal provincialism, social injustice, and polytheistic paganism. However, his call to reverence the one God of both Judaism and Christianity did not sit well with the business leaders of Mecca whose commerce depended, in part, on pilgrimages to a local pagan shrine. Meccan threats to Muhammad's life forced him and his small band of followers to flee to Medina in 622, where he was accepted as their moderator. That flight (*hegira*) marks the beginning of the Islamic calendar.

Muhammad was surprisingly well learned in Judaism including not only Torah, but also rabbinic writings. No one is quite sure how he attained this level of understanding, although his decades of trading most surely brought him into contact with many Jewish merchants. Based on his knowledge and inclination to reverence the Jewish God, Muhammad expected his Jewish "brothers" in Medina to credit his burgeoning prophetic role and assist him in conveying his message to the Arab tribes and the indigenous Jewish tribes of the Arabian peninsula as well. He, apparently, did so from the viewpoint of a "continuator of the great prophetic religions" and propagator of the monotheistic faiths.

In this respect, perhaps Muhammad had a sophisticated understanding of the Jewish covenantal role in the world. But, from the viewpoint of the Jewish elders, Muhammad, an Arab and not a Jew, could only have been seen as an outsider whose claim of admiration for Judaism was fine, but whose claim to be a prophet in the tradition of ancient Israel did not square with the Hebrew Bible. Jesus, who was a Jew by birth and remained a Jew during his short lifetime, they could understand, but Muhammad had no such blood attachment to Judaism.

It was asking too much for these particular Arab-Jewish tribesmen to analogize between the manner in which Jesus and Paul were viewed from the first century by Jews to the way in which they should consider the claim of Muhammad in the seventh century. Further, Jewish tribesmen living on the fringes of Judaism may not even have been well versed in Torah. The position purportedly taken by Gamaliel when Paul appeared before the Sanhedrin would have been unknown to the local Jewish leaders since it was recorded in the Christian Book of Acts of the Apostles.

Therefore, it is not at all surprising that local Jewish leaders acted on this matter without consideration for the past experiences of Judaism in its covenant role. Unfortunately, they allied themselves with detractors, and lost a pitched battle to Muhammad and his followers. For the remainder of his life, Muhammad would resent the attitude of the Jewish community while carrying his new religion to the Arab inhabitants of the Arabian Peninsula and receiving the spoken word that became immortalized in Qur'ân. He died a natural death in Medina in 632.

Qur'ân

Qur'ân, the sacred book of Islam, is the spiritual record of the covenant between humankind and God (Allāh) transmitted to the Prophet through the archangel Gabriel. It provides the ideological base upon which each adherent (Muslim) accepts responsibility to live a life in Allāh. The revelation itself is written in Sura (Chapter) 96 of Qur'ân.

> *Recite (or proclaim) thou, in the name of thy Lord who created; created man from clots of blood: — Recite thou! For thy Lord is the most Beneficent, who hath taught the use of the pen; hath taught man that which he knoweth not.*

Qur'ân is difficult for non-Muslims to understand. It seems to lack a conventional beginning, middle, and ending. Its themes shift without transition from lyrical passages to sacred history, and from law to Muhammad's angst. The suras are not arranged chronologically but rather by length, the longest to the shortest, as are the letters of Paul in the New Testament. The writing is poetic in nature and is meant to be recited and internalized. It is intended as a guide to Muslim life, especially with regard to the importance of one's relationship to God, family, and community.

Qur'ân relies upon the Hebrew Bible to justify its standing in the panoply of monotheistic people. Returning to the vision of humanity that God showed to Abraham in Genesis 15, the same starting point upon which St. Paul depended, Muhammad rationalized that since Jews could not find justification for his prophetic role in their Bible, they must have tampered with the scriptural revelations. Therefore, the Abrahamic version that had been revealed to Muhammad, epitomizing a pure relationship to God was the true one. It followed, that the Hebrew version contained false statements (*tahrif*).

Based on Qur'ânic theology, Arabs traced their descent from Abraham through his first born son Ishmael, the half-brother of Isaac, citing Torah as part of their ancestral history. In Genesis, the angel of the Lord says this to Hagar, mother-to-be of Ishmael:

> *I will greatly increase your offspring, and they shall be too many to count. The angel of the Lord said to her further: "Behold you are with child and shall bear a son; you shall call him Ishmael [God will hear], for the Lord has paid heed to your suffering. He shall be a wild ass of a man; his hand against everyone, and everyone's hand against him; he shall dwell alongside of all his kinsmen."* (Gen. 16:9-12)

Qur'ân speaks to further meetings of significance between Father Abraham and his son Ishmael as this passage exemplifies:

When his Lord made trials of Abraham by commands which he fulfilled, He said, 'I am about to make thee an Imâm to mankind. [As used here Imâm means the person who carries the powers of the prophetic revelation]. And remember when we appointed the Holy House as man's resort and safe retreat, and said, 'Take ye the station of Abraham for a place of prayer'; and we commanded Abraham and Ishmael, 'Purify my house for those who shall go in procession round it, and those who shall abide there for devotion, and those who shall bow down and prostrate themselves ... And when Abraham and Ishmael raised the foundations of the House, they said 'O our Lord! Accept it from us; for thou art the Hearer; the Knower. (Sura 2:118, 120-1)

Abraham is considered by the Qur'ân to be the first "Muslim" by virtue of his complete, unquestioning "surrender" (*islâm* in Arabic) to God's will. In the words of the Qur'ân:

O People of the Book [Jews and Christians]! Why dispute about Abraham, when the Law [Torah] and Evangel [Gospels] were not sent down till after him? ... Abraham was neither Jew nor Christian; but he was sound in the faith, a Muslim [surrendered to God]; and not one of those who add gods to God [idolater]. They among men, who are nearest of kin to Abraham, are surely those who follow him and his prophet [Muhammad] and they who believe on him. (Sura 3:58, 60-1)

Islam presumes that the Arab people had a continuous history from the time of the biblical patriarchs, surviving among other people in a diaspora not unlike that of the Jews. When Muhammad appeared, fulfilling the prophecies of his advent, the people united behind him. From this telling, it is apparent that Islam makes no claim to usurp Judaism or Christianity, although it does believe that both religions lost sight of Abraham's pure monotheism. Therefore, Islam found its own way following the example of Abraham under the direction of Muhammad.

Not unexpectedly, Qur'ân is sometimes decidedly antagonistic toward Jews. A frequently cited example likens Jews to idolaters:

Of all men thou wilt certainly find the Jews, and those who join other gods with God, to be the most intense in hatred of those who believe ... (Sura 5:85)

But in the long run, this hostility did not give rise to serious religious or even social differences between Muslims and Jews as was the case between Christians and Jews. This was because Muhammad claimed neither messiahship nor divinity, and, unlike Jesus, he died a natural death. Muslims had no grounds for blaming Jews for the death of the Prophet. Further, the Islamic ban against depicting religious images took some of the steam out of a potential conflict.

The bitter on-going Jewish-Christian tension over the interpretation of the Hebrew Bible v. Christian New Testament was not present in Islam which had its own book much of which is based on Judaism as it existed at the time of Muhammad. As a result, Jewish-Christian debates were almost nonexistent in the Muslim world.

Religious law (*sharia*), the most fundamental feature of Islam, corresponds directly to and has the same meaning as Jewish *halakhah*. The dietary laws of Islam, include not only the pork prohibition but also a system of ritual animal slaughter which closely resembles Jewish practice, and Islamic manner of speech also betrays recognition of mutually held religious concepts and values.

The manner and frequency of prayer resembles that which the Jews once practiced, as described in the Book of the Prophet Daniel circa 150 BCE.

Christianity, Judaism and Islam

Christians disputed the legitimacy of Islam, contending that Muhammad's mission was not only unmentioned in the Jewish and Christian scriptures, it was not reliably witnessed either by individuals or by miracles. Whereas, the coming of Christ had been prophesied in the Hebrew Bible and witnessed by numerous miracles in the New Testament. These miracles continued long after Christ's sojourn on earth particularly at the graves of martyrs. The very spread of Christianity by the apostles, and the gift of tongues, also present valid testimony to Christian revelation.

Muslims retorted by looking to the New Testament for the foretelling of the Prophet. In this respect, the most pertinent passage is John 14:15-16, in which Jesus says,

> *If you love me, you will keep my commandments. And I will ask the Father, and he will give you another Advocate to be with you forever.*

"Advocate" in Greek, *parakletos*, derives from the same root as the name Muhammad. The Muslims did essentially the same thing in analyzing the Hebrew Bible. Here, they employed the Jewish practice of *gematria* (that is, assigning a numeric value to each letter of the Hebrew alphabet) and applied it to the Hebrew word for "exceedingly" in Gen. 17:20 — *"As for Ishmael, I have heeded you. I hereby bless him. I will make him fertile and exceedingly numerous"* — to yield, again, the numerical equivalent of the name of the Prophet.

In the tripartite debate of the monotheistic religions, Islam takes a shot at Judaism while defining the nature of Jesus (contra Christian theology) in the following passage from Qur'ân:

> *And for their* [the Jews boastfully] *saying "Verily we [Jews] have slain the Messiah, Jesus the son of Mary, an Apostle of God." Yet they slew him not, and they crucified him not, but they had only his likeness. And they who differed about them were in doubt concerning him. No sure knowledge had they about him, but followed only an opinion, and they [the Jews] did not really slay him but God took him up to Himself.* (Sura 4:156)

The Islamic viewpoint of Jesus as expressed in Qur'ân upholds the virgin birth (Sura 3:40-42, 52), celebrates him as *"an apostle to the children of Israel"* (3:43) and a Messenger or apostle (prophet) like Moses and Muhammad (3:138, 4:169, 5:79), and says he was not crucified but taken up by God like Enoch, Moses, Elijah, and Muhammad (Sura 4:156).

However, Jews are said in Qur'ân to have corrupted their own Scriptures as Muhammad surmised from the beginning of his prophecy. Mark R. Cohen avers: "The Torah in the possession of the (then) contemporary Jews was said to be a massive, willful *tahrif* of the original revealed book, lost to the Jews through their sins and the vicissitudes of their history. Eventually, Ezra came along and composed a new Torah which strayed far from the original."

> *And some truly are there among them who torture the Scriptures with their tongues, in order that ye may suppose it to be from the Scripture, yet it is not from the Scripture. And they say, "This is from God"; yet it is not from God; and they utter a lie against God, and they know they do so.* (Sura 3:72)

One example of those "who torture the Scriptures" is in the translation of Deuteronomy 18:15, the passage predicting a new prophet which all three monotheistic faiths claim as their very own. The passage reads as follows in the Hebrew Bible:

> *The Lord your God will raise up for you a prophet from among your own people, like myself [like Moses]; him you shall heed.*

For Jews, this would be Joshua. For Christians, of course, it would be Jesus. For Muslims, the correct translation of the Hebrew is this: *The Lord your God will raise up for you a prophet from among their brothers* [the descendants of Ishmael]. Hence, the Jewish translation (again) constituted *tahrif*, an attempt to deny the coming of Muhammad. Another example is the Abraham-Isaac sacrifice story, called in Hebrew the *Akedah* (Genesis 22), which Muslims believe was written originally with Ishmael as the sacrifice.

Islam censures Hebrew Scriptures claiming it nullifies earlier revelations of the Prophet. Both Islam and Christianity make the spurious claim that what they would like to see in Jewish Scripture is not there because the perfidious Jews knew, with some kind of foresight, that what would be important to Christians and Muslims at a future time should be excised or revised now. Another major theme of Islamic polemics is the Jewish anthropomorphic portrayal of God (attributing human characteristics and/or form to God). However, Muslims do not have the same concern about Hebrew Scriptures as do Christians. The Christians accept Scripture as the true revelation of God, but they disagree with Jews on how to interpret those writings. Since Muslims believe the Scriptures constituted *tahríf*, they don't argue about interpretation.

Growth of Islam

Upon the Prophet's death in 632, a group of his successors known as the Rashidun took up the cause. They were the first of four *khalífahs*, or "designated representatives" of the Prophet. The Rashidun caliphate conquered the Christian Byzantine lands of Mesopotamia, Syria, Palestine, Egypt, Libya, and Tripoli over a twenty-four-year period starting in 632. Jerusalem fell to the Muslims in 638, and the Muslims wasted no time transforming it from a predominately Christian city into a predominately holy Muslim city. But the Islamic conquest of Palestine opened the door for Jewish return, and communities were quickly set up in the Holy Land. Jews were able to survive there for the next four hundred plus years until the First Crusade when those remaining were massacred and their property destroyed.

Meanwhile, Christians began to stir and wonder what the implications might be of this sudden rise of "Arabian" power. Christianity had been evangelizing with great success for some five hundred years. During this time their religion was deeply rooted all over the then-known world with thousands of churches and millions of adherents. It is no wonder that Christians had difficulty grasping the thought that the conquerors of Jerusalem were not simply seeking booty, but were, in fact, the heralds of a spiritually potent religion and architects of a new civilization.

But at this point in the Muslim conquests, the tribal unity that undergirded its expansion was shattered by a dispute over who was the rightful heir to Muhammad. The third caliph, Uthman, was assassinated and succeeded by Ali ibn Au Talib, a cousin of Muhammad who had married Muhammad's daughter Fatima. When he, in turn, was assassinated, his supporters lived on as the *shi'a Ali* or the Party of Ali, known thereafter as the Shi'a, while the remainder of Islam became known as the Sunni, literally "those who follow the way of the Prophet" *i.e.*, traditionalists.

Lest we wonder what all the internecine slaughter between Shiites and Sunnis is all about, let us not forget the rivalry between Christian Catholics and Christian Protestants which started during the time of the Reformation in the early 16th century, and continued to contemporary times in Ireland. Over a period of some five hundred years, an estimated ten million died as a result of those religious wars. Basic to these conflicts were issues of social standing, religious theology, and power. The present stance of Islamic "terrorists" also show the same concerns.

He who is without sin among you, let him be the first to throw a stone...
(John 8:7)

The next wave of Islamic conquest was directed by The Umayyads, an Arab caliphate that ruled from Damascus, Syria for nearly a century. They extended Muslim hegemony over Christian lands for the first time from Tripoli to Gibraltar, and then to Spain in 711. By the year 750, at least fifty percent of the world's Christians found themselves under Muslim dominance. This astounding eighty-year period of conquest caused great concern in the Christian West, especially when Muslims established bases in Sicily and southern Italy during the tenth century. This was, in part, an incentive for the crusades.

One of the great achievements of this wave of conquest was the construction in 691 *of Haram al-Sharif*, the Noble Sanctuary, also known as the Dome of the Rock, on the site of the ancient Jewish Temple in Jerusalem (Mount Moriah). Muslims hold this site sacred as the spot from which Muhammad began his night journey (his ascent to God). Jews reckon it as the site of the *Akedah*. From the time of its construction to the present, *Haram al-Sharif* has dominated old Jerusalem for more than thirteen hundred years. The first and second Temples of the Israelites together stood on the same site for about nine hundred and fifty years. Note that inscriptions from Qur'ân encircle the building; these excerpts, having been placed only sixty years after the death of the Prophet, are the oldest known inscriptions from Qur'ân . Imagine the excitement if a building from the First Temple period were unearthed and found to have inscriptions from the earliest Hebrew Bible.

After the Islamic period of great expansion, Arab dynastic families started to feud over control of the new empire. The Umayyads lost their empire save for a small fraction of the Abbasid caliphate, centered in the new city of Baghdad in 750 CE. At its apex in the late 8th and early 9th centuries, the Abbasid Empire would spawn what is known as the Golden Age of Islam a period of great growth in philosophy, mathematics, and science unprecedented until the Renaissance. In addition to the advanced studies promoted by the

Abbasids, was the vital role they played in the development of a rich cultural life.

A radical Shiite dynasty known as the Fatimids brought North Africa, Syria, and Egypt under their control by 1171. This incursion into Egypt was just as disturbing to the Sunnis as the Crusader state in Palestine. Although control of the empire in Baghdad tended to shift periodically, the level of cultural achievement remained high. It was the time of Omar Khayyám and many other writers in ancient Persia, and the classical schools of Islamic law and theology. It was the Fatimids who founded in Cairo al-Azhar, the world's oldest university, about one thousand years ago, two hundred years before the first university was founded in Medieval Europe.

In the mid-13th century, Arab domination of the Middle East was severely curtailed by the Mongols who swept in from Eastern Siberia across Central Asia, capturing Damascus in 1258, and utterly destroying the remains of the Abbasid dynasty. Their advance was stopped by a slave army known as the Mamelukes. But in a surprising turn of events, the Mongolians over a period of about two decades, integrated and accepted Islam as their religion. Still, the entire Islamic realm was badly shaken by this invasion which resulted in a division of the Abbasid dynasty into the Mesopotamian kingdom and the new Mameluke caliphate in Egypt and Syria. However, the Mamelukes, strict Sunni Muslims, supported the arts. During their period of domination, the well-known tales of *The Thousand and One Nights* was written.

Life of Non-Muslims

Islam considered non-Muslims living under their rule (*dhimmís*) to be subject to the jurisdiction of Islamic law. All were subordinates but with internal autonomy in religious and most civil matters. This was equally applied to Jews wherever they resided in the Muslim East, although Sunni Islam, the orthodox and dominant form of the religion, was in general, more tolerant towards Jews and Christians. This is not to say that the Jews were held on an equal plane with Muslims — they and all other non-Muslims were secondary citizens subject to certain pragmatic restrictions including an annual tax (*jizya*). Jews or Christians were seldom singled out by Islamic law, rather they were subsumed under a category of infidels: the "People of the Book," those non-Muslims were recognized by the Prophet Muhammad as recipients of a divinely revealed scripture. The Qur'ân stipulates:

> *Let there be no compulsion in religion ... Whoever [shall] believe in God — he shall have taken hold on a strong handle that shall not be broken.*
> (Sura 2:257)

People of the Book: Jews and Christians and (subsequently) Zoroastrians being in the more prestigious category were raised a step in the overall hierarchical scheme. This category was later expanded to including Hindus and other religious groups. When an Islamic legal compendium singles out one of the *dhimmí* subgroups by name, it was usually the Christians who were much more prominent than the Jews. But the arrival of crusader armies, at the end of the 11th century, became a disaster for the Christian inhabitants of the Arabic countries. Restrictions were tightened as their loyalty became suspect, and many were forced to emigrate. The percentage of Christians in the population of the Muslim lands declined sharply during and after the crusading period.

The religious duty to protect the *dhimmí* is attributed to Caliph 'Umar. He instructed his successor to protect the *ahl al-dhimmi* (the people of the contract): "I charge him with upholding the protection of God and the protection of His Messenger (Muhammad); that he should observe the compact made with them and fight those that attack them and not overburden them with taxes beyond their capacity." Muslim juristic opinion held that the *jizya* payment represented a fee in return for physical protection and residential rights. The Jews of Islam had in the *jizya* a surer guarantee of protection from anti-Jewish hostility than their brethren in the West.

In reality, the regulations of the 'Umar Pact were intended not so much to exclude as to reinforce the hierarchical distinction between Muslims and non-Muslims within a single social order. *Dhimmi* groups preserved their unique individual status in society by observing their required distinctive aspects. Overall, non-Muslims were to remain in their place. They were to avoid any act, particularly any religious act, that might challenge the superior rank of the Muslims or Islam. Non-Muslims were organized on a religious basis and permitted religious/legal autonomy under their own leaders.

Though most hierarchical distinctions commonly applied in economic activities, they also extended to cultural interchange, service in the government bureaucracy, and the medical profession. The presence of Jews and Christians in marginal situations — although there were exceptions — within the hierarchy of Islam was a permanent feature of the social order. In those situations distinctive dress (*ghiyār*) let everyone know who was a Muslim and who was a non-Muslim. Generally speaking, hierarchy more than theology, motivated Islamic law.

Employment of non-Muslims in Islamic administration began in earnest at the time of the Muslim conquests. It was expedient to allow natives to continue administering the conquered territories rather than replace them with Arabs who found honor in fighting rather than state service.

The rabbis had no real objection to Islamic beliefs, finding them not unlike Judaism since Islam was also a religion of law. Intermarriage between male Muslims and female *dhimmís* is permitted with Qur'ânic sanction on the presumption that, as master in the relationship, the Muslim husband would determine the religion of all children. Islamic law requires the husband of a mixed marriage to permit his non-Muslim wife to observe her religious rituals and to pray inside their house; it admonishes him not to prompt her to break the Sabbath or eat forbidden food. The children, of course, must be brought up Muslim.

In addition, Muslims and Jews shared popular religious practices. Both peoples honored biblical figures like the prophets Ezekiel and Ezra, whose tombs were pilgrimage sites for both faiths.

Persecutions

Although periods of unrest were not the norm in the Arab Diaspora, demonstrations, persecutions, and, rarely, expulsions against *dhimmí* groups occurred occasionally during Islam's classical centuries. The first recorded instance of overt pressure against the *dhimma* was by an Abbasid, Caliph al-Mutawakkil, in 850. He ordered the *dhimma* to wear honey-colored outer garments and belts, and he forbade their employment in government offices or in any official business where they might have authority over Muslims. Christians were forbidden to display crosses on Palm Sunday, and Jews were prohibited from chanting in the streets. The caliph also ordered that houses of worship built after the advent of Islam were to be destroyed, and one-tenth of their homes were to be confiscated. All of this was simply a reaction to a *laissez faire* approach to *dhimmi*.

The next episode of overt pressure was the persecution of Christians and Jews in Egypt and Palestine during the reign of the allegedly mad Fatimid Caliph al-Hākim (996-1021), whose arbitrary, erratic, and outlandish acts instilled terror not only in the *dhimmi*, but also in the entire population of Egypt. The persecution began with an order to the *dhimmi* to wear a distinguishing badge on their clothing; what followed was the destruction of synagogues and churches, including the Church of the Holy Sepulcher in Jerusalem in 1009. This event stimulated recruitment for the First Crusade. Contrary to Islamic law al-Hākim also forced *dhimmi* to choose between Islam and expulsion. Many fled although many converted. But al-Hākim is also reported to have permitted any convert, who requested it of him, to return to their original religion.

The most serious persecution experienced by the *dhimmi* in the Muslim controlled countries of the Middle Ages was that of the Berber Almohads beginning in 1140. The Almohads were a militant puritanical sect which turned on both Muslims and non-Muslims. At the time, the Almohads were in control of Muslim territory along the northern shore of Africa east to Egypt. When they swept across the Strait of Gibraltar in 1150, both Jews and Christians were forced to convert or die. Given that choice, and in light of the past history of fair treatment and the relaxation of past demands, most chose conversion. However, some forty years later the Almohads directed renewed persecutions on the descendants of the first generation of forced Jewish converts who, it was correctly suspected, were secretly practicing Judaism.

At this time in Muslim Spain, Christians were uniting to drive back the "Moors" using essentially the same propaganda techniques employed for crusades. An organized "crusade" defeated the Almohads although the Muslim grip on Spain, centered on the City of Grenada, was not finally broken until 1492. But the deeply imbedded Muslims, following centuries of occupation, were not fully expelled from Spanish society for another century.

The Almohad persecution was followed by a fierce persecution in Yemen in 1172, during which the *dhimmis* (essentially all Jews) were forced to convert. This was during the active military reign of Saladin the Great, who had just annexed Yemen to his growing kingdom, and was organizing Arab tribes to retake Jerusalem from the crusaders.

Trading

Traders of Eastern origin appeared on the European scene at a time when commercial exchange over considerable distance was already entrenched in the conquered areas of southwest Asia and North Africa. Prior to that time, Arabs had participated in the caravan trade linking spice-rich southern Arabia with the markets of Egypt, Byzantium, and Syria. Muhammad himself frequented Syria on trading journeys, and Jewish traders living in the Arabian Peninsula were also engaged in trading prior to the Prophetic revelation. Thus, it is not surprising that Islam also asserted a positive attitude toward commerce, and that Jews of the Islamic East were well integrated into the economic life of the larger society during the Golden Years of Islamic domination.

With so much access to world markets, Islamic and Jewish merchants shared the international trade market. By the ninth century, the Islamic world was employing sophisticated instruments of credit. By the beginning of the tenth century, Jewish merchant-bankers were providing loans and other banking and mercantile services to the ruling oligarchy. Through the 12th century when the economy flourished, Jews and Muslims shared the fruits of commerce and banking without concern for economic competition. The development of sophisticated banking services by Jews and Muslims, upheld by legal experts for both and shared by both courts, was a significant step forward in the provision of an infrastructure for a more complex governing system relying on shared investment throughout the world of competing economies. This in turn placed persons of different ethnic backgrounds and religions in an arena in which that effort tended to override individual prejudice. In total, it led to a basic human desire to live in a harmonious society which is emphasized by Muslim philosophers and which is most conducive to strong economic health.

Credit transactions were an integral part of the economy of the Near East. In keeping with the practice of merchants, both Muslims and Jews engaged extensively in these transactions in spite of the appearance of usury. Characteristic of the accommodation of law to economics in Islam, jurists recognized that without such credit arrangements, including deferred payment at a higher price, the economy would be stifled.

Mark Cohen reported the words of an 11th-century Muslim jurist:

> We hold that selling for credit is part of the practice of merchants, and that it is the most conducive means for the achievement of the investor's goal which is profit. And in most cases, profit can only be achieved by selling for credit and not selling for cash.

In the economic transactions between Jews and Muslims, a certain measure of trust and familiarity were presumed, as well as a common respect for religious law, a property that reinforced Muslim confidence in Jewish honesty in economic affairs. The image of the "honest Jew" embodied in the Arabic notion of *sharia,* underlay the justice and the honesty of the entire realm of Jewish-Muslim inter-ethnic intercourse. Hay Gaon (d. 1038), who was considered to be chief justice of the entire Jewish population of Islam at the time, wrote: These Muslims treat us with great solicitude and protection. Compare this to financial dealings in the European countries at that time and note the greater societal benefits that accrued to the Muslims.

Medical Advances

Medical textbooks had been few and precious when the cultural renaissance began in Muslim Spain. Like all physicians and scientists of the time, Jewish doctors were moving toward a fully rational therapy. Medical knowledge acquired from Arabic texts placed Jewish physicians in the forefront of medicine, and their services were used frequently by royalty. Jewish physicians were found in Arab society in numbers disproportionate to the Jewish presence in the population at large. They formed part of the interdenominational circle of physicians working in state hospitals and adjoining Muslim courts. Muslim admiration for Jewish men of medicine abounds in Arabic biographical dictionaries. These encounters provided considerable social opportunity for Jewish-Muslim and Jewish and Christian intellectuals.

A Spanish Jewish scientist, Abraham ibn Ezra, recounts how Arabs received basic mathematical science from India at a time when Muslims deplored the "profane sciences." An Indian scholar was introduced to the king and then taught the Arabs the basis of numbers, the so-called Arabic numerals, 1 through 9 plus 0 (*sifr* in Arabic). The shape of the numbers differed from time to time with the present form evolving in Spain. The zero, of course, was the key to the system, making tens, hundreds, thousands, etc., conveniently possible. The system spread rapidly after appearing in Christian Spain in 966.

Astronomy and astrological instrumentation began with the arrival of Eastern astronomical tables in Andalusia in 822. These tables had been translated from Greek into Syriac (an Aramaic language) and then into Arabic. At essentially the same time, Indian astronomical tables were received as well. In the 12th century, a generation of Jewish rabbis was discovering an interest in scientific matters, particularly astronomy, because of its relationship to theological issues and to practical needs of the religious calendar. Astronomy at the time consisted of three interrelated elements: instrumentation (primarily the astrolabe), astronomical tables, and astronomical or cosmological theory (the origins and workings of the universe) without which further refinements of the system could not take place.

A Jewish-Indian pair translated the astrological tables, and Arab scholars then took an interest and began refining this information. All parties quickly came to the realization that they needed to determine how the basic information was obtained through observation. At this point astrolabe construction was mastered from treatises written in Arabic, Hebrew, and Latin, the earliest such by an Iraqi Jew about 800. In 827 the Caliph al-Mamun had his astrologers calculate the circumference of the earth by empirical means using an astrolabe. They determined it to be 23,200 miles; they were off by only 7 percent. Work on the astrolabe was then taken up by numerous eager hands on all sides devising ever more accurate instruments. At the end of the Middle Ages, Joseph Vecinho, a student of the great Jewish astronomer Abraham Zacuto, provided an improved astrolabe that the Portuguese used in the their voyages of discovery. By 1300 Europeans had devised mathematical methods of preparing extremely accurate maps.

Dominicus Gundissalinus, a Spanish canon deeply involved in the translation movement, gives the following reasons why astronomy was important circa 1150.

> To know why the Most High God rules the world, to know the orders of spiritual angels, to know the law according to which the heavenly spheres are ordered; this knowledge can only be attained if one knows astronomy, and none can acquire the science of astronomy without a knowledge of arithmetic and geometry.

Christian theology for better or worse, was now linked to the new science.

Convivencia

In the 12th century, many Europeans came to Spain, drawn by the knowledge available there. The Church up to this time was the repository for scientific knowledge since it had been, historically, the forerunner of scientific and technical exploration. But, the major advances in the hard sciences spurred by the work of Arab, Jewish and Christian scholars in Spain began to push the Church toward new – and not always welcome – ideas.

The period of "the *convivencia*," a term today's scholars use to describe intellectual and social tolerance in Spain during this period, remains today the greatest achievement of the three monotheistic faiths working cooperatively to better God's world for all. The depth of their intellectual collaboration is remarkable and has probably never been matched in any other period in history. Some of the outcomes of the *convivencia*, likely the greatest scientific undertaking since the time of the Greeks, at least in the western world, were the development of a scientific vernacular, the move away from a religious viewpoint to a secular stance, and the separation of disciplines based on mathematical models. From a Jewish viewpoint, it was the initiative by Jewish scholars to undertake scientific studies for the first time, a harbinger of future vocations. In total, the *convivencia* was a new epistemology that would turn the best minds of the world to the search for universal reality.

From a practical viewpoint, the European countries now had a new base of scientific knowledge which made the Age of Exploration possible and provided a foundation for the scientific revolution and the industrial revolution.

Notes for Chapter Seven

Good detailed history of Islam is available in Mark R. Cohen, *Under Crescent and Cross: The Jews in the Middle Ages*, Princeton University Press, 1994. Karabell, Zachary *Peace Be Upon You*, Alfred A. Knopf, 2007.

The early years of Islam and Muhammad can be understood from Annemarie Schimmel's book *Islam: An Introduction*, State University of New York Press, 1992 also gives a history of Islam to the present. See also Seyyed, Hossein Nasr, *Ideals and Realities of Islam*, Aquarian, 1994 Evans, Helen C *Byzantium: Faith and Power* (1261-1557), The Metropolitan Museum of Art and Yale University Press, 2004.

QUR'ÂN

The sacred book of Islam, Qur'ân, is discussed by Hossen Nasr Seyyed, *Ideas and Realities of Islam*, Aquarian, 1994. There are a number of Qur'ân English translations, including one written by Dr. Muhammad Muhsi Khan, *The Noble Qur'ân*, Darussalam, 1999.

CHRISTIANITY AND JUDAISM VERSUS ISLAM

Vryonis, Speros Jr. *The Decline of Medieval Hellenism in Asia Minor and the Process of Islamization from the Eleventh through the Fifteenth Century*, 1971

LIFE OF NON-MUSLIMS

Masters, Bruce, *Christians and Jews in the Ottoman Arab World*, Cambridge, 2001.

CONVIVENCIA

An excellent book on this famous episode in monotheistic history is from Mann, Vivian B., Glick, Thomas F., Dodds, Jerrilynn D. *Convivencia: Jews, Muslims and Christians in Medieval Spain*, George Braziller in Association with the Jewish Museum New York, 1992. Expensive, hefty book.

INTERESTING OTHERS

For an interesting story of the building of the Dome of the Rock see the semi-historical *The Rock* by Kanan, Makiya, Pantheon Books, 2001.

Untermeyer Louis, *Rubáiyát of Omar Khayyám*, Random House, 1947
Brown, Nancy Marie, *The Abacus and the Cross: The Story of the Pope Who Brought the Light of Science to the Dark Ages*, Basic Books, 2010.
Noble, David F. *The Religion of Technology: The Divinity of Man and the Spirit of Invention*, Alfred A. Knopf, 1998.

Chapter Eight
The Ottoman Diaspora

Lo, I am with you always means when you look for God,
God is in the look of your eyes,
in the thought of looking, nearer to you than your self,
or things that have happened to you.
There's no need to go outside.

        Rumi (1207-1273)

As the Jews were being expelled from Europe in the early years of the 15th century, a major change was about to occur as Muslim power in the personage of the Seljuk Turks infiltrated the eastern reaches of Byzantium. When their presence first became known, they were recruited as mercenaries by the Arab Abbasid caliphate in its recurrent wars with Byzantium. By the 11th century, the Seljuks had replaced the Abbasids as the primary threat to the Byzantines. In 1071, they annihilated the Byzantine army thus opening all of Anatolia and leaving the Turks just a few hundred miles from Constantinople.

The Seljuk tribes were reorganized in the late 14th century and the early 15th century under Osman I and quickly moved westward. During that time the Turks became Sunni Muslims. As they approached Constantinople, some western Christians suggested that aid might be forthcoming if the emperor was willing to pay homage to the pope. This offer was immediately rejected. The ultimate blow to the Byzantine Empire came on May 29, 1453 when Emperor Constantine XI died fighting as the standard of Islam rose above the Byzantine capital.

Ottoman Administration

The Ottomans, having encountered the crusaders militarily during their conquest of Anatolia, were not partial to Christians. They seized Christian churches and converted them to mosques, and forced Christian congregations into mean quarters without priestly leadership. Bishops were prohibited from visiting their churches; the metropolitan was permitted only a small chapel and space in an old home. It was payback time for the Muslims who in some cities were intent on killing or driving out Christian clerics. All though local authorities were forced to intervene, Christians were still deported from some cities or enslaved by Turks or Jews and replaced by Muslims. As a final reminder of which religion now prevailed in Byzantine, Arnott writes, "[G]old coins were minted with Arabic legends carrying a reproach to Christians: There is no god but God alone. He has no companion.

This event marked the transition of Islam from a religion for, primarily, Arabic tribesmen to one encompassing warriors of Turkish/Mongol extraction as well. The repetitive and destructive nature of the Turkish conquests seriously undermined the influence of the Eastern Orthodox Church which was reduced to extreme poverty through the confiscation of the vast majority of its properties, revenues and buildings. In its weakened condition the adherents of the leaderless Christian communities became easy targets for religious conversion.

When Constantinople came under the sway of the Ottoman Sunni Muslim Turks, the majority Christian religious groups were the Greek Orthodox Church (subdivided by languages) and the Eastern Rite Church subdivided into: Alexandrian, Antiochian, Byzantine, Chaldean, and Armenian. Most observers believed that the Ottomans would destroy the Orthodox Church in Constantinople much as they had done in Anatolia. But the sultan, having recently crushed a Crusade on the shores of the Black Sea in 1444, decided that he needed the Greek Church to oppose the strength of the Latin Church in order to insure that Rome would not continue its propensity for crusading.

The conquering Ottomans imposed the same restrictions on the non-Muslim population as the Arab Muslims had done, but applied them more strictly. The "Umar Pact" was enforced even to the point of requiring Christians to remove bells from their (remaining) churches so as not to make an outward religious display, to silence the hourly striking of their clocks, to adopt distinctive dress, to refrain from building churches, monasteries or dwellings for celibate priests, and to halt the repair of ruined churches. Ottoman documents lumped all the various Christian sects together as *kefere* "infidels" whereas Jews were simply referred to as Jews (*Yahudiler*). This was indicative of the favoritism which Jews enjoyed in the Ottoman Empire.

Under Selim I (1512-1520) the Ottomans turned their attention back to Europe and pressed on through Greece, Hungary, and the Balkans, finally reaching the gates of Vienna in 1529 where resided the ultimate prize: the crown of the Holy Roman Emperor. However, as winter approached, they were forced to withdraw to Buda, Hungary. (This was the time of the Little Ice Age.) The high water mark for the Ottoman Empire was 1683, but then Europe finally united to repel a second Sunni attempt to take Vienna.

Jewish Immigration

During the reign of Constantine VI (780-797), Byzantine Ephesus was a center of international trade where Jews carried on commercial ventures using Attaleia, the principle naval base and commercial station in southern Anatolia. Jews took a prominent role in the valuable trade markets between Constantinople and the Far East.

Ashkenazi Jews (principally German diaspora) having then been expelled from European countries began immigrating into the Ottoman Empire in large numbers in 1421 following their expulsion from the Rhineland and Bavaria and, in 1453, from Crete following the conquest of Constantinople. Most came to the renamed city of Istanbul to join Jews forcibly relocated there by the Ottomans. They spoke *Yiddish* a combination of middle German with Slavic touches picked up while in Poland. The great change in the fortune of the Ottoman Jews occurred when Iberian Sephardim (principally Spanish) fled to the Ottoman Empire in the last 20 years of the 15th century and the first quarter of the 16th century, during the period of forced conversions in Spain and Portugal (the inquisition). Initially, the Sephardim, who spoke a Jewish-Spanish language known as *Ladino* or *Judezmo*, preferred to settle primarily in Salonika (Old Thessalonica) which in 1478 housed no Jews. By the early 1500s, Jews constituted the largest religious group, constituting about sixty percent of the population of Salonika. There they found a secure haven with their European Jewish co-religionists.

As the situation in Spain became untenable for even the more secure Sephardim, their destination of choice became Istanbul. They were particularly attracted to the capital city, because the Jewish community there was the largest and most prosperous in the burgeoning Ottoman Empire. Istanbul in the 16th century became a haven for Jewish refugees. What had made Istanbul particularly attractive was its standing as the economic capital of the Empire. Perhaps even more important, it had by far the biggest and most affluent Jewish community in the empire. The Jews of the city could be counted on to assist newcomers who flocked there.

As Ottoman power rose and gradually expanded in western Anatolia and the Balkans during the late 14th century and the first half of the 15th century, Ottoman leaders came to regard Jews, particularly Sephardim, as a productive urban component politically more reliable than the resident Christian Greeks and Slavs who, as military opponents, had been subjugated by the invading Turks. The Ottomans, therefore, preferred to repopulate and rebuild the important urban centers that fell under their control with the conscripted aid of Jews. The forced relocation of Jews and others was undoubtedly difficult for them. However, a guaranteed job awaited along with financial aid. Eventually those who were relocated prospered.

Not surprisingly, resident Greeks were hostile to the Jews, and became more so as the Greeks were replaced in important positions. Jews, of course, recognized the growing hostility of the Greeks and were careful to live in Muslim communities in order not to provoke them. Even so, the Jews were not completely isolated and could expect contempt, verbal abuse, and occasional assault from the Christian population. However, because of the strong alliance Jews had with the Ottomans, they were able to protect their interests.

Jewish communities maintained internal solidarity and extensive political networks. With many employed directly in government positions, they could, as a last resort, bring their case to the central authorities at Istanbul. During the period 1566-1579, for example, Joseph Nasi, a Sephardic Jew, was the "friend and confidant of the sultan." The Sephardic community was also quietly active in United States history, and prominent in government and law and remains so today. (See, for example, Hyam Salomon, financier of the American Revolution, Supreme Court Justice Benjamin Cardoza, and Emma Lazarus, author of "The New Colossus," the poem inscribed beneath the Statute of Liberty.)

In the second half of the 15th century, Jews came to dominate the internal commerce of Istanbul rising as well to importance in international trade. Many then moved on to play major roles in the government-controlled aspects of the empire, including the operation of the custom houses and docks, the minting, distribution and recall of coinage, and the collection of taxes through the award of "tax farming" contracts. Tax farming means contracting ("farming out") with private bidders to collect state income. This method of tax collecting is intended to maximize revenue through competitive bidding.

Under the tax farming system, bidders agreed to pay the bid sum regardless of the actual yield from the revenue source, thereby transferring risk and effort from the government to the tax farmer. The tax farmer is burdened not only with the labor of collecting, but is also responsible (often in advance) for the full contracted sum, even if the revenue source fails to yield it. But, if the revenue yield is higher than the contracted amount, the tax farmer benefits from the surplus which can be considerable. Thus, tax farming is a high-risk/high-yield investment requiring substantial resources to qualify as a legitimate bidder. Jewish entrepreneurs formed partnerships to outbid rivals. And, critically important, successful Jewish bidders could usually count on the government to ensure that the collectors were not hindered in their work.

Prior to their expulsion from Spain and Portugal, Iberian Jews were prominent in international commerce and banking. Those who chose not to convert to Christianity usually were unable to depart with most of their resources. However, those Jews who chose to convert to Christianity (*conversos*), and those who were forced to convert (*Marranos*), weathered the early Spanish expulsions (probably by placing their capital in remote friendly banks) and then, upon departing, retrieving their capital. Once safely in Istanbul or Salonika, and with freedom to pursue their profession, to the greater good of the Ottomans, they forged wider commercial and banking networks and became wealthy. It appears that within twenty to thirty years following the Ottoman conquest of Istanbul in 1453, Jews were able to dominate the tax farming and monetary systems, while capturing a considerable share of the capital's major financial and commercial activity which had been dominated previously by Greeks and Europeans.

In 1493, about forty years after the invention of movable type, the brothers David and Samuel Nahmias founded a Hebrew printing press. In 1494, they published *Arba'ah Turim* (*The Four Columns*), the well-known code of liturgical and societal conduct written by Jacob ben Asher. It was the first book ever published in the Ottoman Empire. European Jews also brought their knowledge of European sciences, medicine, economics, and languages as well as new technologies and methods of production. They were also conversant, in general, with the ways of Europe. The Ottomans utilized this experience to exploit mineral resources and to manufacture textiles, arms, munition, and other products.

Throughout the 16th century and the early decades of the 17th, *marranos* and *conversos* flocked to the Ottoman Empire where they almost invariably returned openly to Judaism. Indeed, they had little choice since their relatives who had been expelled before them were already well settled in commercial enterprises and Jewish religious centers. Place of origin was crucial in the initial formation of Jewish congregations because they were religious homes for families that were related to each other by kinship and marriage or by business interests, friendship, and mutual acquaintances. These immigrants had much more education and experience than most of the resident Sephardim, having had access to the great body of information developed during the studies in Spain after the Muslim conquests. Travelers to the Ottoman Empire from Europe in the mid-16th century were under the impression that Jewish physicians were the most numerous and knowledgeable, and that they dominated the field of medicine.

The most important reason for the ascendency of the Sephardim appears to be their higher educational and cultural standards. In Salonica (or Salonika), for example, the Jewish community maintained a Great Talmud Torah, a religious primary school where hundreds of students were enrolled, many of whom received free daily meals and clothing. In addition to rabbinical institutions, the community also supported a school for secular studies where medicine, astronomy, and natural sciences were taught. And, they introduced new forms of the performing arts. The most distinguished Jewish physicians, scientists, entrepreneurs, and courtiers were Sephardic.

The influx of so many prominent Jewish scholars from different countries representing different traditions and schools, the contacts among them, and the freedom to travel and publish without hindrance, gave birth to a new and highly motivated Jewish intellectual class. These communities were among the most important centers of Jewish scholarship in the world, along with those in Poland and Lithuania; they would remain so until the European Enlightenment in the late 18th century. In sheer numbers, the Jewish emigration to the Ottoman Empire in the 15th and 16th centuries constituted the most important demographic shift in the Jewish diaspora up to that time.

The great majority of Ottoman Jews, however, were not wealthy bankers, tax farmers, or entrepreneurs, but they were an important part of urban life, practicing many occupations, professions, and crafts, including food-processing. Slaughterers, butchers and meat processors, cheese- and wine-makers, millers and bakers were all regulated by the dietary laws. Although for the most part, they served the needs of the Jewish community, some of their Muslim and Christian neighbors chose to buy from them as well. This was in sharp contrast to their prior life in Germany where they were not permitted to own and operate a small business that catered to the resident population. The manufacture of textiles, and related crafts, was another traditional Jewish occupation which was controlled by *halakhah*, for example, against mixing wool with linen. A surreptitious reminder not to marry out of the faith.

The Jewish administration of the Ottoman government, gave them inside information to its financial workings. If it occurs, for example, to one branch of the government that there is a better way of administering a particular department, then discussion could be held among well placed Jewish administrators to foresee this advantage and then discuss it with the government. At the same time, it could be advantageous to the Jewish administrators via an increase in salary, a placement for one of their up-and-coming young men, or greater access to governmental power centers. Over an extended time period, the Jewish administration tightened and controlled the operation of the government to Ottoman advantage and Jewish enrichment. Here they also learned how to use the brain power of their community and train the coming generation. A very important step in carrying out the covenant. And, it might be added, bedeviling would-be competitors. The Jewish administers were so effective that in a single generation they took over the economic control of the empire when they were less than one percent of the population. In the 17th century, Ottomans could look back with satisfaction on a record of Jewish cooperation of more than two centuries, and an empire that was among the most advanced and well-administered in the world. Therefore, they were pleased to provide additional Jewish refugees with a safe haven, expecting in return continued Jewish cooperation in developing "their" Empire. The domination of Ottoman commerce and industry by the Jews was extraordinary considering the Jewish component of the population. By the early 16th century, Muslims accounted for 92 percent of the population,

Christians 7.9 percent, and Jews 0.1 percent. By the early 19th century, Muslims were 79.0 percent of the population, Christians accounted for 16.7 percent, Jews 0.4 percent, and others 3.9 percent.

However, native Ottoman Muslim culture should not be overlooked. One of the great Muslim preachers and writers of the Ottoman period was Rumi (1207-1273), who became the leader of a mystical community in Konya. (His name means "from Roman Anatolia,") During his lifetime and for several centuries thereafter, Rumi exercised a great influence upon religion and culture in Anatolian society. The force of his personality drew persons of many faiths to his following. Rumi is said to have converted eighteen thousand infidels in his lifetime. When he died, members of many different communities and nations participated in the funeral arcade, including Christians, Jews, Greeks, Arabs, and Turks. Conforming to their individual customs, they read verses from the Psalms, Pentateuch, Qur'ân, and Gospels. The head note poem of this chapter celebrates Rumi's empathetic feelings about monotheism.

Jewish Life in the Ottoman Empire

The Ottomans incorporated Palestine into their empire in 1516. For religious Jews, this was an enticement to settle there. For other Jews, it was an opportunity to make a pilgrimage to the Temple site. The Ottomans raised no barriers to Jewish return to Jerusalem. Süleyman the Magnificent (reigned 1520-1566 at the Empire's apex) greatly impressed Jewish emigrants to Palestine by rebuilding the city walls between 1536 and 1542, thereby making a commitment to the restoration of Jerusalem. Quietly and without any outward objections from Muslims or Christians, Jews began what would become a free emigration to the Holy Land that continued so long as the Ottoman Empire existed. In the late 19th century, when the Empire was crumbling, the first *aliyahs* were beginning, and the Arab population of Palestine was becoming uneasy. However, longtime residents of the Empire continued to be admitted to Palestine. But those who took up short-term residence in other communities of the Empire in hopes of immigrating to Palestine, were, as a rule, not permitted to do so.

The majority of the most respected rabbis and legal scholars in the Ottoman Empire in the 16th and 17th centuries appear to have been of Sephardic origin. The ancient processes by which *halakhah* disputes in Jewish communities were resolved was used continually by them during this period. The *responsa* literature of the rabbinate in the Ottoman Empire is vast. In major western Jewish centers during the same time period, there were few compilers of *responsa*, and their compositions remained unpublished. Thus Jewish law and Jewish legal literature blossomed as a result of daily *halakhah* decision-making by the Sephardic rabbinate in the Ottoman Empire during the 17th century.

Judaism was not without its controversies during classical Islamic times. Two main Jewish factions, the Rabbinates (followers of the rabbis) and the Karaites (Torah only, no Talmud) dueled over Torah exegesis. The antecedents of the Karaites can be traced back to Anan ben David in the 8th century. He held that the Bible alone must be their guide, no oral law. He was a descendant of a family of exilarchs, and a learned leader of Babylonian Jewry. Ben David organized a dissident group when, it was rumored, he was passed over for the position of exilarch in favor of his brother. His followers were intellectuals who formulated what was to become the basic Karaite tenets and began preaching them. As outcasts, this group did not survive; but their basic concepts were revived by Benjamin ben Moses Nahawendi (c. 830). At that time, they adopted their name, which derives from the Hebrew *Benei Mikra,* (Sons of the Scripture).

The basis of Karaism was the utter rejection of rabbinical writings and the perfection of Tanakh, the body of which was essentially closed circa 200 CE. The adherents were scholars of distinction in biblical law, Hebrew word derivation and meaning, and philosophy. They made important contributions to biblical exegesis. Their detailed understanding and analysis of Torah was directed at "correcting" the interpretations of *halakhah* by the Rabbinates. The long list of differences included fine calendar distinctions such as dates and extensions of holiday observances, nonobservance of Hanukkah (because it was not mentioned in Torah), variations in food laws (permitted mixing of meat and milk if of different species), different methods of ritual slaughter, shoeless prayer in kneeling position with men and women together, markedly different order of service, marriage within the sect only, etc. These distinctions prevented Karaites from marrying outside their sect or sharing meals with Rabbinates.

The intense struggle between the Rabbinates and Karaites was touched off by an attack written by the Saadia Gaon (ca. 905), the future head of the Sura Academy in Babylonia and the source of Judaic wisdom at the time. The Karaites took root in Jerusalem, then under Arab Islamic rule, where the law of the sect and a book of the non-legal aspects of Torah was written. Here also, a refutation of Saadia Gaon's letter was undertaken. The center of Karaism gradually shifted to Europe and, after the First Crusade, to Constantinople. Karaism lived on in Byzantium where the most important Hebrew document of the sect was written— a theological summary (*Eshkol ha-Kofer*). Here also Aaron ben Joseph wrote a classical commentary on the Bible, *Sefer ha-Mivhar,* and Aaron ben Elijah ("the Karaite Maimonides") wrote *Gan Eden* (literally "Garden of Eden") a systematic codex of Karaite law and beliefs. Karaite communities continued to exist in later Jewish history in Egypt, the Crimea, and Lithuania. Today there are but thirty thousand Karaites worldwide.

The Karaites commissioned what are considered today to be the two most authentic ancient copies of the Hebrew Bible in existence. The oldest is the Aleppo Codex, written about the year 930 CE in Tiberius. It was the work of the most esteemed Masoretic scribes. It resided originally in Jerusalem, then was smuggled into Egypt. In the 14th century, it was moved to the ancient synagogue in Aleppo, Syria. At the time of the 1947 war between Israel and the surrounding Arab countries, it was set afire and a portion destroyed. The remainder was spirited out of Syria and resides today at The Shrine of the Book in Jerusalem. The other venerated codex was commissioned by the Karaites of Cairo in the year 1010 and prepared by a Masorete. It is known today as the famous Leningrad Codex.

The Leningrad Codex had a rather involved history of which very little is known until it was acquired in the early 19th century by a member of the strong Karaite community in the Crimea. When the Russians conquered the Crimea, they favored the Karaites and did not impose on them the rules for all other Jews. As a result, the Karaites of Crimea achieved great wealth and position. As an adjunct to their studies they collected a vast array of ancient Hebrew documents which they later sold to the Museum in St. Petersburg, including the Codex where it resides today as part of the largest collection of Jewish manuscripts in the world. The primary source for the Hebrew Bible upon which most biblical translations are based today is the *Biblia Hebraica Stuttgartensia*, which is published in Stuttgart, Germany and maintained in Jerusalem. It is based on an exquisite copy of the Leningrad Codex made by Israeli experts and such archeological finds that lead to biblical changes.

Decline of Empire

The great Ottoman expansion in the 15th and 16th centuries resulted in the formation of a vast administrative-military establishment. In order to protect their acquisitions in central and eastern Europe, the Ottomans then engaged in reclaiming Christian territory in the Balkans, negotiated a pact with the French in the late 16th century to keep pressure on the west side of the Hapsburg Empire. One outcome of this treaty was the reopening of Roman Catholic missionary work in the Ottoman Empire. The Jesuit order, founded in 1540, took advantage of this opportunity in 1603.

From the beginning of their reign, the Ottomans had looked with indifference on religion *per se*. They did not discriminate by religion or race, but, as has been shown, they used religion as a political weapon. That the Jesuits were openly seeking converts to Latin Catholicism was of small moment to the Ottomans. The success of the Jesuit movement in the Ottoman Empire grew out of their schools which were very popular, although conversions were not numerous. Subsequently, in light of the baptismal controversy in 1755, the pope issued a decree in 1773 suppressing the Jesuit order. However, as control of the Empire slackened, missionaries and evangelicals began to re-enter from the West, and with them, demagogues who would spark enmity between Muslims and Jews.

Following the Muslim rout at Vienna in 1683, the army became a burden on the Ottoman economy. As the expansion slowed down and opportunities for career advancement became limited, the administrative and military establishment became more conservative and resistant to change. At the same time, Europe's rising population and expanding industrial production created a growing demand for grains and raw materials. The high prices these commodities commanded on European markets resulted in a massive commodity flight from the Ottoman Empire to Europe. The resulting shortages in basic foodstuffs and raw materials back home stymied industry and caused severe inflation.

The prominent position that Ottomans held in international trade and commerce began to erode as important new centers developed between Western Europe and the Atlantic seaboard of the burgeoning North American continent. The Ottomans played no significant part in this trade. The wealth from commerce began to flow toward Christian Europe. Trade routes between the Middle East and the Far East, which had been the mainstay of Muslim commerce for almost a millennium, became less significant in world terms, and they too began to fall under European control. Eventually, the internal trade routes of the Empire also were affected. Obviously, these changes began to choke off the Ottoman's income stream and diminish the influence their banks and corporations enjoyed in world-wide trade and economics. As resources diminished, the capability to compete did so as well. Then, finally, the Sephardic knowledge that was once cutting edge became obsolete, and meaningful contemporary education was best sought in Europe.

As maintaining a sufficient cash flow became a pressing concern for the Empire, the government moved to increase taxes and sell a number of state revenue sources to private enterprises in return for cash. Like all governments past and present, it had increased the amount of its currency beyond the value of governmental income and holdings, giving rise to inflation, which had a devastating effect. The result was unrest, disorder, and in some cases outright rebellion. With the military suffering along with civilians, containment of disorder was not a popular task for soldiers. It was now apparent to the world that the Ottoman Empire was sliding downhill at a rapidly increasing pace. (Note: There must be a lesson for America in the preceding paragraphs.)

The Ottoman experience was the first in which highly educated Jews were to test their skills. God had promised to reward the Jews for performing the dictates of the covenant.

> *Remember it is the Lord your God who gives you the power to get wealth, in fulfillment of the covenant that He made on oath with your fathers, as is still the case.* (Deut. 8:18)

The history of the Jewish experience in Islam, as written in the 19th century, typically painted an optimistic picture of a Muslim-Jewish symbiosis in the medieval period and contrasted with the dismal record of Christian-Jewish treatment in Europe. On reflection, it can be said that the most attractive aspect of Jewish life in the Ottoman Empire was the unprecedented measure of freedom they enjoyed. Jews were left to practice their religion without fear of persecution, permitting them to lead "normal lives," and many thrived.

Several conclusions become self-evident from the study of Ottoman Jewry. The emigration of thousands of skilled financiers, artisans, and merchants from the Iberian Peninsula in the 15th and 16th centuries, and their support by the Ottoman government, built a solid Muslim-Jewish symbiosis until the 19th century. This close cooperation drove a successful economic expansion of great strength for more than four hundred years or twenty generations. Here the Jews learned how to use the brain power of their community and train the coming generations. A very important step in carrying out the covenant.

However, the beneficial relationship between Muslims and Jews that had existed for fourteen centuries has today, essentially, ended. Although this relationship seems to have deteriorated over the past fifty years or so, it actually began to decay about a century before in conjunction with the decline of the Ottoman Empire. The opening cracks in the facade of the Empire permitted anti-Judaism to be introduced by Christian priests and translators throughout the old countries of the Empire. Gradually as the Jews became dis-empowered they moved back to Europe, to the Americas, and to Palestine.

NOTES TO CHAPTER 8

A number of good books are available to study Jewish life in the Ottoman Empire.

Masters, Bruce Christians and Jews in the Ottoman Arab World, Cambridge, 2001.
Levy, Avigdor *The Jews of the Ottoman Empire*, The Darwin Press, 1994
Karabell, Zachary *Peace Be Upon You,* Alfred A, Knopf, 2007.

OTTOMAN ADMINISTRATION

Darling, Linda T. Revenue-Raising and Legitimacy Tax Collecting and Finance Administration in the Ottoman Empire (1560-1660), Brill, 1996

JEWISH IMMIGRATION

Barnavi, Eli *A Historical Atlas of the Jewish People*, Schocken Books, 1992

JEWISH LIFE

Meek, H.A. *The Synagogue,* The Phaidon Press, 1995. A beautiful book

OTHER

Barks, Coleman, et al, *The Essential Rumi*, HarperSanFrancisco, 1995.

Chapter Nine
The Enlightenment

Be warned not to change your Jewish names, speech, and
clothing — God forbid ... Never say: "Times have changed!"
We have an old Father — praised be His name — who has
never changed and never will change ... The order of prayer
and synagogue shall remain forever as it has been up to now,
and no one may presume to change anything of its structure.

Rabbi Moses Sofer (1762-1839)

In the late 18th century, times were beginning to change for Jews.
Their ideal diaspora in the Ottoman Empire and the comfortable relationship
with the Arabs were beginning to crumble. The opportunities for using their
entrepreneurship skills were back in Christian Europe. It was the dawn of the
Enlightenment, the reflection of which in the Jewish community was to
become known as the *haskala*. It began for the Jews in Germany in 1781, with
the distribution of Prussian State Councilor Wilhelm Dohm' treatise, *Concerning
the Amelioration of the Civil Status of the Jews*.

An early advocate of the *haskala* movement was Moses Mendelssohn
(1729-1786) philosopher, grandfather of Felix Mendelssohn, friend to Christian
Wilhelm von Dohm, and translator of the Hebrew Bible into German using
Hebrew letters. At this time, the majority of German Jews still spoke Yiddish;
with this translation, they became acquainted with High German. Mendelssohn
was a devoted, observant Jew, and remained so while advocating that Jews
embrace the *haskala* movement. His objective was to transform the Jews into a
people in tune with modern times but untempted by assimilation.

It was generally believed in Europe at this time that the Jews were
inferior because of their breeding, or as a result of their confinement during the
Diaspora. Mendelssohn was an obvious exception to this theory because of his
learning and refinement. The quandary that arose in the minds of the
enlightened in Europe was "Why should a man of such achievements remain a
practicing Jew?" The example that Mendelssohn presented to the Gentile
world was instrumental in bringing about the belief that Jews should have the

opportunity to participate in the "benefits" of the new learning without the necessity of converting to Christianity.

Mendelssohn was instrumental in bringing the long alienation of the Jews to a resounding end at the beginning of the 19th century, when the equality of all humankind (at least the white, civilized, male kind) was proclaimed throughout Europe, Russia, and the New World. Under the axioms of the enlightenment, proponents were obliged to offer political equality to all subjects including the Jews. The Jews who adopted this movement were called the *maskilim*. But one of the pathways of assimilation that tempted wealthy younger Jews was religious conversion. Conversion among wealthy younger Jews became so common around the time of Mendelssohn's death that Jewish community leaders became alarmed. They tried to work out a program that would preserve prayers in Hebrew, but conversion continued in growing numbers.

There were many who were more than a little uneasy about the assimilation of Jews into German society. From the start in 1781, this debate was as much about theology as about universal citizenship. Bringing Jews into a predominately Christian society was sure to give rise to conflict with Jewish purity rules and days of religious observation. This fundamental point was brought up by a Christian who was not a friend of Judaism.

Johann David Michaelis (1717-1791) wrote a forty-page critique of Dohm's proposal, in which

> he insisted that Jewish law was designed to preserve
> separatism and would thus stand in the way of integrating the
> Jews into a modern secular state. Do the laws of Moses
> contain anything that would make it impossible or difficult
> for the Jews to be completely naturalized and melt together
> with other peoples? One should think so! Their intention is to
> preserve the Jews as a people separated from all other peoples
> ... and as along as the Jews retain the law of Moses, as long as
> they, for example, do not dine with us ... they will never melt
> together with us... (Hess, *Germans*)

Much as the German Jews of the late 19th century would have liked to shake off this opinion, they were never fully successful in doing so.

Judaism in German Society

Despite Michaelis, German society was opened to the Jews. This sudden release from the ghettos of Europe, which began in The Netherlands in 1796, had a profound impact on Judaism. Deep opposition to centuries of closely regulated religious practice surged to the surface. Unfortunately, the reaction to the old ways overwhelmed not only the hyper-technical aspects of orthodox liturgy, but also in many cases the basic heritage of Judaism — the Mosaic covenant between God and the Chosen People. In the rush to become one with native Germans, the Jewish people modified their age old traditions and synagogue liturgy and in many cases their religion.

Before describing the various modes of Judaism that figured in the *haskala*, let us keep in mind advice from Professor Neusner.

> No single, unitary, linear "Judaism" ever existed, from the very beginnings to the present, defining an "orthodoxy." Quite to the contrary, a variety of Judaisms — Judaic systems, comparing a way of life, world view, and definition of a social entity, an "Israel"— have flourished. Comparison of one Judaic system with another shows that each is autonomous and freestanding. Each Judaic system appeals to its distinctive symbolic structure, explains itself by invoking its particular myth, sets forth its indicative way of life, accounts for its way of life by appealing to its own world view ... Except in the theological context, there never has been a single, orthodox, unitary and harmonious Judaism, against which all 'heterodox' or 'heretical' Judaisms have to be judged. [Therefore], we recognize that each Judaism is to be described in its own terms, meaning in the context of its literature or other enduring evidences. (*Introduction to Rabbinic Literature*)

As pressure increased to conform to normative (read Christian) life, traditional Jewish family life was shattered.

In the first instance is whether a family will continue to remain in synagogue, observe the high holidays, keep kosher, observe the Sabbath, etc., depends on how many generations coexist in one dwelling. The oldest usually keep all rituals. As for the parents of school age children, if the husband maintains a retail business, he usually feels obliged to be there on the Sabbath. His wife wants him at home. She cooks kosher meals but the children may be in prep school or college where their meals are not kosher.

New Judaisms

A grassroots movement in Germany that began early in the 19th century to organize Jewish congregations along liberal lines became the basis for **REFORM JUDAISM**. A prime reform mover was Israel Jacobson (1768-1828), who founded the New Israelite Temple Society in keeping with the Reform movement in 1810. Two other Reform Temples followed soon after, in Berlin (1815) and Hamburg (1819). The use of the word "temple" is important here, since it denoted the abandonment of the hope for return to the Temple in Jerusalem, and the Temple's replacement with congregational "temples."

German was soon the language of choice in synagogue, and rabbinic training evolved along *maskilim* lines. But given all of this, the modernist rabbis who assembled in synods in the 1840s to define Reform Judaism as a new version of the ancient faith, had as their objective, keeping Jews within Judaism and not succumbing to the secular wave or converting to Christianity.

In 1854, R. Isaac Mayer Weiss (1819-1900), a German immigrant to America, transported the new Reform Judaism to Cincinnati where he established Temple B'nai Jeshurun. Eventually, he would organize a nationwide association of synagogues: the Union of American Hebrew Congregations. He would also establish the first Reform seminary in the US, the Hebrew Union College. Those who created these new congregations had a profound sense of belonging to the Jewish community worldwide, even as they deleted the prayer for the return to Zion from their liturgies.

By 1870, Reform Judaism was the dominant religious sect in virtually all German urban centers. The largest, most pompous Reform synagogues were designed in a garish pseudo-Moorish style, a proud reflection of the Jews of the *convivencia*. The style demonstrated a growing hope for a German "religious symbiosis" similar to that enjoyed among Jews, Christians, and Muslims almost a millennium before in Spain. It was also believed that the Spanish decor served to elevate rich Western Jews above their poor "primitive" coreligionists in Poland and Russia who were also their fore bearers. To make this point more emphatically, some families went so far as to invent a distant Sephardic genealogy. To others, particularly native Germans, the synagogue architectural style merely reinforced the "oriental image" of Jews. In the end, however, the temples of the new Jewish secular middle and upper classes were not their true religious homes. Their beliefs drew them to the opera house, the concert hall, and the art museum.

As the *haskala* gradually became a major force in German Jewry, the most brilliant of the early rabbis for reform, Abraham Geiger (1810-1874), was in the vanguard advocating changes in the ways of Judaism. Geiger, a fearless theologian, was the source of a major scandal. In the mid-19th century he delved into Christian texts and analyzed them from a Jewish standpoint. As Susanna Heschel notes: "Christian theologians, long accustomed to writing treatises dissecting the history and nature of Judaism, were unaccustomed to their own religion being placed for scrutiny under the gaze of a Jewish theologian. For them this was the height of insolence and incivility."

Geiger also took a careful look at Judaism in his time, arguing that the traditional ritual system and isolated Jewish communities had been of great importance in past centuries because it defined the Jews in their role of servant people living in exile. But Jews in the modern age of universalism should endorse the unity of humankind and desist from the ancient ways since they hold no hope for the future. Geiger was speaking from the viewpoint of one caught up in the heady times of the rapidly spreading secular movement and a concurrent decline in all religious affiliations in Europe. However, in fairness to Geiger, we should note that he backed off his hard line position later in life, advocating for the retention of Hebrew in liturgy, keeping *Shabbat* on Saturday (instead of Sunday) and continuing the practice of circumcision.

Rabbi Geiger was also an originator of a historical-scientific study of the Jewish people. This work became the basis upon which a group of ordained rabbis, searching for another way to practice Judaism in the religiously diverse European world, found a key. By studying the history of Judaism, they believed they could understand its evolution and determine which aspects of the religion represented core values, and which could be deemed obsolete. This prompted Rabbi Zacharias Frankel (1801-1875), in his position as head of the Jewish Theological Seminary in Breslau, to commission a monumental *History of the Jews*. From the insights derived through that study, he concluded that the historical covenant of the Jewish people with God should be witnessed in their daily lives through family morality, mutual responsibility, social justice, and charity. This statement laid the basis for 'positive-historical Judaism a form known today as **CONSERVATIVE JUDAISM**.

Conservative Judaism, like Reform, does not require its observant families to keep the dietary laws. It does, however, require food purity (refraining from eating foods forbidden in Torah). Frankel also made ancestors into an object of veneration, since respect for one's ancestors tightens the bonds of Judaism and discourages conversion. R. Frankel defined God as the force that links together the chain of Jewish continuity. His critics maintained, quite correctly, however, that the "historical approach" allowed Jews to remake their historical inheritance in their own modern self-image.

Conservative Judaism was introduced into America in the early 20th century by Rabbi Solomon Schechter (1847-1915) with the core belief that Jewish law should be adaptable to contemporary situations by making appropriate changes through rabbinic decision, but considered valid in all other respects. Rabbi Schechter also believed that the ultimate authority in Judaism was the community of all affirming Jews, and that theirs was the voice of God. Schechter's theology reflected the feelings of people who still cared deeply for the inherited traditions that could no longer be sustained in liberal society, but believed that the *halakhah* should continue to be observed as much as possible. Today in America, Conservatism has about as many adherents as Reform, but like Reform it has few adherents in the State of Israel.

Applying the Principles of Reform Judaism adopted May1999 to a comparison with Conservative Judaism's Statement of Principles (1988) highlights points of agreement and areas of disagreement, as well as voids.

Regarding the points of agreement, Reform and Conservative believe that all Jewish people, irrespective of philosophical or religious persuasion, are linked to all other Jews in every age and place by the eternal covenant and by history. Both movements affirm the importance of studying Hebrew and the lifelong study of Torah and, in the case of Conservatives, Talmud as well. Both affirm the necessity to uphold the highest ethical and moral standards in their relationship with others. Both are committed to full religious, human, and civil rights in the State of Israel (meaning recognition of Reform and Conservative synagogues and equality for the native peoples). Both stand for the unique contributions made by the Jews of Israel and those of the Diaspora, and urge that they aid and enrich each other. Both seek to understand and dialogue with other nations and faiths.

The major points of disagreement begin with the difference between the centrality of the synagogue in the life of Reform Judaism and the necessity to consider the revision of sacred obligations as a result of unique contemporary contexts. In fact, Reform Judaism considers rabbinic *halakhah* obsolete and much of Talmud relegated to civil authorities. Nevertheless, the Reform movement continues to rely upon *responsa* (considered opinions of a rabbinic board in response to a congregational or rabbinic inquiry), but rejects it as binding. The thrust of Conservatism is to maintain the law and practices of the past as much as possible and prevent rash revisions. Conservatives have, in the past fifty years, committed to carrying on the rabbinic tradition of preserving and enhancing *halakhah* by making appropriate changes through rabbinic decision in the orthodox model but with the emphasis on historical criticism. Conservatives reject fundamentalism and literalism which do not admit a human component in revelation.

Reform speaks to the inclusion of varied kinds of families, all persons regardless of sexual orientation, those who have converted to Judaism, and the intermarried who strive to create a Jewish home. Reform does not discriminate by gender with regard to clergy nor does Conservatives. However, Conservatives remain split on the blessing of gay unions. Thus, the matter of ordination and same sex blessings is left to the individual seminaries and congregations. Reform voted in June1990 to admit acknowledged, sexually active homosexuals into its rabbinate.

Conservatives speak forthrightly to the necessity of adhering to the covenant obligations and suggest that its fulfillment is vital not only for Israel's continued existence, but for the well-being of all humankind. They speak also of the necessity for every human being to live as if he or she individually has the responsibility to bring about the messianic age. In their May 1999 reaffirmation of their Statement of Principles, Reform declared, "We are obligated to pursue justice and righteousness, and to narrow the gap between the affluent and the poor, to act against discrimination and oppression, to pursue peace, to welcome the stranger, to protect the earth's biodiversity and natural resources, and to redeem those in physical, economic, and spiritual bondage." This statement upholds the principles of the covenant and points the pathway to peace and equality to all inhabitants of this planet.

Conservatives affirm survival of the spirit or soul after death and in the resurrection of the body as well. Reform asserts: We affirm the reality and oneness of God, even as we may differ in our understanding of the Divine presence.

Unfortunately, the statement of principles is not universally applied in either the Reform or Conservative movements. The Conservatives admit as much in the publication of a survey which "illustrates numerous areas in which the majority of Conservative Jews do not uphold the practices and philosophies of the Conservative Movement." To a certain extent, this appears to be true for the Reform movement as well.

The Reform and Conservative communities are an important part of the contemporary Jewish world. They provide a context in which busy, concerned, and observant Jews can continually refresh their understanding of the commandments and the covenant, and to uphold these ideals in their work. Their achievements in perfecting the world and working in strong cooperative relationships with those who profess another religion, are very important in bringing the world to an understanding of its life under God. This fundamental charge to the Jewish people not only honors the covenant, but keeps the Reform and Conservative sects from turning inward.

MODERN ORTHODOX is a movement within the range of Orthodox Judaism that attempts to synthesize traditional observance and values with the broader Jewish community and the secular world. The general term "orthodox" denotes a conservative and ritualistic religious outlook. It was first applied derisively to Jewish conservatives by a liberal polemicist in an article published in1795. This date is coincident with the start of the Enlightenment when change was very much in the air. The designation, however, caught on and a century later became standard when the traditional congregations of Europe formed the "Free Union for the Interests of Orthodox Judaism." In a sense, this was a stubborn stand to uphold the old ways (see header to this chapter). Orthodox Judaism is the least centralized and most diverse movement in Judaism. Within the broad definition of orthodox, there is a wide range of matters on which its various sub-groups diverge.

Modern Orthodox traces its roots to the works of Rabbi Samson Raphael Hirsch (1808-1888) whose pronouncement on the purpose of Judaism is on the cover of this book, and, especially, R. Azriel Hildesheimer (1820-1890). The latter's approach represented "unconditional agreement with the culture of the present day; harmony between Judaism and science; but also unconditional steadfastness in the faith and traditions of Judaism." In the former respect it stands opposed to the ultra-Orthodox. In the U.S., "Centrist Orthodoxy" is the most common form of Modern Orthodoxy. Centrist

Orthodoxy as it is formulated today is the product of the doctrine and philosophy of Joseph Soloveitchik (1903-1993) at Yeshiva University who taught that Judaism believes the world is "very good." He enjoins humankind to engage in *tikkun olam* (the perfection of the world).

Modern Orthodox rabbis have been criticized for attempting to modify *halakhah* and the Codes of Jewish Law in the name of adapting to the needs of the modern world. Within the sect today adherents take pains to distance their "reforms"— those which could be justified as based on the *Shulkhan Arukh* (compilation of Jewish law) and *posekm* (rabbinic interpretation) — from those of the Reform Jewish movement. Ultra-Orthodox, on the other hand, hold that Modern Orthodox is secular in its approach to upholding Jewish beliefs.

The **ULTRA-ORTHODOX** Haredim and Hasidim live in enclaves in both Israel and America. The name "Haredim" comes from the Hebrew root for "tremble" and means "those who tremble in the presence of the Lord." The rabbi is the center of Haredim community life. The Hasidim, "pious ones," live in rabbi-centered communities as well, but are more active in the pursuit of messianism and, to a differing extent, the practice of Kabbalism (see Chapter 10). Hasidic communities carry the name of their place of origin in the Pale of Russia. It is generally true that both Hasidim and Haredim in America are somewhat more tolerant in their approach to the secular world than their compatriots in Israel.

It is the primary belief of ultra-Orthodox Jews that their ancestors entered into the covenant of their own free will, and that the ancient covenant obligates all Jews for all time in their role as servant people. God will not abandon the covenant, and neither can the individual Jewish person abandon the obligation to God even if he or she fails to discern its terms or chooses to pray in a different faith community. As Samuel Heilman points out, in *Defenders of the Faith: Inside Orthodox Jewry,*

> the Haredim ... consider the world beyond their insular
> enclaves ... to be fraught with insidious temptation as well as
> moral and spiritual pollution. They believe that the survival of
> the Jewish people, of which they consider themselves to be
> the true representatives, depends on their own capacity to
> survive without change. They remain convinced that what is
> truly valuable and enduring is already within their grasp,
> handed down by tradition and custom and protected by their
> way of life. It is the objective of the Haredim to produce
> scholars who are great believers, as well as, people of kindness
> and virtuosity who find it possible to live with the Holy One
> from birth to death. Their minimum is to observe all God's
> commandments with devotion and intention. And like all

defenders of the faith, they await the miraculous rebuilding of God's Holy House [the Temple in Jerusalem].

Ultra-Orthodox also believe that life in this world is just a "passing shadow, a fleeting dream." The only enduring reality is the immortal soul. Therefore, they focus their lives on their relationship with God, and on individual preparation for eternity.

Regarding the modern state of Israel, the ultra-Orthodox do not believe that the people can claim a right to the Holy Land or hold it by force; nor do they believe that Israel can be a Jewish state when a near majority of the Jewish population (43 percent) is secular.

American Haredim are far less militant and scrupulous in their struggle to remain apart from the surrounding culture. Some members of Hasidic communities work in the secular world. Misfits and troublemakers in the Israeli Haredi society are often sent to an American enclave. Opposition of the Haredim to contemporary forms of Judaism is firm and unrelenting. As an example, The Synagogue Council of America which represented the rabbinic and congregational associations of the three major denominations — Orthodox, Conservative, and Reform — was disbanded when the ultra-Orthodox insisted that they could not work with Reform and Conservative rabbis on religious issues because it might be regarded as: "legitimizing the destroyers of Judaism."

The ultra-Orthodox community is exclusive, basing membership on matrilineal descent; a mixed marriage within the community is not possible. Converts are accepted under the same conditions imposed during the period of Jewish proselytism: the convert must be willing to assume the burdens of the covenant, and male circumcision is necessary. In the matter of reproduction, childbirth is, essentially, unregulated in ultra-Orthodox communities.

Reform Judaism lives within the secular world and is part of the landscape of that world. Religious beliefs are not its primary concern; the daily concerns of the world are paramount. If those who believe in and carry out the rules of the covenant pay homage to that cause. The urge to compromise religious obligations is strong, and the time to study Torah/Talmud is brief. Orthodox believe the law is divine and cannot be compromised. One cannot be a practicing Jew in the orthodox sense and still be involved in the daily give and take of a secular world. That is why the ultra-Orthodox community, particularly in Israel, is so important to Judaism today. The life of a committed Jew to study, prayer, and good works is a necessary continuation of the life under God, and it is also a training for those who leave the Orthodox community and carry that understanding into the secular world there to inspire and lead the process of *tikkun olam*.

In addition to the older sects in Judaism, there are as well relatively new contemporary forms. R. Mordecai Kaplan (1881-1983) began **RECONSTRUCTIONIST JUDAISM** in 1922, with the conviction that Reform, Conservative, and Orthodox Judaism were not viable solutions to contemporary Judaic problems.

Reconstructionists hold that all Jews, whether by birth or by choice, are members of the extended Jewish family. On the other hand, "Jews [first] need to know why they should be Jewish at all." The answer to this unique conundrum for Jews-by-birth is that they carry the DNA of their ancestors. That cannot be changed.

Reconstructionists believe that God is the source of all meaning, and it is the duty of each Jew to question and study in order to find his or her exclusive path to the divine. Jews, generally speaking, do not act individually, but rather as a community or cult. Still, rare occasions arise in which individual Jews must act for the preservation of the faith (or faithful) or for God's covenant purposes. However, Jews who cultivate their own pathway to God may have only a tenuous relationship to God and Judaism, and that may make the recognition of a "call" less likely. But it can be said, on the other hand, that God cherishes each of us individually and calls us to His service in accordance with our abilities and commitment.

A Reconstructionist Jew has strong commitments both to tradition and to the search for contemporary meaning. Torah has been the strong central core of Judaism and its instrument in spreading the name of God. Members of this movement believe that "when a particular Jewish value or custom is found wanting, it is the obligation of Reconstructionists to find a means to reconstruct it— to find new meanings in old forms or to develop more meaningful, innovative practices. This, indeed, is the essence of Reconstructionism.

It is not clear if one set of guidelines is offered to all Reconstructionist congregations for an up or down vote, or whether it can be modified by each congregation. As for individuals preparing discourses on the adaption of Jewish tradition to new circumstances, this can only lead to congregational anarchy. In essence, this approach drains all meaning from *halakhah*, and it belies the Reconstructionist own theme that each member of that sect has a strong commitment to tradition.

Does the covenant have any meaning to Reconstructionists? Their theology "affirms the uniqueness of the Jewish people and its heritage among the peoples of the world." But "uniqueness" is not defined. If it means the people chosen by God in accordance with the covenant, then the statement aligns with classical Judaism. "We dream of a Jewish people [who] will overcome divisions and realize its commitment to the single goal of transforming the world into one where all people are respected as bearers of the divine image." This can be taken as one honest interpretation of the covenant statement. But, it is a big statement for a small sect.

SECULAR HUMANISTIC JUDAISM was found by Rabbi Sherwin T. Wine (1928-2007) in 1963 for atheistic Jews. For the purposes of this society, a Jew is a person of Jewish descent or any person who declares himself/herself to be a Jew and who identifies with the history, culture, ethical values, ceremonies, civilization, community, and fate of the Jewish people.

It is difficult to summarize the beliefs of contemporary secular Jews. One suspects that their beliefs range over a very wide continuum, from "I live life without regard to Judaism or the ethical concepts of Judaism; I do whatever feels right to me," to "I believe in the Law and I keep the holidays, but I find the synagogue services and activities unrewarding." So rather than explore that line, let us look at an organizations that upholds secular concepts that is intended primarily for Jews.

This group does not believe in a god, but espouses "natural spirituality" as opposed to "supernatural spirituality." They hold that an afterlife of reward or punishment cannot be trusted to improve our lot on Earth. It is their belief that at death we will be punished or rewarded by the results of our behavior toward those influenced by our actions. Their objective is to help each other and make the world a better place. Each affiliated community has a commitment to a religious and ethical emphasis, family life and ethical education.

Secular Jews who organize in communities preserving various aspects of Judaism may be looked upon as the far left wing of modern Judaism: far removed from the ultra-Orthodox on the right, but not far beyond Reconstructionist Jews. In their religious world, there is little talk about Torah/Talmud and none about the covenant to make God's name known throughout the world.

Hertzberg has remarked that he "would say to those Jews who ask me to condone their agnosticism: What are you teaching your children and your grandchildren that they must continue to do as Jews? The ancient rabbis had the boldness to put this very idea in the mouth of God: "would not mind if they forsake Me provided they adhere to my commandments."

Notes for Chapter 9

EARLY GERMAN-JEWISH HISTORY

Hess, Jonathan M. *Germans, Jews, and the Claims of Modernity*, Yale University 2002

Sacher, Howard, *A History of the Jews in the Modern World*, Alfred A. Knopf 2005.

Bilski, Emily D. *Berlin Metropolis: Jews and the New Culture*, U. Of California and the Jewish Museum, 1999 [recommended]

Elon, Amos, *The Pity of it All: A History of the Jews in Germany 1743-1993*

Dorff, Elliot N. *Conservative Judaism: Our Ancestors to our Descendants*, United Synagogue of Conservative Judaism, 1998

Segal, Eliezer *Varieties of Orthodox Judaism*, University of Calgary,

Heilman, Samuel *Defenders of the Faith: Inside Orthodox Jewry*, University of California Press, 1991

Hirsch, Ammiel and Reinman, Yosef: *One People, Two Worlds*, Schocken Books, 2002

JEWISH LIFE IN GERMANY

Richarz, Monica, ed. Jewish Life in Germany: Memoirs From Three Centuries, Indiana University Press, 1991

OTHER

Goldfarb, Michael, *Emancipation*, Simon and Schuster, 2009

Heschel, Susannah, *Abraham Geiger and the Jewish Jesus*, University of Chicago Press, 1998

Chapter Ten
Russian Jewry

Awake my people, how long will you slumber?
The night has passed, the sunlight is dawning.
Awake, cast your gaze near and far,
Recognize your moment and your opportunity...

"Hakizah Ami," Judah Leib Gordon, 1863.

As the *haskala* movement spread across central and Western Europe from Budapest to London in the early 19th century, very little real reform was occurring in Russia where several million Yiddish speaking Jews lived in what was known as the Pale of Settlement, the largest Jewish community in the world at that time. "Pale of Settlement" derives from the Latin *palus*, meaning a stake driven into the ground to which a barrier could be attached. The western area of Russia amounted to one large ghetto extending from the Baltic Sea in the north to the Black Sea in the South. Here progress toward the enlightenment was dependent upon the attitude of the tsar.

The deeply embedded traditional form of Judaism was carrying on as best it could. Quietly, without any hubris these *shtetls* (towns) were incubating some of the most influential rabbinic voices in the modern history of Judaism. In the late 17th century, Rabbi Israel ben Eliezer (1698-1760) was born. He would come to be known as the Ba'al Shem Tov (Master of the Good Name). It was he who started the modern Hasidic movement. Several decades later, Moses Sofer was born (1762-1839). He founded the ultra-conservative, *haredim* form of Judaism.

The Russian tsars did not have a "Jewish problem" until the partitions of Poland in 1772, 1793 and 1795, when they inherited a significant number of Jews in their new territory. Tsar Nicholas I, who ascended to the throne in 1825, considered the Jews to be heretical parasites. His most abominable measure was the conscription of unmarried Jewish males at age twelve and older for twenty-five years of military service. In order to avoid service, young Jewish males were married when conscription was threatened. This strategy backfired and resulted in the drafting of boys as young as eight. Raised in squalid, crowded and smoke-filled hovels, most of these pre-adolescent boys lasted about six months. Residency restrictions by Nicholas led to severe crowding and economic over-competition within the Pale. The problem was compounded by rapid Jewish population growth in the 19th century.

By the 1830s a small group of Jewish merchants managed to become important players in the Russian economic world with direct access to the tsar. They were the Russian *maskilim,* who seized control of the Jewish institutions in the Pale, and established modern Jewish schools and German-style synagogues. In 1863 in St. Petersburg, a group of *maskilim* joined to form the Society for the Dissemination of Enlightenment. Their objective was to bring as many Jews as possible into the greater Russian society through the study of the Russian language and the pursuit of secular careers. This developing group, which enjoyed the privileges of full Russian citizenship, adopted the same attitude toward the host country as their coreligionists in France and Germany, by urging those who had been educated in the secular schools to embrace "our good mother Russia."

Traditional Judaism

Deeply entrenched traditional Judaism opposed the inroads into community life advocated by the *maskilim,* and continued to resist the reforms that were sweeping through central and Western Europe. Opposition to the position of the purveyors of the *haskala,* the *maskilim,* soon crystalized under the leadership of Rabbi Moses Sofer. In 1819, he wrote *A Reply Concerning the Question of Reform.*

> They [the *maskilim*] have added to and deleted from the prayers, substituting texts of their own invention ... they have also discarded [the benediction for] the flourishing of the House of David our messiah, and for the rebuilding of Jerusalem the Holy City [*i.e.,* the Temple]. The choicest statements [included in the Talmud] ... issued from the mouths of wise and discerning men, whose minds were full of knowledge and ideas and who possessed a profound understanding of all the sciences. Over the centuries these ideas have been recurrently clarified by thousands of sages. ... Therefore, let [the Reformers] stand up and be counted with the sages of our generation; may the grace of the Lord be upon them! ... If they say: " ... we do not accept the sages of the Talmud and their authority," they shall bear the burden of the words of Maimonides: "He who repudiates the Oral Law ... is classed with atheists [whom any person has a right to put to death]."

In sharp contrast to the *maskilim* or reformers, who opted for acculturation in one way or another, were the traditionalist Jews who were repelled by the values and ways of the world outside their own and wished, on the contrary, to stress the values in aboriginal ways of life, and to move aggressively toward the restoration of those ways. These Jews brought into consciousness and confrontation with one another two opposite things: the spiritually negative character of the contemporary world and the spiritually positive character of the past tradition. Their fundamental belief was to preserve themselves as Jews which required them to preserve their traditional practices ... Ritual, study of Jewish texts, observance of ceremonial, custom, even certain folkways were not dispensable husk but rather the vital kernel of Jewish life.

> *You shall be holy to Me, for I the Lord am holy, and I have set you apart from other peoples to be Mine.* (Lev. 20:26)

The traditionalists will evolve into the ultra-Orthodox of today. "But by the mid-nineteenth century, secular books began to be smuggled into the yeshivas of the Pale and read on the sly, their forbidden contents eagerly examined by students as they chanted the Talmudic singsong." A few rabbis were ready to receive the new learning of the West, but, in the main, the Russian rabbinate felt that any large infiltration of Western thought would be their undoing, and they were right.

Tsars Alexander II and III

Then, in 1855, Tsar Nicholas died. He was succeeded by his son, Alexander II, whose first edict was the abolition of juvenile conscription. In 1861, Jews who graduated from secondary school were permitted to live outside the Pale, and became eligible for state employment. Other reforms were passed by Alexander II, the most far reaching being the emancipation of the serfs in 1864. Although strongly opposed by the aristocracy, the tsar said: "I would rather free them from the top, then have them free themselves from the bottom." The primary character of serfdom is its tie to the land. When emancipated, many former serfs left baronial estates and gravitated to the cities. This, of course, is why it was strongly opposed by the aristocracy. The flood of cheap labor worsened the employment prospects of Jews living in the cities of the Pale. In 1874, the tsar reduced the term of military service to four years for all male citizens, but to only one year for those who had graduated from secondary school.

These reforms in conjunction with the *maskilim* activities brought a gathering flood of eager young Jewish men into the universities until the tide represented 15 percent of the entire Russian student university enrollment. In

Odessa, 70 percent of the Jewish students were in Russian schools by the mid-1870s. These aspirations were given voice by Judah Leib Gordon in his inspirational ballad *Hakizah Ami* (Awake My People) published in 1863, a stanza of which is quoted in the header to this chapter:

> Awake, my people! How long will you slumber?
> The night has passed, the sunlight is dawning.
> Awake, cast your gaze near and far,
> Recognize your moment and your opportunity ...
>
> This paradise is now open to you,
> Its sons now call you "brothers."
> How long will you dwell among them as a stranger?
> Why do you spurn their friendship?
> So lift your head high, stand upright,
> Regard them now with love.
> Open your hearts to knowledge and reason,
> Become an enlightened people, speaking the[ir] tongue.
> To the welfare of the state bring your own contribution,
> Bear your share of its wealth and opportunity.
> Be a man in the streets and a Jew at home,
> A brother to your countrymen and a servant to your ruler."

This became the "most widely celebrated positivist work of Hebrew literature ever produced in 19th century Russia." Recognize the use of the term "brother," an aspect of the Enlightenment.

A government decree permitted more Jewish business men, as well as more skilled Jewish artisans, Jewish university graduates, and also discharged Jewish veterans to move into the Russian interior. It was the tsar's expectation that Jewish capitalists would be attracted to Russian industrial ventures, that Jewish artisans would provide useful services for Russia's backward rural population, and that educated Jews might invigorate Russia's liberal professions. In considerable measure, the tsar's expectations were fulfilled.

The year 1881 was critical in the history of eastern Jewry. In March, Alexander II was about to finalize a new constitution giving voting rights to the people. Just before he signed the papers, he was assassinated by a member of a terrorist group. That ended the liberal reforms, as his successor, Tsar Alexander III, was far less amenable to the movement. Anti-Semitic pressures had begun to build in the Russian imperial government about ten years earlier, as young Jewish men moved through the secular universities and became important players in the professions and economic markets.

Shortly after the assassination of Alexander II, the first of many pogroms in the years 1881-84, broke out in the Ukraine. The imperial minister of the interior blamed the riots on the Jews, citing their alleged control over commerce and industry. Alexander III took this opportunity to impose severe economic restrictions on the Jews in order to "defend the principal population from Jewish exploitation." Apparently, the prior efforts of Alexander II to build a working relationship between the educated Jews and the Russian professionals in the rural areas had been too little/too late.

At this time, the western border of Russia was opened to those Jews who wished to emigrate. Politically more secure and more favorable economic conditions beckoned. At that time, Germany, and Berlin specifically, became the most attractive place to live because of its acculturation, social integration, educational opportunity, and day-to-day tolerance. On the other hand, anti-Semitism was generally thought to be most virulent in France. Nearly two million Jews fled Russia between 1880 and 1910, with up to 100,000 crossing Germany every year on their way to North Sea ports and safer havens in North and South America.

Native-born German Jews were repelled by the sight of the threadbare Easterners. Their traditional appearance caused the integrated German Jews to fear being identified with the immigrants by native Germans. Nevertheless, the German Jews rallied, and in 1882, alone, Jewish charities spent nearly one million marks either to help move the emigrants through Germany in sealed trains, or to finance their repatriation to Russia. This massive population transfer was handled with military efficiency. The telling slogan of the *Hilfsverein* [aid association] was "German thoroughness and Jewish heart." It would not be the last time that German thoroughness would engineer a mass Jewish emigration in sealed trains.

Back in Russia, those who survived the pogroms continued their daily lives working at occupations they learned from their fathers and grandfathers. Their living quarters, which often doubled as workshops, were primitive and overcrowded. Their routes of escape were extremely limited. For the vast majority, escape meant moving to an industrial city and joining the ranks of the Jewish proletariat. Their dreams of immigrating to more hospitable countries were dashed by the exclusionary quotas imposed in America and Palestine. By the beginning of the 20th century forty percent of the remaining Jewish population in the Pale was partially or fully dependent on charity as a result of the tsar's severe restrictions.

A spokesman for the tsar told a Jewish delegation in 1898 that one-third of the Jews would die out, one-third leave, and one-third be assimilated. The Jews attempted to deal with the progressive decline in their economic conditions, the discriminatory laws, and the pogroms by several means: migration to a more enlightened country or revolutionary change through education and social action. And for the younger Jewish generation, in particular for students, a cultural, secular life compatible with their political aspirations for a Jewish national homeland. They would eventually achieve some degree of success in all these aspirations.

The massive upheaval caused by pogroms in the Pale of Settlement, forced many of the Jewish intelligentsia, in Russia and in Central and Western Europe, to rethink the benefits of the *haskala*. Since it was now probably impossible to reverse the advances made by the *maskilim* since the turn of the 19th century, the question turned on how aggressive would the host countries become in limiting, or actually preventing, Jews from making further inroads into their economic structure. Potential hosts would then blame this restriction, of course, on the perceived "pushiness" in the professional trades. Also lingering in the minds of the *maskilim* was the suspicion that perhaps all would not go well with liberated Jews both in Eastern and Western Europe. Would the Gentile communities of their adopted countries turn against them in a rising tide of anti-Semitism as had already occurred in Russia? It was this concern that spurred a movement to return to the ancient homeland.

Messianism

While these musings were starting to evolve into a movement to return to the Holy Land, most of Russian-Jewry living in abject misery and deplorable conditions yearned for the coming of the Messiah to lift them to a better place. Messianism, which is usually signaled by the return of a Davidic heir, has a long history in Judaism. Its origin can be found in the following passage from the Book of Isaiah, written about two hundred years after the death of King David (c. 750 BCE).

> *A shoot shall grow out of the stump of Jesse*
> *(father of David),*
> *A twig shall sprout from his stock.*
> *The spirit of the Lord shall alight upon him:*
> *A spirit of wisdom and insight,*
> *A spirit of counsel and valor,*
> *A spirit of devotion and reverence for the Lord.*
> *He shall sense the truth by his reverence for the Lord:*
> *He shall not judge by what his eyes behold,*
> *Nor decide by what his ears perceive.*
> *Thus he shall judge the poor with equity*
> *And decide with justice for the lowly of the land.*
> (Isa. 11:1-4)

The rabbis of late biblical times were generally considered to have been indifferent to messianism. So far as the rabbis were concerned, a Jew was called to the service of God, and rabbinic Judaism was the correct way to express that service. Until the true Messiah came, all speculation or "prophecy" about what God would do next was essentially non-Jewish. However, in Talmud there are more than sixty instances in which the Messiah is referred to one or more times. Most of the entries are simply references to the end time (e.g., *"in the days of the Messiah"*). But, a few have interesting information. There is no doubt in Talmud that the Messiah is of the Davidic line.

In summary, we learn from Torah/Talmud that it is God's intention to see a just and righteous world under a messianic leader whose values are God's own. Second, we learn from Talmud that the time of Messiah (b. Pesah. 54b) and the name of Messiah (b. Pesah. 54a) are hidden from humankind. Third, the arrival of Messiah will be announced by the Prophet Elijah (see Malachi 3:23 OT) on a day that is neither a preparation for the Sabbath or a feast day (b. 'Erub. 43b). Fourth, one may expect Messiah after a seven-year cycle beginning with insufficient rain to sustain all crops, followed by an insufficient harvest, then true famine and a falling away from Torah, then a partial return of the harvest followed by a bumper crop and a return to Torah, and then heavenly sounds and war. Fifth, the Messiah, son of David, will come when all people perfectly keep the covenant, or when none do (b. Sanh. 97a).

Over the long course of Jewish history starting in the first century CE, many men have tried to follow in the footsteps of Jesus of Nazareth. The best known is Simon Bar Kochba, who led the insurrection of 132-135 CE. During the Arab conquests and subsequent reign, three more false messiahs drew many followers. In the 12th century, Maimonides wrote his letter to the Yemenite Jews, cautioning them against self-proclaimed messiahs.

A second and more profound wave of messianism began with one David Reuveni, in early 16th-century Europe, who claimed to be a descendant of King David. He sought to free Jerusalem from the Muslims. Drawing upon Christian crusading techniques, he appealed to Pope Clement VII for aid. His efforts awoke the passion of a *marrano* who reverted openly to Judaism, taking the name Solomon Molcho. They made an unsuccessful appeal to the Holy Roman Emperor, in punishment for which both were killed. But they drew many followers in Spain, Portugal and Italy, and as far east as Poland.

This episode was a preamble to what followed in the mid-17th century. The Jewish community in the Ukraine was decimated by pogroms instituted by Bohadan Chmielnicki, a Ukranian military leader and educated member of the gentry, who led a successful war against the Poles. Following his success, Chmielnicki joined with the Polish peasantry to massacre more than 100,000 Jews. This outrage triggered a desperate longing for Messiah.

The answer to the prayer for Messiah to come and save the Jews of the Pale was answered by Shabbetai Zevi (1626-1676) a brilliant talmudic student. He was born on the western coast of Turkey and moved to Jerusalem where he met the well-known Kabbalist, Nathan of Gaza. Because of the timing and predictions rampant in Kabbalism, Nathan decided that Shabbetai was the promised Messiah and became his prophet. Shabbetai's success in drawing followers not only in Russia, but also throughout Germany, Italy, France, and the Ottoman Empire was immediate. He also attracted the attention of Ottoman authorities who gave Shabbetai the choice of either converting to Islam or death. To the amazement of his startled followers, he chose the former. Nathan was able to explain this transformation by saying that Shabbetai converted in order to descend into Islam and destroy it from within. On this basis, the belief in his divinity lived on.

In the 18th century, a disciple of Shabbetai Zevi named Jacob Frank appeared as his reincarnation. Frank, whose influence covered much of the Pale and northern Germany, advocated conversion to Christianity as a means of attaining the secret knowledge of that sect. In this respect, he was following his progenitor's lead. Thousands of his followers did so, but when the church determined that Frank's view of the trinity was not in line with theirs and that he still regarded himself as Messiah, he was sent to prison for 13 years. During that period his flock continued to grow. Over the years, his followers became respected figures in the Church and married into Polish aristocracy. Their descendants include Adam Mickiewicz, Poland's national poet.

In 1796, Shneur ("elder") Zalman (1745-1812), founder of the Lubavicher Hasidic sect, published a systematic account of his religious teachings. The Book, known as the *Tanya,* is Zalman's teaching about Messiah. He held that Messiah will come to an exhausted people to lift it beyond long centuries of despair. "The *Tanya* teaches a radically different doctrine: the image of Messiah is extraordinarily optimistic. The Messiah will come soon to bring the world to perfection." The wave of messianism diminished by about the first quarter of the 19th century, but never completely died. In our time, it arose once again in the Hasidic community upon the death of the Lubavicher Rebbe, Menahem Mendel Schneersohn in 1994.

It is central to Jewish belief that at the "end of days" Jews will be around to experience the miracles and wonders of the coming of the Messiah. This can only happen if all Jews uphold the covenant in their daily lives, and demonstrate concern for the needs of all people. Should this occur, the Messiah need only marvel at what can be accomplished. Therefore, Jews should not wait for Messiah to lead, but should turn to the task themselves and pave the way for Messiah. It is within the power of each Jewish individual to bring the redemption closer by the godliness of his or her life. By doing so, the whole world will be redeemed for all humanity. Individual concern for others on the part of Jews or anyone else is not necessarily religiously based, but it is firmly based on the reality of God and God's covenant negotiated with Moses at Mt. Sinai.

How did Talmud speak of messianism to the rabbis of the late 19th century? Certainly we can say that at the end times, when all people observe the commandments of God, we will see the Messiah on Earth. That time is not now in view. But look upon the fourth talmudic point as metaphorical: "one may expect Messiah after a seven-year cycle beginning with insufficient rain to sustain all crops, followed by an insufficient harvest, then true famine and a falling away from Torah, then a partial return of the harvest followed by a bumper crop and a return to Torah, and then heavenly sounds and war." Compare the first part of that passage with the plight of the Jews in Diaspora, followed by a return to Torah in mid-19th century, heavenly warning sounds, and war. Elijah in his prophetic role would then warn of the dangers to come and point the way for a true Messiah. When the people arise in messianic expectation, the potential Messiah will come from the people, and have their backing and support. The question is: will God send a prophet to warn God's people?

Kabbalism

The Kabbalah ("tradition") is a form of Jewish mysticism that emerged suddenly in the early 13th century. The earliest version of the Jewish mystical phenomena in the medieval world was the Chassidei Ashkenaz movement (Pietists of Germany) which existed in the 12th and 13th centuries. The impetus for this movement was the emerging conflict between religion and the societal values then undergoing rapid economic development and urbanization. The Hassidei applied the special abilities of the learned and pious scholars to interpret *rezon ha-bore* ("the will of the Creator") which, according to them, was expressed only partially in the commandments. Wonders and miracles, they believed, truly revealed God's nature. Therefore, their literature is greatly concerned with magic and demonology.

The impetus for this movement was the desire of many to have a closer personal relationship with God than that which could be attained though rational, intellectual studies, and liturgies. In essence there were two forms of Jewish mysticism: that which relied upon interpretation of biblical text and talmudic sayings while also viewing them as mystical cult symbols, and that which put writings aside and sought closeness to God "through visions, dreams, revelations of celestial powers and intuitive reflection." The significance of the Kabbalist movement cannot be overestimated. In the final centuries of the diaspora, it affected a majority of world Jewry, primarily those living in the Pale.

One of the more important legacies of the German Pietists is their contribution to what was to become the first anthology of Kabbalist methods: the *Sefer Bahir* (Book of Light). It was written in the form of a *Midrash*, replete with lectures (or sermons) on biblical verses, probably in the 13th century. *Bahir* appears to be a compilation of mystical *sefirot* (a channel of divine energy or life force), "the ten emanations through which the Godhead manifests itself" each of which has been given a kabbalistic name. Soon after its compilation several commentaries were written elucidating its concepts. The unorganized and, in places, interrupted presentation of *Bahir* was soon clarified by the appearance of the *Sefer Zohar* (Book of Splendor) the classic work of Jewish mysticism. *Zohar* was written by Moses de León (c. 1250-1305) and his circle of practitioners in Castile, Spain near the end of the 13th century. Like the *Bahir* it is written as a midrashic commentary on the Pentateuch. Many of these concepts were widely distributed to the Jewish community and infused with novel mystical ideas by the distinguished Rabbi Moses ben Nahman (Nachmanides) (1194-1270) in the second half of the 13th century from his residence then in Israel.

During the terminal years of high Jewish society in Iberia (the late 15th century), kabbalists wrote "intensely messianic works" which survivors of the Spanish expulsion expanded during their years in the Ottoman east. The Kabbalah of Isaac Luria (1534-1572) flourished, more-or-less secretly, in the great Jewish Sephardic center of Safed. The operating basis of Kabbalism in those times was the esoteric interpretation of Torah using the symbols delineated in *Bahir*, but with unique interpretations common to a particular school. Each school or group could glean through their specific knowledge the truth that lay behind the biblical words. Lurianic Kabbalism retained a belief in the coming of *haMashiach* (the Messiah).

It was the Lurianic form of Kabbalism that took root and flourished in the 16th century. This form was premised on the myth that all humans in this world were exiled from the Divine presence because of a flaw in the creation permitting evil to exist. The Jewish people were created to repair that flaw and thereby be redeemed. By reasoning in this manner, Luria gave purpose and credence to Kabbalism and brought the mystical forms of Judaism into the open. *Zohar* was printed twice in the 16th century; the second printing, in Mantua, Italy became the basis for all subsequent editions which were expanded over the years. As viewed today, kabbalists work to bring disparate aspects of a particular problem together to find wholeness or truth in the repair. This is the work of *tikkun olam*, repairing the world.

In the time of the Chmielnicki massacre, Jewish leaders could no longer assure their people that they would be protected in the future nor could they answer questions about why the people were made to suffer. Therefore, many turned away from traditional Jewish observance and sought solace in Kabbalah. It was through *Zohar* that they recognized signs of the imminent end of the present age and the probable coming of *Mashiach*. Thus, a century after the death of Isaac Luria, his charismatic leadership was taken up by Nathan of Gaza (1643-1680), the highly respected rabbi of the Kabbalah who, in 1665, identified Shabbetai Tzevi as the long-awaited Messiah.

The Ba'al Shem Tov did not agree with some of the basic concepts of Lurianic Kabbalism. On the assumption that God had created all that is in this world, he took the position that the mystery of creation should be celebrated, but the basic tenets of Judaism should be preserved and strictly observed. So influential did this form of Kabbalism become, that the *Zohar* became the third most important book in the life of Judaism after Torah and Talmud. During the 18th century, Hasidism and the traditional Orthodox clashed frequently, particularly with regard to the messianic inclination of the former. During the 19th century, Kabbalism was toned down, but it has seen a resurgence since the last quarter of the 20th century.

Famous Jews of the Pale

The Jews of the Pale during the second half of the 19th century, left a rich and expressive literary and artistic heritage in Hebrew and Yiddish. The best loved of the classical Yiddish writers is Sholem Aleichem ("Peace be with you") née Shalom Rabinovitz (Ukraine 1859-New York 1916). His literary production was vast. From his first Yiddish story in 1883 until his death, he produced forty volumes of stories, novels, and plays, and he established a distinguished literary journal, *Die Yiddishe Folks Bibliotek* (the Jewish Peoples' Library). He immigrated to the US in 1905, after the Kiev pogrom.

Sholem Aleichem's world is the Eastern European *shtetl*. His best known fictional figures were Tevye the milkman, Menahem Mendel the promoter, Hapke the maid, and many named farm animals. He loved them with all with their follies and foibles. His humorous tales of life among the poverty-ridden and oppressed Jews of the *shtetls* have been adapted often for the stage, the best known adaptation being *Fiddler on the Roof* in 1964.

Another leading figure in the cultural renaissance at the turn of the century and one of the founders of modern Yiddish literature, was Isaac Leib Peretz (1851-1915), a contemporary of Sholem Aleichem. Peretz believed that it was his mission to create modern national literature by blending his socialist philosophy with his fascination for Jewish folklore and Hasidic tradition. His novels embody his belief that modern progress was the path that shtetl Jews must follow to greater freedom and enlightenment. His belief as a writer was, "To find the essence of Jewishness in all places, at all time, in all parts of a people scattered throughout the world ... and to see it illuminated by the prophetic dream of man's future— this is the task of every Jewish artist." Peretz characterized the plight of the shtetl Jews like Khaim the porter, Shmerl the woodcutter, and, most famously, Bontsche Shvayg the silent.

Medele Mokher Seforim (1835-1917) a writer contemporary to both Peretz and Sholem Aleichem, also was a mentor to many young, upcoming writers including David Pinski, Abraham Reisen, Joseph Opatoshu, and Sholem Asch. Sholem Asch (Poland 1880-London 1957) wrote plays which are among the highlights of Yiddish drama. Asch's novels and stories offer a true, though sometimes romanticized, picture of Jewish small town life and the religious world of Eastern Europe. Asch gained international renown when Max Reinhardt produced his play *Gott de Rache* ("God of Vengeance") in Berlin in 1910.

The best known of the generation that followed these classical Yiddish writers was Alter Kacyzne (1885-1941). He published his first work in Yiddish in 1918, followed by a sizable body of work including poetry, plays, short stories, a novel, film scripts, cultural and social essays, travel journals, and news articles. He was founder, editor, and columnist for several important publications, chairman of the Yiddish PEN Club, as well as executor and editor of Peretz's literary estate. Kacyzne also made important contributions to Yiddish literature as a dramatist for the Yiddish stage. But his greatest gift to the Jews of Poland was his brilliant and powerful photographic portrait of that once-vital Jewish world.

Kacyzne had close ties to Di Khalyastre ("The Gang"), a group of modernist Yiddish writers including future bestselling novelist Israel Joshua Singer (brother of Isaac Bashevis Singer), the future bard of Hebrew poetry, Uri Zvi Greenberg, the poet Melekh Ravitch, and the artist Marc Chagall who was, without question, in his manner, in his form of expression, and in his inborn kabbalistic mysticism, a specifically Jewish artist. Standing alone and largely unrecognized in his time was Bruno Schulz (1892-1942) a Polish writer of remarkable ability assassinated during the Holocaust years.

Yiddish theater in Poland goes back to 16th century Purim plays. The poet Abraham Goldfaden (1840-1908) founded the first modern Yiddish theatrical ensemble in Romania in 1877. In 1883, the czar banned such groups, and many emigrated to Berlin or New York. Those remaining in the Pale were permitted to restart their ensemble groups in 1900, when many new Yiddish plays were written. The Moscow theater offered samples of overwhelmingly intense scenic art which symbolized the New Russian spirit in the age-old Jewish life style. The "Wilnär Truppe," founded in 1916, was the genesis for the "The Jewish Art Theater" in America. Another group, which originated in Leningrad in 1918, evolved into the "Jewish Academy Theater" in Moscow. Poland had as many as fifteen Yiddish theater groups in 1934. The "Habima" ensemble was founded in Moscow in 1916, and toured Europe and the US. In 1927, many members of that group went to Palestine, becoming the basis for the National Theater in 1956.

The Yiddish film industry in Warsaw grew out of the Yiddish theater with famous stage actors playing crucial roles in its development. Between 1923 and 1938, Zygmont Turkow and his wife Ida Kaminska produced classics in Yiddish plus original Yiddish plays which they later filmed. In 1936, Joseph Green achieved his greatest success in *Yidl with the Fiddle* starring Molly Picon. The Yiddish film industry and theater productions continued until [the German invasion in] September 1939. Yiddish theater also influenced the

German Jewish theater and film industry during the early 20th century as many of the actors from the Pale gravitated to Berlin.

The most striking aspect of the Jewish experience in the Pale of Russia during the 19th century was the tremendous pressure under which Jews were placed by the Russian authorities starting in the 1880s. Including limited educational opportunity, a very tight job market resulting in poverty conditions for a large percentage of these unfortunate people, and, the most extreme measure, the periodic pogroms abetted by the government. Almost two million Jews left the Pale to find more hospitable conditions in Central Europe, North America, and South America. Jews who remained in Russia and Poland during the first third of the 20th century entertained and uplifted their brethren through Yiddish literature, stage, and eventually film. Even under terrible conditions, this original work influenced both the stage and film industries in Germany and, subsequently, in America.

The Russian-Jewish movie business in America began in the New York Bowery in 1906-07 when the motion picture craze hit, and most of the old Yiddish music halls were converted into movie houses. One of the first to see the opportunity were the brothers Minsky, Abe and Billie who combined vaudeville with moving pictures. The Minskys stayed in the vaudeville business, but Louis Mayer, Benjamin Warner, and Samuel Goldwyn (née Goldfish) all born in the Pale, founded the great movie studios of Hollywood. Although we may no longer recognize their influence today, they created the Broadway and Hollywood legends in the 1920s and 30s.

The most important outcome of the Russian Jewish experience was the overwhelming urge of the people to find a Messiah who would lead them back to the Holy Land (*Eretz Israel*). In the 19th century the most prominent men devoted to this cause were Tzevi Hirsch Kalischer (1795-1874) and Rabbi Judah Alkalai (1798-1878). Kalischer was born in Posen, western Poland. Alkalai was an Orthodox Rabbi who had lived in Jerusalem when he was young and later became leader of the Jewish community in Semlin, Serbia.

Both Kalischer and Alkalai based their notion of a homeland in Palestine on religious, not secular, imperatives. In fact they looked with great suspicion upon the objectives of the Enlightenment and relied instead on the Bible and Kabbalah. Neither had much knowledge of the practical aspects of emigration. Both attempted to raise funds from wealthy European Jewish families with very little success, although Kalischer was able to establish an agricultural school outside of Jaffa in 1870 with Rothschild help. Neither man would have made a significant impact on the history of *Eretz Israel* had it not been for one interesting fact: one of Rabbi Alkalai's devoted followers was the paternal grandfather of Theodor Herzl.

The Russian Jewish experience is of intense interest to most American Jewish families of Russian extraction. The grandparents and in some cases their great grandparents spoke often of their home in Russia. Also, they had seen actors familiar to us in American movies, whom they knew from European plays or movies by their Eastern European names, *e.g.*, Edward G. Robinson (Emanuel Goldenberg). And they read books about their *shtetl* life, particularly those of Sholem Aleichem. As the U.S. and European countries gradually permitted Jews to merge with the native population and become important players in the economic and cultural scene, Russian Jews remained penned up in the Pale of Settlement subject to the whims of the reigning Tsar.

Russia is an amalgam of three major ethnic groups: Ukrainians, Belorussians and Russians. They tolerated their "blood brothers," but clashed as well from time to time. The same could not be said of the Jews or the Poles. The Jews survived as best they could but had no means of defending themselves against pogroms during which loss of life and property was appalling. The younger generation particularly wanted out and a chance to make a decent family life hopefully in Palestine. The Russians were more than happy to watch them leave.

As the Russians opened their western border, a great surge of Jewish emigrants overwhelmed the German state of Prussia. Their haggard appearance and unique dress stunned the native Germans and rattled the integrated Jews. The German Jews quickly organized to insure that the newcomers were either shipped out to America or Argentina, where immigration (to a certain extent) was permitted, integrated into German-Jewish enclaves, or returned to Russia. A small percent, who had made a place for themselves in the Russian economy remained. As pogroms, with government approval, became more frequent, the educated Jews would become the drivers for a Jewish state.

The old-time religion in Russia came under increasing pressure from the new forms of Judaism in Europe, from the great population lost to emigration, and to the anxiety of anticipating the next pogrom. The Russians rabbis sought to uphold their religious authority, but stricter forms of Judaism had to be developed to insure that the old ways would prevail. In addition other religious aspects gave Russians hope such as Kabbalism which brought mystical forms of the religion and messianism which gave them hope for a peaceful future.

Meanwhile, Yiddish tour groups of Jewish performers entertained in Russia, and then spread across the Atlantic to America where Yiddish theater was joyfully received on the lower East Side of New York City in more than two hundred such theaters And just in time for the nickelodeon films to take over the theaters. It was the beginning of the movie business quickly recognized by Jewish entrepreneurs who would rapidly come to dominate the national appetite for entertainment.

Let us remember some of the Jews of the generation who made a great new America.

Felix Adler professor of education and philosophy

Hannah Arendt political and social philosopher

Barney Balaban motion picture pioneer

Jack Benny entertainer on radio and in movies

Irving Berlin composer and lyricist of music for stage and screen, wrote *God Bless America*

Emil Berliner long distance telephony

Leonard Bernstein composer and conductor, wrote *West Side Story*

Bruno Bettelheim, teacher for children with severe psychological problems

Felix Bloch Nobel Prize in Physics for nuclear induction 1952

Konrad Bloch Nobel Prize in Physiology or Medicine for cholesterol mechanisms 1964

Louis Brandeis Supreme Court Justice

Arthur Burns, economist and adviser to four presidents, chair of Federal Reserve 1970-78

Melvin Calvin Nobel Prize in Chemistry 1961

Benjamin Cardozo Supreme Court Justice

Aaron Copland classical music composer

Walter Damrosch classical music conductor

Jo Davidson sculptor

Babette Deutsch writer and consultant to Library of Congress

Edgar Doctorow writer and college teacher

Barney Dreyfuss baseball executive and creator of the World Series

David Dubinsky labor leader and president of the ILGWU

Gerald Edelman Nobel Prize for Physiology or Medicine in 1972

Albert Einstein professor of theoretical physics at Institute for Advanced Studies

Erick Erikson Harvard professor of human development and psychiatry

Howard Fast writer of historical novels, *e.g., April Morning* about the Battle of Lexington

Jules Feiffer playwright and cartoonist

Edna Ferber novelist, *e.g.,* wrote *Show Boat*

Abraham Flexner founder and organizer of Institute for Advanced Studies at Princeton

Felix Frankfurter Supreme Court Justice

Erich Fromm psychoanalyst and social philosopher

George Gershwin composer of music for stage, screen, opera, classics such as *Rhapsody in Blue*

Allen Ginsberg poet

Donald Glaser Nobel Prize for Chemistry for work on bubble chambers 1960

Arthur Goldberg Supreme Court Justice and UN Ambassador

Rube Goldberg cartoonist

Samuel Goldwyn movie pioneer founder of Goldwyn Pictures Corporation

Samuel Gompers trade unionist, founder and president of AFL

Peggy Guggenheim art patron, important influence on modern art in U.S. and Europe

Oscar Hammerstein II lyricist for *Show Boat* and five Rogers shows, *e.g.*, *The Sound of Music*

Moss Hart playwright, e.g., You Can't Take it With You

Jascha Heifetz violinist

Joseph Heller novelist, *e.g.*, *Catch-22*

Lillian Hellman playwright

Laura Hobson novelist, *Gentlemen's Agreement*

Sol Hurok ballet impresario

Erica Jong feminist and writer, *Fear of Flying*

Louis Kahn architect and professor at U. of Pennsylvania

Theodore Von Karman aerodynamics expert on jet aircraft and rockets

Max Kohler defender of legal rights of immigrants, naturalized citizens, and aliens

Walt Kuhn painter, organized the Armory Show of modern art in 1913

Simon Kuznets awarded Nobel Memorial Prize in Economic Sciences 1971

Carl Laemmle film pioneer, founded Universal Film Company, rescued many German-Jews

Edwin Land invented the Polaroid Camera

Emma Lazarus poet wrote *The New Colossus* inscribed on the Statute of Liberty

Joshua Lederberg professor of genetics awarded Nobel Prize for Medicine and Physiology 1958

Herbert Lehman director-general of UN Relief and Rehabilitation Fund 1949-1957

Max Lerner writer taught at Harvard, Williams, and Brandeis

Mervyn Leroy worked in film industry from 1919, directed *Wizard of Oz*

Fritz Lipmann shared Nobel Prize in Medicine and Physiology 1953

Walter Lippmann journalist founded *New Republic*, editor of the *New York World*

Peter Lorre movie actor appeared in many films, *e.g., Casablanca*

Bernard Malamud novelist wrote, among others, *The Fixer*

Groucho Marx comedian in films, Broadway and television

Louis Mayer film pioneer founded Louis B. Mayer Pictures

Yehudi Menuhin violinist, president of International Musical Council of UNESCO

Eugene Meyer banker, newspaper editor, and publisher

Albert Michelson award Nobel Prize in Physics 1907

Henry Morgenthau, Jr. Secretary of Treasury in Roosevelt administration

Richard Neutra architect

Louise Nevelson sculptor

Adolf Ochs publisher purchased New York Times in 1896

Clifford Odets playwright, many plays including *Waiting for Lefty*

Eugene Ormandy music director

Dorothy Parker author

Jan Peerce opera singer

Sidney Perelman humor writer, won Academy Award for *Around the World in 80 Days*

Molly Picon Yiddish actress, visited displaced person camps after WW II

Otto Preminger film director of many well-known movies including *Exodus*

Isidore Rabi awarded the Nobel Prize for Physics 1944

Simon Rawidowicz philosopher

Hyman Rickover, admiral USN, conceived idea of nuclear powered submarines

Jerome Robbins choreographer, shows included *Fiddler on the Roof*

Richard Rodgers composer of show music, *e.g., Carousel*

Sigmund Romberg, light opera music composer, *e.g., The Student Prince*

Billy Rose composed many popular songs, *e.g., Without a Song*, produced *Aquacade*

Anna Rosenberg consultant on labor issues, appointed Assistant Secretary of Defense

Samuel Rosenberg edited Public Papers and Addresses of Franklin D. Roosevelt

Julius Rosenwald merchant and philanthropist, President of Sears, Roebuck and Co.

Henry Roth author of classic book on immigrant life *Call it Sleep*

Mark Rothko artist of modern themes

Helena Rubinstein designer and manufacturer of cosmetics for women

Abraham Ribicoff, Governor of Connecticut, Secretary of Health, Education and Welfare, U.S. representative and senator

Abraham Sachar first president of Brandeis University

Jonas Salk research scientist developed anti-polio vaccine

Paul Samuelson awarded Nobel Prize in Economics 1970

Edward Sapir leader in study of human life development

David Sarnoff first general manager and subsequently president of RCA

Jacob Schiff banker, business man, and philanthropist

Joseph Schlossberg journalist and trade union leader

Rose Schneiderman help found National Trade Union Women's League

B.P. Schulberg film producer. Paramount Studios named a building for him

Julian Schwinger awarded Nobel Prize in Physics in1965

David O. Selznick film producer, *e.g.*, *Gone With the Wind*

Ben Shahn painter and graphic artist

Isaac Bashevis Singer author awarded Nobel Prize for Literature 1978

Raphael Soyer artist of New York City street scenes

Sam Spiegel produced many films, *e.g.*, *Lawrence of Arabia*

Gertrude Stein novelist, art patron

David Steinman engineer designed and built more than one hundred steel bridges

Joseph Sternberg film industry pioneer editor, producer, director

Alfred Steiglitz pioneered photographic techniques and photo art forms

I.F. Stone journalist published influential newsletter of current affairs

Lee Strasberg actor and artistic director, founded Theater Institutes in NY and LA

Nathan Straus philanthropist established milk, coal, and food distribution stations in NYC

Leo Strauss philosopher wrote studies on political philosophy and religion

Lewis Strauss business man, philanthropist, rear admiral USN, served on Atomic Energy Comm.

Gerard Swope electrical engineer and president of International General Electric Co.

Herbert Swope journalist exposed Klu Klux Klan, crime in New York, and labor conditions in FL

Leo Szilard physicist conceived the nuclear chain reaction and co-invented the nuclear reactor

Irving Thalberg film producer, supervised production at MGM

Michael Todd film producer, produced *Oklahoma!*

Louis Untermayer writer, compiled anthology of *Modern America Poetry*

Selman Waksman received Nobel Prize in Medicine and Physiology 1952

Lillian Wald public health nurse, established Henry Street Settlement

Irving Wallace novelist, *e.g., The Prize*

Max Weber painter and sculptor

Jerome Weidman prolific writer of short stories, plays, and novels

Norbert Weiner mathematician taught at MIT

Eric Werner musicologist, studied ancient musical forms from Greek to Renaissance

Eli Wiesel author, humanities professor awarded Nobel Peace Prize in 1986

Jerome Wiesner scientist, assistant to President Kennedy, president of MIT

Herman Wouk novelist, *e.g., The Caine Mutiny*

Anzia Yezierska writer of short stories and novels

Florenz Ziegfeld impresario of Broadway shows and film

Adolf Zukor film executive and founder of Paramount Studios

The contributions of many Jewish women and men helped make America great.

Persons on this list were American born or naturalized citizens generally in the last third of the 19th or early years of the 20th century. Most died by 1980. (Primary Source: Dan Cohen-Sherbok *Dictionary of Jewish Biography*, Oxford University Press, 2005.)

Notes for Chapter Ten

During and after the collapse of the Ottoman Empire, Jews scattered throughout Europe, Palestine, and the Americas while several million remained in Russia. Many Russians yearned to return to the Holy Land, but strong leadership was lacking. In addition the eastern European rabbinate adhered firmly to the centuries old rules for synagogue while western rabbis, for the most part, turned to the new, looser forms of Judaism. Great books describe the documentary history of these years.

Mendes-Flohr, Paul and Reinharz. Jehuda, *The Jew in the Modern World*, Oxford University Press, 1995, second edition. (All you ever wanted to know about the Jews from 1655 to 1970.)

Hertzberg Arthur, *Jews: the Essence and Character of a People*, HarperSanFrancisco, 1998

Howe, Irving, *World of Our Fathers* Harcourt, Brace, Jovanovich, 1976

Salamander, Rachel, *The Jewish World of Yesterday 1880-1938*, Rizzoli, 1991

JEWISH LIFE IN EASTERN EUROPE

Alter, Polyn, *Jewish Life in the Old Country*. Metropolitan Books, 1999

EMIGRANTS FROM RUSSIA TO AMERICA

Eisenberg Ellen, *Jewish Agricultural Colonies in New Jersey, 1882-1920*, Syracuse University Press, 1995.

Buhle, Paul, *From the Lower Eastside to Hollywood: Jews in America Popular Culture*, Verso, 2004

Gaber, Neal, *An Empire of Their Own: How the Jews Invented Hollywood*, Anchor Books, 1988

Hoberman J. and Shandler, Jesse, *Entertaining America: Jews, Movies and Broadcasting*, Princeton University Press, 2003

OTHER

Abraham, Pearl *The Seventh Beggar*, Riverhead Books, 2005

Butwin, Julius and Frances, trans. *Favorite Tales of Sholom Aleichem*, Avenel Books, 1993

Lazarus, Emma, *An Epistle to the Hebrews*, Jewish Historical Society of New York, 1987

Chapter Eleven
Rise of Zionism

*Yea, Prophesy, the Lord hath said. Again
say to the wind, Come forth and breathe afresh,
Even that they may live, upon those slain,
and bone to bone shall leap, and flesh to flesh.
The Spirit is not dead, proclaim the word,
where lay dead bones, a host of armed men
stand!
I ope your graves, my people, saith the Lord,
and I shall place you living in your land.*

The New Ezekiel, Emma Lazarus, 1882.

In 1850, there were more than four million Jews in Eastern and
Central Europe and more than five million in Palestine. By 1900, there were
more than 8.5 million Jews in Europe and 1,175,000 in America, and more
than eighty million in Russia. Pressure began to build and to purchase land in
Palestine and turn the country into a Jewish paradise.

Jewish Immigration

The issues in the 1880s were whether emigration of more than 1.5
million Russian Jews should be aided and if so, should they go to Palestine or
America. The imperatives for colonizing a religious or a secular Palestine were
debated. Traditional rabbis prayed continually for God to look upon the
suffering of the people, redeem them from their exile, and return them to the
Holy Land. This was to happen, of course, in Gods time, as a religious
imperative. The rabbis looked with suspicion upon "impious interference in
the unfolding of the divine master-plan."

As to the issue of migration to America, the assimilationists viewed the
educational and economic benefits as an opening to participate in the
opportunities of the modern world. But the Orthodox were deeply suspicious
of these aims based on centuries of distrust of Gentile intentions, and the
obvious danger of shattering a traditional way of life with its fixed liturgy. They

also feared that the migrants would be lost from the ranks of strict observers. This proved to be true, as the Conservative and Reform movements ultimately counted more adherents in America than traditional Orthodox.

During the course of this debate, the Jewish population of the Ottoman empire became an important pool for the colonization of Palestine. Movement to the Promised Land started in earnest about 1840 at the rate of about ten thousand per year and continued until the 1880s, when the inflow increased to 25,000 annually because of the pogroms in Russia. The first groups to move were deeply religious Ashkenazim who established a religious settlement (*yishuv*). Longtime resident Ottoman Jews became the largest religious community in the 1840s, and after1860 they constituted a majority of the population of Jerusalem. Enjoying full citizenship rights, some Ottomans purchased shops and land in the area. They also engaged in financial transactions, as they had in Anatolia, which permitted them to acquire economic power in a very short time.The philosopher Moses Hess (1812-1875), speaking of Jewish assimilation into German society, wrote in *Rome and Jerusalem*, "Germans as a whole in spite of its collective intellectuality, in its practical and social life is far behind the rest of the civilized nations of Europe." This was because of the German belief in the superiority of the *Volk* (the common folk) in comparison to other races, especially as it regarded Jews. Hess wrote,We shall always remain strangers among the nations. They may tolerate us and even grant us emancipation, but they will never respect us. Nor would the Germans be tolerant of the national aspirations of others... The Jew in exile who denies his nationality will never earn the respect of the nations among whom he dwells.

Hess's book calls for the establishment of a Jewish socialist commonwealth in Palestine, in line with the emerging national movements in Europe, as the only way to respond to anti-Semitism and assert Jewish identity in the modern world. Therefore, they had to return to their own country, to Palestine. Hess proposed a modern secular Jewish State, a nation like any other but not a religious one. This movement to Palestine, was already then underway.

An early member of the Russian Jewish Society for the Dissemination of Enlightenment was Yehuda Leib (Leon/Leo) Pinsker (1821-1891). Pinsker was a physician living in the southern reaches of the Pale in the city of Odessa, territory of Ukraine. Pinsker had studied in secular high school and college (University of Moscow). Highly respected as a physician, he was honored by the tsar for his services during the Crimean War. Dr. Pinsker was one of the driving forces in the integration of Russian Jews into Russian society. But Pinsker lost his home in Odessa as a result of the pogrom of 1881, and began a journal called *Auto-Emancipation: A Warning Cry to His Fellow Jews by a Russian Jew*, in which he declared, "the proper ... remedy would be the creation of a

Jewish nationality as a nation among nations by the acquisition of a home of their own."

Pinsker's writings energized Russian Jewry to organize a society which they called *Hibbat [Hovevei] Zion* (Lovers of Zion), and to found a series of agricultural settlements in Palestine under the leadership of Pinsker, the most well-known of which was Rishon le-Zion. The French overtone to the naming of these settlements was a result of financing by the French branch of the Rothschilds. Beginning in the 1880s, as Pinsker's movement developed a strong base of supporters among the middle class, Hibbat Zion clubs spread throughout the Pale.

Meanwhile in America, Emma Lazarus (1849-1887), whose poetry forever changed the spiritual meaning of the Statue of Liberty, read Pinsker's pamphlet and took up the cause of what will become Zionism. She was one of the early greeters of Russian Jewish immigrants at Ward's Island, NY, in March 1882 and was impressed with their education, determination, and physical capability. She noted that such a large number (a million or more) could not easily be accommodated in existing countries, and must, therefore, have an ensured and unrestricted right to their own territory. Between November 1882 and February 1883, Lazarus wrote fifteen installments for the *American Hebrew* advocating the emigration of Russian Jews to Palestine in order to rebuild their national home and insure their permanent protection.

Detractors arose immediately from the influential Reform German-Jewish community, and from the wealthy and deeply assimilated American Jews. They protested "romantic notions of race, nation, and Holy Land Restoration." Lazarus responded that wealthy Americans and Western European Jews were so thoroughly denationalized that they would not accept the Holy Land as a free gift, if with it were coupled the odious necessity of living among their co-religionists." She also claimed that assimilated Jews in America felt that the assumption of responsibility for Russian Jews would compromise their loyalty to their country.

This public disagreement prompted American Reform Judaism to adopt a "Declaration of Principles" at its 1885 Pittsburgh Conference.

> We recognize, in the modern era of universal culture of heart
> and intellect, the approaching of the realization of Israel's
> great messianic hope for the establishment of the kingdom of
> truth, justice, and peace among all men. We consider
> ourselves no longer a nation, but a religious community, and
> therefore expect neither a return to Palestine, nor a sacrificial
> worship under the sons of Aaron, nor the restoration of any
> of the [Talmudic] laws concerning the Jewish state [*e.g.*, the
> rebuilding of the Temple in Jerusalem.]

Whereas the key phrase in Pinsker's *Auto-Emancipation* is "Jewish nation," the "Declaration of Principles'" the key phrase is "religious community." The Reform declaration is in line with the principles of the Enlightenment with which Diaspora Judaism has always had an internal conflict as pointed out by Michaelis. Of course, the messianic hope, expressed best in the Isaiah 2:4, is God's ultimate objective for the world:

> *Thus He will judge among the nations and arbitrate for the many peoples,*
> *And they shall beat their swords into plowshares and their spears into pruning hooks.*
> *Nation shall not take up sword against nation, They shall never again know war.*

But what American Reform Judaism, influenced by Jews of German background, is saying here is what the Reform Jewish congregations of Germany stated some decades before in order to assure their host country that they were not a nation within a nation.

The Reform movement saw no need for restoration of the ancient covenant in the biblical homeland, since veneration of Torah could certainly continue in America. Thus, any passage of Torah referring to the restoration of Jews in the Promised Land was to be ignored or looked upon as a relic of ancient history. The Reform statement agrees with the ultimate objective signaled by the arrival of the Messiah, but not active participation in bringing that about. This decision is the crux that differentiated Reform Jews in America from most Orthodox Jews, and may account, even today, for Reform Judaism limited influence in Israel. The question of whether the United States was concerned, as were the Germans, about the nation-within-a nation problem was yet to be analyzed.

Apparently, secular leaders of the Hibbat Zion program gave little thought to religious concerns that had to be addressed by Jews immigrating to Palestine. The question of whether the imperative to colonize Palestine should be religious or secular continued unanswered. However, there was an alternative to the program of territorialism in Palestine: migration to agricultural colonies in other countries, sponsored by wealthy Jewish commercial and banking firms. The two most prominent such efforts were the Baron de Hirsch's Argentinian agricultural communities in the last decade of the 19th century, and the *Am Olam* (Eternal People) movement, a Russian organization founded by Peter Smolenski (1840-1885) that advocated communal agrarian settlements by Jews in the US for the physical and spiritual rehabilitation of the people.

By the second decade of the 20th century, the Jewish emigrants in Argentina comprised thirteen colonies with a total population of 33,135, of whom 20,382 were farmers. The *Am Olam* movement settled about two thousand Russian Jews in agricultural communities in southern New Jersey starting in May1882. Smolenski wrote in his monthly *HaShahar* warned in 1872 of a coming breakdown in Jewish loyalties.

Theodor Herzl

Would these solutions have signaled the beginning of the end to Judaism as a definable purposeful religion? Was God calling the Jews back to their biblical homeland? Why did secularists feel an attachment to Palestine if their personal religious aspect was undeveloped? The answer to these questions hinge on the fact that the pressure for the return was coming from Eastern Europe. There traditional Orthodoxy and Hasidism, as well as lingering aspects of messianism, were major factors. It is understandable, considering the flood of pogroms, that Russian Jews adhered to the biblical imperative to return to the Promised Land. Their strongly-held conviction on this matter lent considerable weight to the Palestinian alternative, making other alternatives difficult or impossible to fully realize.

The Orthodox rabbinate at this point had not taken a unified position on these issues; indeed, it was always difficult to obtain a unified position. Rabbis in assembly act as a deliberative legislative body usually seeking unanimity without regard to a timetable. The basic issue dividing the Orthodox was whether Hibbat Zion was a signal from God to return to the Holy Land, or whether it was a chimera. This debate split more or less along Eastern/Western European rabbinical lines. In 1883, Emma Lazarus warned, "The lesson of discipline and organization is the last one that the Jews will learn; but until they have mastered it, they cannot hope to secure by desultory, independent and often mutually conflicting efforts, equal conditions and human rights for their oppressed brethren." Looking into an uncertain future, she wrote, "Where are we to look in America for the patriotic Jew whose intellect is sufficiently expanded to accept all the conclusions of science, and yet whose sense of the moral responsibilities and glories bequeathed to him by his ancestors is sufficiently vivid to kindle him into a missionary and a prophet?"

At this point in the development of Zionism, Theodor Herzl stepped on to the stage. He was born May 2, 1860, in Budapest, Hungary, the only son of Jakob and Jeannette Herzl. He had one sibling, Pauline one year older. His parents were not particularly religious, but observed the Sabbath and holidays. They gave Theodor just enough Jewish education to undertake his *bar mitzvah*. However, his paternal grandfather Simon Herzl, an Orthodox Jew, was a follower of Rabbi Judah Alkalai who, in 1839, published a book stating the need for Jewish colonies in the Holy Land. Simon Herzl visited his son and family annually, and was held in tender affection by Theodor.

In 1878, Herzl's beloved sister died of typhoid and the family moved to Vienna where Herzl studied law at the university. Anti-Semitism in Austria was more than ordinarily high at the time, and Herzl encountered it in his fraternity which participated in an anti-Semitic demonstration. He forthwith resigned stating:

> I would not think of launching a polemic here against this repressive fashion of the day. I merely wish to mention in passing that even if I were not a Jew, from the standpoint of my love of liberty I would have to condemn this movement.

Following graduation in 1884, his doting parents sent him on an European tour during which he wrote travel articles for the Vienna *Neue Freie Presse*, a Jewish-owned newspaper that employed him upon his return.

Herzl's parents in 1889, arranged a marriage for him with Julie Naschauer, an attractive but unstable woman of comparable social position. Within a short period of time, two girls and a boy were born to the couple. But in 1891, when Herzl accepted the position of Paris correspondent for his newspaper, he spent very little time with his wife and children. The children, who needed their strong father, suffered most grievously. Pauline, named for his sister, committed suicide as did Hans on the twentieth anniversary of his father's death after converting to Christianity, and Margarete (Trude) died in a Nazi concentration camp.

We do not see in Theodor Herzl's early years a dedication to the mission of salvation of Russian Jewry. Despite his *bar mitzvah*, he was a non-practicing Jew. He was also uninformed of any attempt to resettle Jews in Palestine or any other place. However, under the growing pressure of anti-Semitism caused by emigrating East European Jews who crowded the streets of Vienna, together with the feelings of non-Jews who were finding it more difficult to compete in the business world and the professions with newly trained Jews, Herzl began to despair that assimilation would work. This attitude took root in him and developed.

The year 1892, was pivotal in the development of Herzl's religious zeal. In June, one Captain Mayer, a Jewish officer in the French Army, was killed in a duel by a notorious anti-Semite. Mayer's funeral, over which the chief rabbi of the city presided, was a public event of great note to the Jewish community in Paris. The chief rabbi, in his eulogy, assured France of the unswerving loyalty of its Jewish sons. It was also the year that the term "Zionism" was coined by Nathan Birnbaum, founder of *Kadimah* [Forward-Eastward] an early Zionist movement and publisher of Pinsker's journal *Auto-Emancipation*. The May 18, 1893 issue of *Auto-Emancipation*, changed its header from "Organ of the Jewish Nationalists" to "Organ of the Zionists"

At the time, however, Herzl "could not have named a single settlement in Palestine, was embarrassingly ignorant of Judaism and Jewish history, knew next to nothing about East European Jewry except to disdain it, and, had the word been uttered in his presence, could not have said what 'Zionism' was." Further, Herzl did not yet believe in a homeland for the Jews. He wrote that

> [t]he lot of the factory worker is similar to that of the Jews who had to live in an anti-Semitic era. Jews of the future will see better times; those living in the present have simply tough luck. The Jews themselves must cooperate in order that these better days may materialize, not through founding organizations to fight anti-Semitism, not through the publication of newspapers, but through the complete regeneration of Jewry, by a thoroughgoing assimilation.

At this point, Herzl, on the verge of prophecy, was comparable to Saul before his transformation to St. Paul.

Herzl's transition from disinterested observer of Jewish emigration to concerned philo-Semite to dedicated Zionist occurred over a decade. In 1894, he wrote a play called *The New Ghetto* in which he clearly envisioned the outcome of the German attitude towards its Jewish citizens. Thereafter he assumed responsibility to lead the expatriate Jews to the Promised Land. Herzl devoted the remainder of his life to attaining the goals of Zionism. During the period, June 1895 to his death in July 1904, he maintained a diary of his prophetic work which was published in the original German and later translated into English. The edition to which reference will be made here is the Lowenthal English translation, which provides insights into Herzl's attitude, concerns, and methods.

In the following passage, Herzl relates his calling:

> I have been pounding away for some time at a work of tremendous magnitude. I don't know even now if I will be able to carry it through. It bears the aspects of a mighty dream. For days and weeks it has saturated me to the limits of consciousness; it goes with me everywhere, hovers behind my ordinary talk, peers at me over the shoulders of funny little journalistic work, overwhelms and intoxicates me ... Title: *The Promised Land*. The question gnawed and tugged at me, it tormented me and rendered me profoundly unhappy ... In fact, I always came back to it whenever my own personal experiences — their joys and sorrows—lifted me to a higher plane.

Thus said the Lord, the God of Israel: Write in a scroll all the words
that I have spoken to you. For the days are coming ... when I will restore
the fortunes of My people ... and I will bring them back to the land that
I gave their fathers and they shall possess of it. (Jer. 30:2-3)

Herzl is also quoted by a close associate as saying:

This work is for me and the rest of my life of the greatest
importance, perhaps also for all men. For what makes me
assume that I have planned something valuable is the fact that
not for a second did I think of myself working as a literary
man but always of other people who are suffering gravely.

Herzl then confided this vision for a Jewish homeland in his diary:

During our two thousand years of dispersion we have been
without united political leadership. I hold this to be our chief
misfortune. It has done us more harm than all the
persecutions. It has rotted and ruined us from within. There
has been no one ... to train us in true manhood. On the
contrary. We have been dragged into the shabbiest
occupations and we have been locked up in Ghettos where
side by side we have degenerated. And when the gates were
opened we were expected suddenly to have all the traits of a
free people.

If we had a united political leadership ... if ... we possessed
this leadership, we could proceed to the solution of the
Jewish question ... The aim we would have in view, once we
possessed a center and a head, would determine the means to
be pursued. We can have but two aims — either to remain
where we are or to emigrate somewhere else. For either, we
need to educate our people ... even if we decide to emigrate, it
will take a long while before we can reach the Promised Land.
Moses needed forty years. We require perhaps twenty or
thirty. In any case, new generations will arise whom we must
educate.

The matter of education became of extreme importance. The question
was the *manner* of education. Was it to be strictly secular, or strictly religious, or
a combination of both?

Hark back now to these words of Emma Lazarus in 1883: "Where are we to look in America for the patriotic Jew whose intellect is sufficiently expanded to accept all the conclusions of science, and yet whose sense of the moral responsibilities and glories bequeathed to him by his ancestors is sufficiently vivid to kindle him into a missionary and a prophet?"

She found him in Vienna.

The Jewish State

Obsessed with his vision of a homeland for the Jews, Herzl followed the conventional route of appealing to the very wealthy for aid. Unsuccessful in his approach to Baron de Hirsch and the Viennese branch of the Rothschilds, Herzl heeded the advice of his father to found his movement not upon those whose livelihood depended upon assimilation, but rather on the oppressed masses. To reach these people, Herzl needed a convincing pamphlet. In 1894, he wrote *Der Judenstaat (The Jewish State)* in a creative fury. In February 1896, *Der Judenstaat* was published in an edition of 3000. "It became as significant for Zionism as was the *Communist Manifesto* for socialism." Today, it is considered one of the most influential books of the 19th and 20th centuries.

The Jewish State was a summation of Herzl's position on Zionism, "the restoration of the Jewish State." He disclaims any originality in presenting this concept, but he does provide a plan for meeting his objective. This was the difference between Herzl and his predecessors. He spent little time in theological contemplation of the problem; rather, he spent his time devising strategies to achieve his objective. He assumed that the objective would be achieved, saying that:

> I am absolutely convinced that I am right, though I doubt whether I shall live to see myself proved to be so ... I ask the cultivated men whom I am addressing to set many preconceived ideas entirely aside. I shall even go so far as to ask those Jews who have most earnestly tried to solve the Jewish Question to look upon their previous attempts as mistaken and futile ... I shall therefore clearly and emphatically state that I believe in the practical outcome of my scheme, though without professing to have discovered the shape it may ultimately take. The Jewish State is essential to the world; it will therefore be created.

The Jewish State was likely a book inspired by divine revelation. Those things for which we feel a strong compulsion and which are done in recognition of a need of others and which stretch our abilities either physically or mentally, may be attributed to the strength of our conscience or to an irresistible urge. In either case, it may be as close to God as we can expect to be. Herzl's explanation for writing the Jewish State met these criteria.

Herzl did not believe that he alone could accomplish this momentous task but hoped that

> ... our ambitious young men, to whom every road of progress is now closed, seeing in this Jewish State a bright prospect of freedom, happiness and honors opening to them, will ensure the propagation of the idea ... The Jews who wish for a State shall have it, and they will deserve to have it.

This appeal to what is basically a patriotic objective obscures the issues of responsibility that attach to the *Eretz Israel* (Land of Israel) movement. From this point on, we can view Herzl's work as that of a prophet in the same sense as other biblical prophets. That being the case, we might ask to what purpose was Herzl's ministry? The answer, which is clear in his writing, is to save a remnant of Judaism from the coming Holocaust, and to plant it in the Promised Land there to renew the biblical imperative to live out God's covenant.

Dwelling on the goal of assimilation and the realities of anti-Semitism in Europe, Herzl wrote,

> We are a people— one people. We have honestly endeavored everywhere to merge ourselves in the social life of surrounding communities and to preserve the faith of our fathers. We are not permitted to do so. In vain are we loyal patriots, our loyalty in some places running to extremes; in vain do we make the same sacrifices of life and property as our fellow-citizens; in vain do we strive to increase the fame of our native land in science and art, or her wealth by trade and commerce. In countries where we have lived for centuries we are still cried down as strangers and often by those whose ancestors were not yet domiciled in the land where Jews had already the experience of suffering ... It is useless, therefore, for us to be the loyal patriots ... If we could only be left in peace ... But I think we shall not be left in peace.

Anticipating the protests of the assimilated Jews, particularly to his opening phrase above, and using French Jews as an example, Herzl said,

> if all or any of the French Jews protest against this scheme on account of their own "assimilation," my answer is simple: The whole thing does not concern them at all. They are Jewish

Frenchmen, well and good! This is a private affair for the
Jews alone. The movement towards the organization of the
State I am proposing would, of course, harm Jewish
Frenchmen no more than it would harm the "assimilated" of
other countries. It would, on the contrary, be distinctly to
their advantage. For they would no longer be disturbed in
their "chromatic function," as Darwin puts it, but would be
able to assimilate in peace, because the present anti-Semitism
would have been stopped forever. They would certainly be
credited with being assimilated to the very depths of their
souls, if they stayed where they were after the new Jewish
State, with its superior institutions, had become a reality.

Herzl warned that Jews were always in danger, but promised that they
would always survive as a people.

... The distinctive nationality of Jews neither can, will, nor
must be destroyed. It cannot be destroyed, because external
enemies consolidate it. It will not be destroyed; this is shown
during two thousand years of appalling suffering. It must not
be destroyed, and that, as a descendant to numberless Jews
who refused to despair, I am trying once more to prove in
this pamphlet. Whole branches of Judaism may wither and
fall, but the trunk will remain.

This has the sound of Paul's olive tree. However, Herzl who knew
little of the Hebrew Bible, probably knew less of Paul's letters. But the threat
only underscored the need to return to Palestine.

Is it not true that in countries where we live in perceptible
numbers, the position of Jewish lawyers, doctors, technicians,
teachers, and employees of all descriptions becomes daily
more intolerable? Is it not true, that the Jewish middle classes
are seriously threatened? Is it not true, that the passions of the
mob are incited against our wealthy people? Is it not true, that
our poor endure greater sufferings than any other proletariat?
I think that this external pressure makes itself felt everywhere.
In our economically upper classes it causes discomfort, in our
middle classes continual and grave anxieties, in our lower
class absolute despair ... Can we hope for better days, can we
possess our souls in patience, can we wait in pious resignation
till the princes and peoples of the earth are more mercifully
disposed towards us? I say that we cannot hope for a change

in the current of feeling. The nations in whose midst Jews live are all either covertly or openly anti-Semitic.

Palestine is our ever-memorable historic home. The very name of Palestine would attract our people with a force of marvelous potency ... We should there form a portion of a rampart of Europe against Asia, an outpost of civilization as opposed to barbarism. We should as a neutral State remain in contact with all Europe, which would have to guarantee our existence. The sanctuaries of Christendom would be safeguarded by assigning to them an extra-territorial status such as is well-known to the law of nations.

The appeal of this passage is to the political concerns of middle European countries; it does not speak to the religious responsibilities of the new state. However, Israel still remains, in the minds of western world leaders, "an outpost of civilization in the Middle East."

Regarding the matter of negotiating for territory in Palestine and financing the exodus of Jews eager to colonize, Herzl set up in *The Jewish State* two agencies, "The Society of Jews" for the former concerns and "The Jewish Company" for the more practical concerns.

[The] Society will be ... authorized to confer and treat with Governments in the name of our people. Externally, the Society will attempt ... to be acknowledged as a State-forming power. The free assent of many Jews will confer on it the requisite authority in its relations with Governments. Internally, that is to say, in its relation with the Jewish people, the Society will create all the first indispensable institutions; it will be the nucleus out of which the public institutions of the Jewish State will later on be developed.

Our first object ... supremacy assured to us by international law, over a portion of the globe sufficiently large to satisfy our just requirements. This is necessary because a [gradual] infiltration [of immigrants] is bound to end badly. It continues till the inevitable moment when the native population feels itself threatened, and forces the Government to stop a further influx of Jews. Immigration is consequently futile unless we have the sovereign right to continue such immigration. The Jewish Company will have the following responsibilities: "convert into cash all vested interests left by departing Jews." It will also "take over ... abandoned estates till such time as it

can dispose of them to the greatest advantage ... The
Company will endeavor everywhere to facilitate the
acquisition of land by its tenants, who are Christians. In the
land to be settled, the Company will acquire large areas for its
own needs and the needs of the people at reasonable prices. It
will also sell building sites at reasonable rates ... for the
construction of homes.
The Jews once settled in their own State, would probably
have no more enemies ... [although] I think the Jews will
always have sufficient enemies, such as every nation has. But
once fixed in their own land, it will no longer be possible for
them to scatter all over the world. The diaspora cannot be
reborn, unless the civilization of the whole earth should
collapse; and such a consummation could be feared by none
but foolish men. Our present civilization possesses weapons
powerful enough for its self-defense.

Herzl believed that the settlement of Palestine by the Jews would be a
boon to the native population as well. And, indeed, it might have been if a
working relationship had been established from the beginning.

The *Jewish State* describes in some detail the purchase of land
through equitable negotiation, the provision of dwelling
places, a seven-hour work day, free market commerce,
promotion of industry, methods of raising capital, etc. The
plan covers most practical areas of concern. Herzl believed in
the entrepreneurial spirit of young Judaism and urged that it
be encouraged in every possible way. The book concludes
with this uplifting statement:

Therefore I believe that a wondrous generation of Jews will
spring into existence ... Let me repeat once more my opening
words: the Jews who wish for a State will have it. We shall live
at last as free men on our own soil, and die peacefully in our
own homes. The world will be freed by our liberty, enriched
by our wealth, magnified by our greatness. And whatever we
attempt there to accomplish for our own welfare, will react
powerfully and beneficially for the good of humanity.

This bold statement reflects one of the duties under the covenant.

Impact of the The Jewish State

The *Jewish State* arrived like a bombshell in the lives of assimilated European Jews. The Jewish pacifist-humanist writer Stefan Zweig (1881-1942) recalled its impact.

> I was still in the "Gymnasium" [high school] when this short pamphlet [*The Jewish State*], penetrating as a steel shaft, appeared; but I can still remember the general astonishment and annoyance of the bourgeois Jewish circles of Vienna. What has happened, they said angrily, to this otherwise intelligent, witty and cultivated writer? What foolishness is this that he has thought up and writes about? Why should we go to Palestine? Our language is German not Hebrew, and beautiful Austria is our homeland. Are we not well off under the good Emperor Franz Josef? Do we not make a decent living, and is our position not secure? Are we not equal subjects, inhabitants and loyal citizens of our beloved Vienna? Do we not live in a progressive era in which in a few decades all sectarian prejudices will be abolished? Why does he, who speaks as a Jew and who wishes to help Judaism, place arguments in the hands of our worst enemies and attempt to separate us when every day brings us more closely and intimately into the German world? The rabbis thundered passionately from the pulpits, the head of the *Neue Freie Press* forbade the very mention of the word Zionism in his "progressive" newspaper.

Others said, "How was it possible that such a man should be the author of a serious political brochure, offering a solution of the Jewish problem, especially as, so far as most people were aware, he had never belonged to any Jewish society nor concerned himself with Jewish affairs?" But, it was the anti-Semitic press that now praised Herzl.

The initial reaction from *Hibbat Zion* was one of suspicion.

> Who was this stranger, of whom they had never heard before, and what did he want? Was he serious about the business? Why this tremendous trumpet blast of a proclamation, why this gigantic political program which had no prospect of realization within measurable time? Might he not, with his tactless openness, antagonize the philanthropists on whose money the work [of colonization] depended, irritate and alarm

the Turkish government, whom they were constantly
reassuring of their non-political intentions, and thus bring
danger on the colonization itself, the one thing that mattered?

And with regard to the assimilationists:

From Berlin to San Francisco wherever emancipationist
rabbis and Jewish communal leaders began to realize that the
move to establish a Jewish state was serious, Herzl's efforts
were immediately understood to be a mortal blow to the
world they had created for themselves. What difference would
it make how much they emphasized that their Judaism was
merely a faith, without political implications? The very
existence of a Jewish state — even the existence of a political
movement for the creation of one — would render all their
protestations meaningless.

Not all responses were critical. David Wolfsohn recognized the futility
of assimilating and felt the immense strength of the vision, and the new world
that could be possible for the Jews. He was a successful business man and a
believer in a Jewish state. Wolfsohn would become Herzl's right hand and
immediate successor to the presidency of the Zionist organization.

A door had been flung open for them, light streamed in.
Clarity, dignity, strong faith and a prophetic, appealing pathos
lifted out of the dreariness of the daily reality. That flutter of
eagles' wings [Exod. 19:4] which, as Herzl told later, he had
felt above his head when he wrote *The Judenstaat*, became
audible now to these of his readers. Now they suddenly saw
before them a goal, a great and attainable goal, and the steps
which led to it.

And from the poet Richard Beer-Hofmann:

Even more than to the contents of the book I was attracted
to its implications. At last there comes again a man who does
not carry his Judaism with resignation like a burden or
misfortune, but is proud to be the legal inheritor of an
immemorial culture.

Then there were those who rejected both assimilation and nationalism.
"Never before have I felt so liberated by Judaism as I do now ... I have never
wanted the Jews to become a nation again and humiliate themselves by

entering the contest of rival realities. I love the diaspora and affirm it as the sense of Judaism's idealism, as the principle behind its vocation for world citizenship and universal humanity." Stefan Zweig

Hazony in summarizing the impact of *Der Judenstaat* noted that, "So far as I am aware, Herzl's [book] constituted the only systematic theory ever advanced to explain how a Jewish state could be made real and permanent. As such [it] continues even in our own time to be critical for understanding what has been done until now for the sake of this cause and what has not."

As thrilling and promising the *Judenstaat* was, primarily to Eastern Jewry, its place in the covenant was uncertain. Would it be a country in which the Jewish people could finally demonstrate what it means to live in a society under God? Or would this movement by a non-practicing Jew result in just another European type single national people? Obviously, this was in sharp contrast to America where many national types were learning to live together. But what of the Arabs long since living in Palestine? Will they coexist with the Jews, just as the Jews tried to coexist, for example, with the Germans? And what impact will a Jewish State have on international Jewry?

All of these questions, and many others not yet posed, remain to be answered. Judaism awaited Herzl's next move.

Notes for Chapter Eleven

The desires long held by Russian Jews to return to *Eretz Israel* started to take shape under Theodor Herzl, who worked ceaselessly to place on the table a well-thought-out plan which he published in book form in 1896. *The Jewish State*, (Dover Publications, 1988) is considered to be one of the most influential books of the 19th and 20th centuries. The impact on those who were against it as well as those who supported it was staggering.
Diefendorf, Elizabeth, *Books of the Century*, Oxford University Press, 1996
Herzl dominated the movement to establish a Jewish state in Palestine. Soon after his death in1904 biographies started to appear by writers who knew him.
Bein, Alex, *Theodore Herzl, A Biography*, Jewish Publication Society of America, 1941
Cohen, Israel Theodor, *Herzl, Founder of Political Zionism*, T. Yoseloff, 1959
Patai, József, *Star over Jordan, the Life of Theodore Herzl*, Philosophical Library, 1946
Mendes-Flohr and Jehuda Reinharz, *The Jew in the Modern World: A Documentary History*, Oxford, 1995.
Lowenthal, Marvin, *The Diaries of Theodor Herzl*, The Dial Press 1956
Many other books on Herzl have been written since. The ones I consulted are:

Goldberg, David, *To the Promised Land*, Penguin, 1996

Hazony, Yarom, *The Struggle for Israel's Soul*, New Republic, 2001

Lowenthal, Marvin, *The Diaries of Theodor Herzl*, The Dial Press, 1956

Shmoni, Gideon, *Zionist Ideology*, Brandeis, 1995

Sacher, Howard M. *A History of Israel from the Rise of Zionism to Our Time*, Alfred A. Knopf, 2001.

T. Yoseloff, *Founder of Political Zionism*, M W Books, 1959

For related reading:

Lazarus, Emma, *An Epistle to the Hebrews*, Jewish Historical Society of New York, 1987

For inspirational writing by a champion of Herzl, read Emma Lazarus' 1883 poem for the dedication of the Statute of Liberty which spoke to so many Jewish refugees:

> Give me your tired, your poor,
> Your huddled masses yearning to breathe free,
> The wretched refuse of your teeming shore.
> Send these, the homeless, the tempest-tossed to me.
> I lift my lamp beside the golden door.

Chapter Twelve
The Zionist Congress

The aim of Zionism is to create for the Jewish people a home in Palestine secured by public law.

First Zionist Congress, Basel, Switzerland

While alienating the rich and powerful with his *Jewish State* pamphlet, Herzl was making converts among some of the less influential but well connected Jews in Europe. He realized that his support was from the desperate people, and he turned his attention to them. His master stroke was calling the people together in congress to set a program for their deliverance. By doing so, he made the issue public and took some of the sting out of anti-Semitism. But at the same time he put the European Jewish assimilationists at greater risk.

As the Zionist movement became current news, heads of state began to show interest in a Jewish state in the Middle East. This led to a meeting with the Grand Duke of Baden (uncle to the Kaiser) in April 1896, and shortly thereafter an ill-fated visit to the court of the Ottoman sultan who had jurisdiction over Palestine. After being shuffled from one vizier to another without obtaining an audience with the sultan, Herzl realized that the only interest the sultan may have had in him was the utilization of Herzl's influence in the sultan's own behalf.

Interest Grows

On the journey via rail to Constantinople in June 1896, Herzl was overwhelmed by a joyful demonstration of Jews at the Sofia train station in Bulgaria.

A gripping scene awaited me in Sofia. Lining the platform, where our train drew up, stood a great throng — who had come on my account ... Men, women, children were massed together, Sephardim and Ashkenazim, mere boys and white-bearded patriarchs ... a lad presented me with a wreath of roses and carnations. Dr. [Reuben] Bierer [leader of Bulgarian

Zionists] delivered a speech in German. Then Dr. [Joseph] Caleb [Zionist leader in Sofia] read out an address in French, and finally, despite my resistance, kissed my hand. In this and subsequent speeches I was hailed as Leader, as the Heart of Israel, etc. in extravagant terms ... Everyone pressed around me to shake hands. As the train got underway "they cried *leshonoh haboh b'rooshaolayim!* ["Next year in Jerusalem!"] I too was deeply moved." (Lowenthal, *Diaries*)

Shortly thereafter, upon his return to England, Herzl once more attempted to enlist the great wealth of the Rothschilds by meeting directly with Baron Edmund in France on July 18, 1896. He was rebuffed. The wealthy and influential made it clear to him that they were not about to grant authority over the fate of European Jewry to a man of no real means, and one who was a suspect publicist at that. But once more Herzl was brought up short by the devotion of the common Jews to his cause:

In the evening, my mass-meeting at the Working Men's Club in the East End [of London]. ... [The] club-house was packed. People crowded into every corner. ... I talked for one hour, in the fearful heat. Great success. Succeeding speakers extolled me. One of them, Ish Kishor compared me to Moses, Columbus, etc. The chairman, Chief Rabbi [Moses] Gaster, delivered a fiery speech. Finally, I thanked them with a few words, in which I deprecated their exaggerations. Great jubilation, hat waving, and cheering that carried over into the street. Now in truth it depends solely on myself whether I shall become the leader of the masses ... As I sat on the platform of the Working Men's stage last Sunday I underwent a curious experience. I saw and heard my legend being made. The people are sentimental; the masses do not see clearly. I believe that by now they no longer have a clear image of me. A faint mist is beginning to rise and envelop me, and may perhaps become the cloud in which I shall walk.

First Zionist Congress

Herzl knew then it was only possible to succeed through the immediate organization of the masses, and turned his attention to convening the First Zionist Congress. Nothing quite like this had ever been attempted among the Jews since ancient times. Not since Ezra had the Torah been read to the people more than 2,300 years before. Lowenthal notes that "The instrument for political and financial action [was] itself a novel and untried experiment in Jewish life." The effort to bring about this momentous event tested even the hard driving Herzl who had been told a year before that his heart was being affected by his strenuous life. Early in 1897, he encountered resistance from influential Jews in England, France, and Russia. He despaired for the success of the movement, and contemplated his own death. But, recognizing then that he alone was the master of this movement, Herzl moved ahead with all his strength to make the First Zionist Congress a reality. This is the beginning of a movement which he would lead to change the face of Judaism forever.

In a lecture at the Israelitic Union, Herzl laid out his goals:

> Not merely prevention of persecution of Jews is the aim of Zionism, but the fulfillment of an inner mission. The atmosphere of the Jewish spirit and Jewish character, in which so many strong generations developed, must be reestablished. The persecutions steeled the character of the Jews, and their inner unity gave them strength for endurance and resistance. The generation that withdrew from Jewry lacks inner unity and therefore cannot count either on the past or the future. That is why we must be Jews again and never leave this fortress ... We shall be respected as other people are, if we have ideals as they have.

The "inner mission" of which Herzl speaks is, basically, the reestablishment of an individual and collective spirit that with other like-minded Jews seeks to make for themselves a free and strong society. It has no clear connection to their covenant duty. Continuing, he said:

> Many think this is just an old whim which we have taken over. It is, on the contrary, something entirely modern, as modern as our everyday sufferings and fates. We have always had to suffer from something, and we have withstood everything. Now we live in times in which it is easier to have fortitude ... Just as people were pleased when Greece rose from the ruins, so a cry of astonishment will be heard when the Jews, at present degraded and lying in the dust, rise from their degradation. This is why I think we must stick together, even if we differ on some details, because the fight is waged against us all. I don't know whether this generation will live long enough to see the liberation from humiliation and misery. But I do know that wandering on this road alone will make different people of us. We shall win again our lost inner unity and, with this, our character. Not a loaned, untrue

character but our own. Only then do we want to vie with other decent people in justice, love for our neighbors and high liberalism. We want to be active on all fields of honor, to try to advance in the arts and sciences so that the glory of our deeds reflects upon the poorest of our people.

Whether the challenge to seek justice and offer love to neighbors constitutes the admission of a covenant duty is debatable. This passage, however, is reminiscent of Micah 6:8

> *And what the Lord requires of you: Only to do justice, and to love goodness, and to walk modestly with your God.*

In March 1897, Herzl met with like-minded Jews from Austria and Germany, gaining their support for the Congress. Continuing dissension and increasing attacks upon his plans grew to a general assault in the spring of 1897, but Herzl, driven by the cause, broadcast his new slogan: "The Congress will take place!"

Bein reports that the assimilated rabbis protested against the

> nonsensical distortion of the meaning of Judaism and of the ideals of the confessors of the Jewish faith as implied in "the calling of the Zionist Congress and in its published agenda." The aims of the "so-called Zionists" contradicted the 'prophetic message of Jewry and the duty of every Jew to belong without reservation to the fatherland in which he lives. Religion and love of the fatherland, no less than our regard for the welfare of Judaism, lay upon us the duty to repudiate the aims of Zionism and to ignore the call to the Congress. The Congress document was an unworthy, cowardly concoction "one of those contemptible utterances which play into the hands of our enemies."

Herzl replied to these public attacks with devastating effectiveness. Using his own funds, he decided to start a weekly publication to be called *Die Welt (The World)*, the masthead of which displayed a Star of David and the coastline of Palestine between the title's two words. It became the instrument to lead Judaism "out of our times into happier times." Herzl began his reply

> by pointing out that those who did not feel that they belonged to a Jewish people had no business to interfere in its affairs. "To belong to Jewry, to exploit this relationship as it were professionally, and to fight it at the same time" was

something monstrous. For 'Zionism is not a party. Jews of
every party can enroll in the movement, just as the people
contains within itself all parties. Zionism is the Jewish people
on the march. [But] When they speak of Zion they mean, in
God's name, anything but Zion."

The union of German rabbis replied to Herzl's article in the *Berliner
Tagblatt* of July 6, 1897:

> We can say to our fellow countrymen with complete
> conviction that we comprise a separate community solely with
> respect to *religion*. Regarding nationality, we feel totally at one
> with our fellow Germans and therefore strive towards the
> realization of the spiritual and moral goals of our dear
> fatherland with an enthusiasm equaling theirs... Eighteen
> hundred years ago, history made its decision regarding Jewish
> nationhood through the dissolution of the Jewish State and
> the destruction of the Temple
> ...
> We ask the Zionists then, in whose name and by what
> authority do they speak? Who gave them a mandate to call for
> a congress ... We are protesting against the organizers who
> claim to speak for all Jewry, but behind whom stands not one
> single Jewish congregation.

Herzl's proposed Congress was frightening to those who worked to
assimilate because it undermined their position. Having had almost a century to
assimilate into their host country, many such Jews were economically secure,
and, therefore, threatened by this new movement. How could they continue to
justify their position as Germans first and Jews second when the growing
Zionist movement was broadcasting Jews first?

However, the arguments of the German Jewish community did not
advance their own cause to assimilate into the German Gentile society. Their
defense that Jews must work toward the assimilation of their brothers and
sisters in all countries speaks to a certain unity of social purpose for all Jews in
Diaspora. But what was never clear about the assimilation movement was its
ultimate goal. Is there an unwritten agenda? Will this movement pursue
assimilation in all aspects of social life (excepting religious belief), including the
ultimate dissolution of Judaism through intermarriage and the gradual
breakdown of religious practices?

On August 29, 1897, the first Zionist Congress assembled in Basel,
Switzerland. Delegates arrived from Russia, Germany, Austria-Hungary,
Bulgaria, Romania, England, Holland, Belgium, Palestine, America, Algeria,

and the Scandinavian countries as well. Missing were delegates from Lebanon, Syria, Persia, and Egypt, the Sephardim from Ottoman countries. The delegates totaled 197. The largest delegation (70) was from Russia. Herzl arranged the agenda and all of the accessories including the dress of the delegates, which was white tie and frock coat, and the new flag: a white field with two blue horizontal stripes and the Star of David, basically the flag of Israel today. Many of the delegates took it for granted that this was the old Jewish flag. The familiar *Hatikvah* was written for this event; the song later became the Israeli national anthem.

Imagine yourself in that hall in 1897, when world Jewry renewed its national purpose. Secretaries able to speak the language of any delegate, most importantly Yiddish, were on hand and prepared to translate each day's activities from German into native languages. The Russian delegation prepared a Yiddish report of the daily discussions for their delegates. World press outnumbered the delegates on the floor, and spectators crowded the balconies. The Congress was a masterful propaganda coup.

The Congress met for three days. "This was not a mere gathering of practical men," Jacob de Haas reported at the time, "nor yet a mere assembly of dreamers; the inward note was that of a gathering of brothers meeting after the long Diaspora ... it was for the first time, after more than eighteen hundred years of dispersion throughout the world, that Jews had been called together to deliberate upon measures for their rehabilitation as a nation."

The Congress came to order and Herzl arose and, calmly, completely self-possessed, erect, walked over to the tribune, the focus of attention. Then in the words of Ben Ami, the *Hovevei Zion* and Hebrew writer, he became his own legend:

> It was extraordinary! What had happened? This was not the
> Dr. Herzl I had seen hitherto ... Before us rose a marvelous
> and exalted figure, kingly in bearing and stature, with deep
> eyes in which could be read quiet majesty and unuttered
> sorrow. It is no longer the elegant Dr. Herzl of Vienna; it is a
> royal scion of the House of David, risen from among the
> dead, clothed in legend and fantasy and beauty. Everyone sat
> breathless, as if in the presence of a miracle. And in truth, was
> it not a miracle which we beheld? And then wild applause
> broke out; for fifteen minutes the delegates clapped, shouted
> and waved their handkerchiefs. The dream of two thousand
> years was on the point of realization; it was as if the Messiah,
> son of David, confronted us ...

The perception both of the working men of London who yearned for a country in which their abilities would be fully rewarded, and of the downtrodden Jews of the Pale who wanted only to be free and live without fear, was that a new Moses had come to lead them back to the Promised Land. Perhaps they saw as well the promised Messiah, but surely the delegates to the First Zionist Congress did not doubt that they had seen a miracle: the Messiah, son of David standing before them. It was surely one of the greatest moments in Jewish history.

Without loss of words [Herzl] set forth, in a single sentence, the task of the Congress:

> We are here to lay the foundation stone of the house which is to shelter the Jewish nation ... In this epoch, in other respects one of such high achievement, the Jews were everywhere surrounded by the ancient Jew-hatred in modern form: anti-Semitism. It had hit hardest just those Jewish elements which it had probably not wanted to reach primarily: The modern educated de-ghettoized Jew, who felt himself stabbed to the heart. Today we can say this calmly, without being suspected of making a play for the tearful compassion of our enemies. Our conscience is clear. The world has always been badly misinformed about us. The feeling of unity among us, which the world so often and so bitterly throws up to us, was in the process of dissolution when the tide of anti-Semitism rose about us. Anti-Semitism has given us our strength again. We have returned home: Zionism is the return of the Jews to Judaism even before their return to the Jewish land.

"Judaism" is the monotheistic faith of the Jews. The word denotes both a religious and a national concept. Whether Herzl intended a religious aspect to the use of this word, we do not know.

Here we see that Judaism is gathering its strength from the rising tide of Anti-Semitism. Herzl continued:

> In this Congress we procure for the Jewish people an organ which till now it did not possess, and of which it was so sadly in want. Our cause is too great for the ambition and willfulness of a single person. It must be lifted up to something impersonal if it is to succeed. And our Congress shall be lasting, not only until we are redeemed from the old state, but still more so afterwards ... serious and lofty, a blessing for the unfortunate, noxious to none, to the honor of all Jews, and worthy of a past, the glory of which is far off, but everlasting.

The most important outcome of the First Congress was Herzl's introduction to Russian Jewry.

> ... at the Basle (*sic*) Congress there rose before our eyes a Russian Jewry the strength of which we had not even suspected. Seventy of our delegates came from Russia, and it was patent to all of us that they represented the views and sentiments of the five million Jews of that country. And what a humiliation for us, who had taken our own superiority for granted! All these professors, doctors, lawyers, industrialists, engineers and merchants stand on an educational level which is certainly not lower than ours. Nearly all of them are masters of two or three languages, and that they are men of ability in their particular lines is proved by the simple fact that they have succeeded in a land where success is particularly difficult for Jews ... They do not assimilate into other nations, but they exert themselves to learn the best that there is in other peoples. In this wise they manage to remain erect and genuine. And yet they are ghetto-Jews! The only ghetto-Jews of our time! Looking on them, we understood where our fore-fathers got the strength to endure through the bitterest times.

Herzl's new-found respect for the educational and vocational achievements of the liberated Russian Jews was magnified many times over. This new insight focused Herzl's determination to insure that these people would have an opportunity to apply their abilities in a free society.

The New York Times reported from Basel on August 31, 1897:

> The Zionist Congress opened at Basel yesterday with 200 delegates in attendance from various parts of Europe. Dr. Theodor Herzl the so-called "New Moses" and originator of the scheme to purchase Palestine and resettle the Hebrews there, was elected President and Dr. Max Nordau was elected Vice President of the Congress. Dr. Herzl has only recently come into prominence. He seeks to float a limited liability company in London for the purpose of acquiring Palestine from the Sultan of Turkey and thoroughly organizing it for resettlement by the Hebrews. He has, it is said, already won converts to the Zionistic movement in all parts of the world.

When asked to outline his plans, Dr. Herzl said:

> My plan is simple enough, We must obtain the (*sic*)
> sovereignty over Palestine our never-to-be-forgotten,
> historical home ... At first we shall send only unskilled
> labor— that is, the very poorest, who will make the land
> arable. They will lay out streets, build bridges and railroads,
> regulate rivers, and lay down telegraphs according to plans
> prepared at headquarters. Their work will bring trade, their
> trade the market, and the markets will cause new settlers to
> flock to the country. Every one will go there voluntarily, at his
> or her own risk, but ever under the watchful eye and
> protection of the organization.

It will surprise no one that at this point in Herzl's rush to Palestine others did not entirely approve of this venture. One of the most vociferous critics was Asher Ginsburg (1856-1927) who wrote under the pen name Ahad Ha'am (One of the People). He was born in the Kiev Province of the Pale to a well-to-do merchant family. He believed that as the various European cultures engulfed the Jews, their distinctiveness would be obliterated, leaving them scattered remnants without a common element. He therefore supported a return to the Holy Land, but with a difference.

Ahad Ha'am's visits to *Eretz Israel* in 1891 and 1892 convinced him that the Zionist movement would face an uphill struggle in its attempt to create a Jewish national home. In particular he warned of the difficulties associated with land purchase and cultivation, the problems with the Turkish authorities, and impending conflict with the Arabs. But Ahad Ha'am also believed that the creation in *Eretz Israel* of a Jewish cultural center would act to reinforce Jewish life in the Diaspora. His hope was that, in this center, a new Jewish national identity based on Jewish ethics and values might resolve the crisis of Judaism. He returned in 1922, to spend the last five years of his life in Tel Aviv.

Ahad Ha'am's vision for return was to be known as Cultural Zionism. In 1894, he defined it as a kind of rebirth.

> This is the conception of Judaism on which our literature
> must be based. We must revitalize the idea of the national
> renaissance, and use every possible means to strengthen its
> hold and deepen its roots, until it becomes an organic element
> in the Jewish consciousness and an independent dynamic
> force. Only in that way, it seems to me, can the Jewish soul be
> freed from its shackles and regain contact with the broad
> stream of human life without having to pay for its freedom by
> the sacrifice of its individuality.

Years later, in 1897, he predicted worldwide benefits from this rebirth.

> This Jewish settlement, which will be a gradual growth, will
> become in the course of time the center of the nation,
> wherein its spirit will find pure expression and develop in all
> its aspects up to the highest degree of perfection of which it is
> capable. Then from this center the spirit of Judaism will go
> forth to the great circumference, to all the communities of the
> Diaspora, and will breathe new life into them and preserve
> their unity; and when our national culture in Palestine has
> attained that level, we may be confident that it will produce
> men in the country who will be able, on a favorable
> opportunity, to establish a State which will be a Jewish State,
> and not merely a State of Jews.

The disinterest of Zionist leaders in religious observance was in line with their secular attitude. Most were unfamiliar with the Bible and the religious traditions of Judaism. Some had never even entered a synagogue according to a knowledgeable writer in the London Times. Yet, it was the secular, in the main, who decided that the Jews must have a home of their own in Palestine so that they could live free of oppression. The secular imperative will become a major concern as National Zionism progresses into General Zionism, and finally into Zionism.

The finale of the First Congress was a statement of the objectives of National Zionism. Following is the official program of the Zionist movement as printed in the *Jewish Chronicle* on September 3, 1897:

> The aim of Zionism is to create for the Jewish people a home
> in Palestine secured by public law. The Congress
> contemplates the following means to the attainment of this
> end:
> 1. The promotion, on suitable lines, of the colonization of
> Palestine by Jewish agricultural and industrial workers.
> 2. The organization and binding together of the whole Jewry
> by means of appropriate institutions, local and international,
> in accordance with the laws of each country.
> 3. The strengthening and fostering of Jewish national
> sentiment and consciousness.
> 4. Preparatory steps towards obtaining government consent
> where necessary, to
> 5. The attainment of the aim of Zionism.

The first objective does not speak to the higher achievements possible in industrial, scientific and cultural realms. It does undergird what will become, about a decade in the future, the beginning of Labor Zionism. The second goal, binding world Jewry in support of Zionism, is directly opposed to the (unorganized) assimilationist goal of assisting world Jewry to blend into the society of their host country; it does have a possible overtone of Cultural Zionism. The third goal, "strengthening and fostering Jewish national sentiment and consciousness," is a world-wide aim to organize Jewish opinion in support of a national homeland in Palestine. American Jews soon rallied to the cause of Zionism, although that enthusiasm did not result in a ground swell of American immigrants to Palestine. The fourth objective is a call for continuation of diplomatic efforts in order to insure support for Zionism by legitimate governments with an interest in the protectorate of Palestine.

In commenting upon the success of the First Congress, Lowenthal reported that Herzl said:

> If I were to sum up the Congress in a word — which I shall take care not to publish — it would be this: At Basel I founded the Jewish State. If I said this aloud I would be greeted by universal laughter. In five years perhaps, and certainly in fifty years, everyone will perceive it.

The year of the Congress was 1897. Fifty years later, in 1947, the United Nations adopted a resolution declaring that separate Arab and Jewish States be established in Palestine no later than October 1948.

> *I will restore the fortunes of my people Israel, and they shall rebuild the ruined cities and inhabit them; they shall plant vineyards and drink their wine, and they shall make gardens and eat their fruit. I will plant them upon their land, and they shall never again be plucked up out of the land that I have given them, says the Lord your God.* (Amos 9:14-15)

By making the Jews' solidarity a public political issue ... Zionism triumphantly proclaimed the national solidarity that the anti-Semites alleged, thus the heirs of the ideology of the *haskala* had to strive all the harder to deny it. The "Jewish Problem" was now, for the first time, on the world agenda.

Second Zionist Congress

Following the First Congress Herzl gave his full attention to the establishment of a Jewish bank which was to be the depository for funds contributed by the wealthy and the masses for their emigration. But opposition continued from financiers, and the attempt to raise funds for the proposed exodus had little success. Herzl's reaction was to return to Basel for a Second Zionist Congress. His supporters tried to dissuade him, fearing that fewer delegates would turn out, but Herzl persisted, and the Second Congress turned out to be more successful than the first as the Zionist movement began to accelerate. On August 28, 1898, Herzl addressed his opening remarks to the Second Congress before 360 delegates from 913 affiliates world-wide, and nearly five hundred observers including a young Chaim Weizmann, destined to become the first President of the State of Israel. The Second Congress resolved to establish the Jewish Colonial Trust.

Max Nordau (1849-1923) delivered an address on the position of the Jews during the past year. He was born in Pest, Hungary, and was brought up in an Orthodox household; his father was a rabbi. Nordau was educated as a physician, but was noted for writing plays and newspaper reports. He also authored cultural and political tracts, as well as novels. Nordau settled in Paris in 1880, where he became a committed backer of Herzl in 1895, and thereafter worked closely with him. Nordau was a notable at the first eleven Zionist Congresses, delivering the keynote address at the first ten. He was a firm defender of Herzl's political Zionism throughout the remainder of his life. Nordau defined political Zionism as reprised by Shimoni:

> The premise of political Zionism is that there is a Jewish nation. The New Zionism, known as political Zionism, distinguishes itself from the old, religious, messianic form, in that it disavows all mysticism and no longer identifies itself with messianism. It does not expect the return to Palestine to be brought about by a miracle, but rather seeks to accomplish it by its own efforts.

The stand taken by Nordau at the Second Congress to separate political Zionism from religious Zionism was a declaration of intent to dissociate from the rabbinate and make this mission a secular enterprise. Indeed, Nordau seems to be saying that the return to Palestine can be accomplished only by men of action, never intimating or considering that the men of action were in a leadership position just because they *could* carry out the Lord's work. (Just like Saul/Paul and Muhammad)

Whether Herzl would have agreed wholeheartedly, we do not know. Denying that the new Israel would be on the road to messianism is a serious statement. Did Nordau mean that the new settlers would not follow God's way, but rather their own? If so, they would be headed the wrong way. On the other hand, it is not at all certain that God was not directing the hand of Herzl. The signs seem to point to a prophetic ministry, which Nordau did not flatly deny. So, if Herzl is a prophet of God, then the new Israel is intended to exist under the covenant. And if the new Israel is under the covenant and acts accordingly, the Messiah eventually will come.

One of Nordau's more productive efforts was his espousal of physical education for formerly ghettoized Jews to develop bodily health along with higher education. It was his influence that resulted in the demonstrated physical ability of young middle European Jewish men and women in various sporting events, and later their ability to withstand the difficult tasks of colonizing Palestine.

Soon after the Second Congress, Herzl received an unexpected letter from the sultan of the Ottoman Empire expressing his thanks for the (politically) kind words in behalf of their protectorate of Palestine, and a letter from the Kaiser's uncle suggesting that a meeting with the Kaiser was possible. There followed preliminary conferences leading to the highly anticipated meeting. In early October 1898, Herzl suffered a mild heart attack, but went ahead with a planned speech to working men in London that same night. He then worked through the night to codify his plan for the Kaiser, even though he appeared to have suffered another mild heart attack.

Kaiser Meeting

At the time of Herzl's audience with the Kaiser on October 18, 1898, Wilhelm II had control of the reins of power in Germany. He worked well with Jewish men of business and finance, but was disdainful of the Jewish press and chose not to socialize with Jews. Even so, some of the most powerful Gentiles in Germany felt that the Kaiser was too friendly with Jews. Herzl wished to enlist the Kaiser in an alliance to undermine the authority of the Ottoman Empire in Palestine, now in long decline and known as the "sick man of Europe."

Germany had been working for about thirty years to control the center of Ottoman power. Herzl and other leaders of the Zionist movement were German-speaking Jews who felt most comfortable dealing with Germans. Should their movement succeed they would be introducing a German cultural element into the Orient. Therefore, Wilhelm had more than a passing interest in what Herzl had to say. The two met in Constantinople, both on their way to visit the Holy Land.

The content of the meeting is contained in Herzl's diary and may be summarized as follows. The Kaiser seemed to approve of Herzl's land company and the idea of a German protectorate of Palestine. The Kaiser apparently had been following the Dreyfus case closely and was of the surprising (to Herzl) opinion that Dreyfus surely was innocent. Wilhelm seemed taken with Herzl's suggestion of an overland rail route from the Mediterranean to the Persian Gulf, thence by ship to India, a plan consistent with the German initiative to build a railroad from Berlin to Bagdad. (Neither man could have then envisioned the importance that the Middle East would take on when the first oil-fueled battleship, the *Dreadnought*, was built by the British in 1909.) At the close of the meeting, the Kaiser invited Herzl to submit in writing his request regarding what was to be asked of the Sultan.

The Kaiser's reason for visiting Palestine was primarily political in order to advertise Germany's desire to be a presence in the area. Overtly, the reason for the trip was the dedication of the German-built Church of the Redeemer in Jerusalem. Herzl's trip was exploratory. Palestine was in a primitive condition in 1898, sparsely populated and cultivated. There were at the time eighteen Jewish colonies, of which only four could be considered villages. About four thousand rural Jewish settlers lived in those communities, most sponsored by *Hibbat Zion* and maintained by Edmund de Rothschild. About 45,000 people lived in the cities, some dependent on alms. Herzl visited essentially all the rural enclaves.

Herzl was impressed with the ancient beauty of the City of Jerusalem but dismayed by the foulness and filth.

> I would cordon off the old city with its relics, and keep out all ordinary traffic; only places of worship and philanthropic institutions would be allowed to remain inside the old ramparts. And ... with greenery, there would gradually rise a glorious New Jerusalem. The elite from every part of the world would travel the road up to the Mount of Olives. Loving care can turn Jerusalem into a jewel. Everything holy enshrined within the old walls, everything new spreading round about it.

A final audience with the Kaiser and Herzl's party occurred on November 2, 1898 a few days before Herzl's departure as reconstructed by Lowenthal. The Kaiser was in good spirits and received Herzl's address regarding his plan for the settlement of Palestine. The Kaiser responded, "Your movement, with which I am thoroughly familiar, is based on a sound healthy idea." They spoke briefly and agreeably about the need for water and shade as well as attention to medical conditions. Members of Herzl's party spoke of their plans for solving these problems. Herzl departed Palestine on the fifth of November, feeling that his trip produced fairly good results.

Third and Fourth Zionist Congresses

Recognizing the political importance of the annual Congress, Herzl moved ahead with plans for the Third Zionist Congress to be held in Basel in August 1899. The number of affiliates had grown from 913 to more than three thousand, with the largest increase occurring in Russia. Sick and declining in health, Herzl presided but with a noticeable loss of charisma. Nevertheless, the Third Congress saw the establishment of the Jewish Colonial Trust (Bank) for which each voting delegate was required to contribute one shekel (25 cents by the exchange rate at the time). But the Zionist movement was losing momentum in conjunction with Herzl's physical decline.

The next year (1899-1900), passed unproductively for Herzl. He spent a good deal of his time trying to arrange an interview with the Ottoman Sultan. He also met with the American ambassador to Turkey who personally favored a homeland for the Jews in Mesopotamia. The ambassador did point out that it was useless to talk to anyone except the Sultan. Meanwhile the situation of Eastern European Jews worsened as pogroms spread to Romania, news which spurred Herzl to move more quickly to insure a homeland in Palestine.

Herzl arranged for the Fourth Congress to be held in London on August 13-15, 1900. As was his custom, Herzl delivered the opening address to what the London Times called "Many hundreds of delegates of both sexes ... from nearly every country in Europe as well as from Palestine, Canada, the Transvaal [South Africa], Rhodesia, and the United States." (The Congress reported more than four hundred delegates present.) Herzl's address was in German, but he did speak partly in English. The opening speech as reported in the London *Times* follows:

> He declared that the Zionist movement meant not only much for the Jews but it also meant something for others. It not only opened up to every country a settlement of the Jewish question in a manner worthy of mankind, but it likewise contained the elements of a great perspective for the Orient. The Asiatic problem grew from day to day more serious, and would for some time be deeply tinged with blood. It was of increasing importance to civilized nations, therefore, on the shortest road to Asia there should be set up a post for civilization, which would be at the service of civilized mankind ... Such a post was Palestine, and the Jews were ready with their blood and their substance to provide that post for civilization. Thus would the Jews be helped, but the greatest gainer of all would be the Turkish Empire, under whose suzerainty the Jewish state would be set up.

Other speakers followed, the main topic being the situation of the Rumanian Jews. We see here Herzl's continuing main thrust of providing a safe haven for worldwide Jewry in immediate danger, and also his tilt toward Palestine as that haven. He was shrewd enough to point out subtly the advantage to those countries to whom Turkey was indebted, and to Turkey as well, of having serious Jewish money involved in this enterprise. Near the close of the Fourth Congress a motion was made "that the congress should only meet once every two years. The resolution was defeated by an overwhelming majority."

A wan and sick Herzl was fawned upon by the British gentry, but could not, for reasons of health, chair the Congress for long. At the same time, as he reported in his diary, "I would have gladly enjoyed seeing this beautiful English garden, but I was smothered under royal honors. People gaped at me in admiration while I drank a cup of tea. They presented their children and introduced their ladies; old men wanted to kiss my hand. During yesterday's afternoon session I handed over the gavel to Gaster [R. Moses] and Nordau and slipped away to the Kensington Gardens where, in charming surroundings and with a view over the water, I took a cup of tea in peace." To the Jewish world that was excited by the Zionist movement, Herzl was an other-worldly figure: the new Moses, a prophet, perhaps even a Davidic Messiah. In any case, he was looked upon as one sent by God.

Looking back over the Fourth Congress, Herzl wrote in his diary about a week later: "The Fourth Congress is at an end. There was much noise, sweat, and drum-beating. Of work, there was naturally nothing, and yet the results were excellent. We had manifested before the English world, and our manifestation had been remarked. On the whole, the English press published the kind of reports we needed and still need."

It is of interest to note that the Fourth Congress was supported by the Reform Jewish community in New York City under Rabbi Stephen S. Wise. This, despite the fact that the American Reform rabbinate had, in 1885, taken a stand diametrically opposed to colonization in Palestine. Rabbi Wise was a founder of the New York Federation of Zionist Societies in 1897, which led in the formation of the national Federation of American Zionists, a forerunner of the Zionist Organization of America. At the Second Zionist Congress, he was a delegate and secretary for the English language. Obviously, the drumbeat for the return to Palestine had just become more insistent. Jewish pride was on the rise and the third objective of the First Zionist Congress, "The strengthening and fostering of Jewish national sentiment and consciousness" was becoming a reality. Rabbi Wise would become the leading spokesman for Zionism in America.

The Zionist congress served as the leading edge of the Zionist movement from the time of Herzl until interrupted by the First World War. Starting in 1921, it met every other year until a government was set up for the country of Israel in 1948. It gave voice to all viewpoints and direction to the leadership. It was, in effect, the final gift of a defiant Herzl to the Jewish world. But was it harmful to the assimilationists?

To answer, we would have to look at each country that was admitting Jews. The prime example, of course, is Germany and Austria. But anti-Semitism in the Germanic countries was well underway long before the Zionist movement became a serious alternative. Therefore, it probably was not the cause of the German Jews' ultimate fate. Many young people who foresaw an increasingly dangerous future, left to make a life in Palestine— an alternative that they probably would not have had were it not been for Herzl.

Notes for Chapter Twelve

As Herzl pushed relentlessly to make a Jewish homeland in Palestine, he sacrificed his remaining gift of life in daily units stretching it to the ultimate. Each day was productive and, so far as we know, none were given to self-care.

The books listed as supplemental reading for the prior chapter apply to this chapter as well. In addition, we have several more books.

Ahad Ha'am (nee Ginsburg, Asher) *The Jewish State and the Jewish Problem,* 1897. (Try www.zionismontheweb.org)

I. Zangwill, *Dreamers of the Ghetto,* Harper and Brothers, 1898. (Reproduction available from Amazon, also Kindle Edition.)

Those who are interested in the British development of an oil-fueled navy (briefly mentioned in the meeting with the Kaiser) can read Massie, Robert K, *Dreadnought: Britain and Germany and the Coming of the Great War,* William Morrow and Co. Random House, 1991.

Chapter Thirteen
Prophet of Zionism

As Mirah had gone on speaking she had become possessed
with a sorrowful passion — fervent, not violent. Holding her
little hands tightly clasped and looking at Mrs. Meyrick with
beseeching, she seemed to Deronda a personification of that
spirit which impelled men after a long inheritance of
professed Catholicism to leave wealth and high place, and risk
their lives in flight, that they might join their own people and
say, "I am a Jew."

George Eliot, *Daniel Deronda*

Herzl's work for unimpeded immigration into Ottoman-controlled
Palestine neglected to prioritize forging a mutual understanding with the
indigenous Palestinian Arab population. As the influence of the empire
declined, European countries became influential through Ottoman economic
capitulation which resulted in the granting of trading privileges. Gradually, the
Ottoman Empire became dependent on European loans to run its affairs, the
total of which became staggering.

Many Palestinian farmers were involved in communal ownership with
Greek landlords. The Palestinians assumed this arrangement to avoid heavy
property taxes and military service imposed on landowners of record. But
ownership reverted to the absentee landowners who paid the annual tax. The
most prominent Greek families purchased approximately 57,500 acres. With
other families, they had a potential to purchase about 250,000 more acres.

When extensive Jewish colonization began in 1882, the majority
landowners were the ones who sold land to the *Habbat Zion* settlements. The
fact that land was readily available from the indigenous people made Herzl's
mission to the Sultan superfluous. However, without funds the Zionist cause
could not take immediate advantage of that situation.

Fifth Zionist Congress

Herzl assembled the Fifth Congress in Basel for five days in December 1989. More than one thousand delegates were in attendance, representing every country in the world with the exception of Australia. Herzl opened the proceedings of the Fifth Congress with this quotation from the English poet and novelist Hall Caine:

> If I were a Jew myself, I should be very proud of this fact; proud of belonging to a race that has produced some of the greatest men in history; proud of a nation that still plays a role in the shaping of history even though it has no throne, no king, no soldiers, not even an inch of land; proud of a literature that culminated in the Holy Scripture that was never rivaled by any other masterpiece of human spirit. I should be proud to have an opportunity to join a movement that intends to change Palestine, a land of deserts, into a land of fertility and prosperity. But I should be even prouder of the opportunity that Jews now have, namely that they can be active in behalf of the poor and oppressed among their people and are intent to materialize the religious hope that has maintained them for 3000 terrible years.

Herzl then went on to say:

> That is how the Christian poet thinks. Is it possible that Jews would not understand it? Are we stripped of all pride and dignity? Or don't Jews believe in success? Why are the colonizations of Baron Hirsch and those of Rothschild failures? Because both started on a wrong basis. They thought: In the beginning was money. No, in the beginning was the idea. With money one can get hirelings. One cannot stir up a people that way. Only an idea can do that.

The most important official outcome of the Fifth Congress was the establishment of the Jewish National Fund for the purchase of land in Palestine. But the Fifth Congress is remembered also for the reactionary movement called *Mizrahi* (an acronym from the Hebrew words *merkaz ruhani* meaning "spiritual center"). This movement arose in response to a speech by Max Nordau in which he declared

> the Jews to be the poorest people under the sun, as they possessed less than any other people, yet they had all the wants of modern civilization and expended much on religious culture further to lower their economic position.

That speech gave rise to a resolution by a small group called the Democratic Faction which included both Chaim Weizmann and Martin Buber. Buber was an influential philosopher and later Professor of Philosophy and Religion at Hebrew University (1938-1951). This faction urged "that the education of the people in the spirit of Jewish nationalism was an important aspect of Zionist activity and an obligation for every Zionist."

Buber urged the inclusion of ethical and spiritual values in Zionism and was a strong advocate of Jewish-Arab understanding. He was also a champion of Jewish artists whose work expressed Jewish history and culture. In this respect he encouraged artists and displayed the work of a half-dozen at the Fifth Congress. Although a strong advocate of ethical Judaism, the Democratic Function espoused secularism and opposed the Orthodox Hasidim to the point that Reuben Branin, Herzl's Hebrew-language secretary, wrote "that he had not witnessed such a terrible attitude ... toward popular Orthodoxy among the most radical parties in all Europe."

This strong movement to stamp Zionism as a secular movement and further to insure that it remained so through the education of emigrant Jewish youth, was a red flag in the face of the eastern Orthodox rabbinate. They responded through Mizrahi which, under the leadership of Rabbi Yitzhak Yaakov (Isaac Jacob) Reines (1839-1915), had become a permanent part of the world Zionist organization. It remained so right up to the time of the establishment of the nation of Israel after which it became the National Religious Party. The motto of the new party was, "The land of Israel for the people of Israel according to the Torah of Israel." This was a badly needed balance to offset the strong secular movement of the Zionist Organization. The Democratic Faction of Weizmann and Buber lasted only two years, but the attitude and influence of its prominent members would return to haunt the birthing of the State of Israel.

The official manifesto of Mizrahi was issued in 1902 from Vilna, Lithuania.

> In the lands of the Diaspora the soul of our people — our
> Holy Torah — can no longer be preserved in its full strength,
> nor can the commandments, which comprise the entire
> spiritual life of the people, be kept in their original purity,
> because the times are besieging us with difficult demands. It is
> impossible for us to respond to those demands without
> ignoring the holy treasure entrusted to us at Sinai without,
> God forbid, turning it into a thing of little value in our eyes,
> as each of us strays further and further away from the other.
> Against his will each loses his Jewish self in the [non-Jewish]
> majority, for only in their midst can he fulfill all those secular

requirements which the times demand of him ... It has therefore been agreed by all those who love the spirit of their people and are faithful to their God's Torah, that the reawakening of the hope of the return to Zion will provide a solid foundation as well as lend a special quality to our people. It will serve as a focus for the ingathering of our spiritual fortress for our Torah and its sanctity.

Competing Interests

Although Mizrahi's manifesto states the need to maintain the morality of the commandments and Torah in the daily life of Jews, it makes no messianic statement. Because the Mizrahi is in agreement with the need to initiate large scale Jewish immigration into the Holy Land, they must see in the political Zionist movement a sign that God is calling them home, lest they be accused of simply protecting the religious element that joined in the Herzl movement without due thought to the implications of the covenant. If God is calling them home, then all those who heed the call will be under the covenant.

To understand the Mizrahi position, we turn to the writings of Rabbi Reines.

Upon the ruins of our world a strange, new world is rising; where once our vineyards flourished we now plant strange fruits. The day is near when not a single scholar will be found among us, and the honor, glory and genius of Judaism will turn to dust. Soon, the vital and vivid Judaism we still find among the Jews of Russia will suffer a fate like that which befell her in France. A dreadful disaster is imminent!

Most regrettably, the fathers, even those who have remained faithful to their God and to the ways of Judaism, are bringing, with their very hands, this disaster upon themselves and upon their sons. They send their sons out at a tender age to face the temptations of the world, to be educated in the secular schools, to earn a living in industry and commerce. What are we to expect then from our offspring who are nurtured upon foreign soil, who are not nurtured by a proper study of Judaism? The future awaiting us is grim, indeed. A horrible fate awaits Judaism, the very Judaism which has valiantly fought for her survival these thousands of years.

Our wise men took this situation to heart, and gathered together to contemplate a solution to the crisis. They understood that the new situation demands a new outlook, that it would be a crime before God and the nation to sit idly by while the crisis grows and worsens. They agreed that the present day realities must be reckoned with and may not be ignored, and that one must take into account the changing needs of the people. To this end, they decided to establish a new yeshivah, a yeshivah which will permit our sons to remain in the temple of the Torah and yet acquire the sort of knowledge and understanding that would assure their future well-being. The yeshivah will grant its pupils the moral authority to be rabbis and equip them with enough worldly knowledge to assure their acceptance as leaders of their generation. The yeshivah will not only educate talmudic scholars, but will seek to give a rich Jewish education to those who will find their future in practical, mundane spheres. The yeshivah is intended for the good of the Jewish people and for the preservation of Torah learning.

Rabbi Reines opened a new age yeshiva in Vilnius, Lithuania in 1905. The motive of the Mizrahi seemed to be the acceptance of an inevitable mass emigration to the Promised Land and the need to insure that those who go are educated in the way of the Torah as well as the new secularism (read "modernism"). In Israel, Mizrahi and the Religious Zionist Movement are the dominant Modern Orthodox sects. The Modern Orthodox rabbis of the Mizrahi understand the emigrants will be under the ancient covenant. The Religious Zionist Movement upholds essentially the same belief, but filters it through a kabbalistic lens. This approach represented a major comprise between the traditional orthodox and the radical new secularism, one that was sorely needed to bring God's presence into the Zionist organization.

Meanwhile the Democratic Faction, representing National Zionism turned to the building of a new society through education of the young based on the principles espoused by Ahad Ha'am. Speaking at the time of the Fifth Congress, Ahad Ha'am had this to say about future educational programs:

Conquer the schools! In the synagogue we have to deal with the parents, in the schools with the children. To conquer the parents, to infuse a new spirit into grown men who have already settled down into a certain way of life ... would be a matter of more labor than profit; the small results would not generally be worth the expenditure of energy. Surely, it [would be] better for our purpose to lay out this energy on the conquest of the children. In them we have a clean sheet on which we may write what we will. If in the course of time we can put into the field a large squadron of younger men to

fight their elders, the products of the school against the
leaders of the synagogue, where will the victory lie? History
bears witness that in a war of parents and children it is always
the children who win in the end; the future is theirs.

This proclamation, which takes the religious education program out of
R. Reines' yeshivah, will have a major impact on the development of the
(secular) higher education system of pre-Israel about a quarter century later.
Meanwhile, Buber and other members of the Democratic Faction disappear
from the scene for a decade. At essentially the same time, a new name is
introduced, one of the most highly respected rabbis of the Kabbalah: Rabbi
Avraham Yitzhak Ha-Cohen Kook (Abraham Isaac the priest 1864-1935). He
was born in Latvia and settled in Palestine in 1904, where he was appointed
rabbi of the congregation in Jaffa. He served there until 1914, then became the
first Chief Rabbi of the Ashkenazi community in 1921, in which position he
served until his death.

Having been brought up in an Eastern European *shtetl*, R. Kook
understood that the situation in the Pale was fundamentally different from that
in Germany. In the Russian controlled areas, Jews tended to gravitate to
political causes such as socialism and communism in the manner of militant
secularists. That attitude and the pressing conditions of life in the Pale led to
Eastern European support for political Zionism.

Rabbi Kook recognized that Jewish life in the Pale, which was
centered about religious communities, offered in macrocosm the life
envisioned for Jews in Torah. However, with the breakdown of society that
occurred during the *haskala* and the subsequent pogroms, it was no longer
possible to continue that life. In order to provide a venue in which a full Jewish
life could take place, the only alternative was to rebuild a Torah-observant
society in the ancient homeland of Judaism. He expressed himself on this
subject as follows:

> *Eretz Israel* is part of the very essence of our nationhood; it is
> bound organically to its .very life and inner being ... In the
> land of Israel one draws upon the light of Jewish wisdom,
> upon that quality of spiritual life which is unique to the
> people of Israel, upon the Jewish world view and way of life
> which are essentially derived from the dominance of the
> world of unity over the divided world.

Jonathan Sacks speculates that for Rabbi Kook, the essence of
Kabbalist religious belief is the unity of God's creation. Evil is not part of that
creation but arises when one sees elements of creation as separate components.
The appearance of evil subsides when the separate parts find their proper place

in God's unity. Applying this theology to the *Eretz Israel* movement yields the concept that secular Zionism taken as a separate element is evil when nationalism becomes an end, but "it is essentially holy because it embodies a self-transcending love for the Jewish people." The diaspora has separated the Jews and caused them to think of Judaism as various disparate elements, but Israel is the "world of unity "which will harmonize these elements including the secular and sanctify the whole" *Arguments for the Sake of Heaven*).

From his viewpoint then, R. Kook felt that the return to Israel would be the beginning of the reunification of Jews with Judaism, a viewpoint expressed by Herzl as well. To accomplish this end, R. Kook believed that the secular had to be sanctified, including, agricultural labor, the arts and sciences, and the political process. He pointed out that the culture must in essence be Jewish. Here he blends, more-or-less, with Ahad Ha'am. R. Kook, however, draws a veil of religious sanctity over all aspects of Jewish life in the Holy Land to insure a specific culture of Judaism, while Ahad Ha'am ignores the religious aspects and strives to define a Jewish culture by blending various tradesmen, laborers, scientists, and artists whose creativity and respect for traditional beauty will give rise to a spirited cultural rebirth.

Further, R. Kook believes that secular immigrants to Israel should be considered an instrument of God's plan to reestablish the Chosen People in the Promised Land. God's task for the rabbinate is to educate each immigrant in his or her duty to live a godly life and contribute to the radiance of the community, thus to revive the spirit of Judaism. Secular Zionists believed that contemporary education would lead to a society that can compete on the world stage. So, from the start, secular Zionists joined Religious Zionists in support of a return to the homeland, but only the latter supported the return to Judaism.

With the gathering strength of the secular Zionists, the Religious Zionists took comfort in the words of R. Reines and R. Kook, and stood aside as the movement for a homeland in the ancient Promised Land gathered strength. As much as the rabbis prayed for the return to their people's homeland, they believed that they were unable in a practical sense to assist God in making that happen as reflected in these words of Rabbi Shmuel Mohilewer (1824-1898), one of the first members of the *Hibbat Zion* movement:

> Obviously persons who devote all their days to Torah study
> and worship, and know naught outside the walls of the house
> of study, are not capable of conducting efforts by natural
> means for our redemption. This task was up to 'the worldly
> wise,' the ministers of state, the wealthy, those fit to come
> into the courts of kings.

Modern Orthodox rabbis like Mohilewer believed that cooperation with the *maskilim* was necessary, but they also felt that their religious influence should be incorporated within the nationalist movement.

British Support

In June 1902, Herzl's father died. His support was important to Herzl, and his death was a major blow. Shortly thereafter, Herzl was called back to London by Lord Rothschild who announced his support for the planned exodus to Palestine. In July 1902, Herzl was asked to testify before the Royal Commission on Alien Immigration. He testified,

> The Jews of Eastern Europe cannot remain where they are now. Where are they to go? If they are not wanted here, then a place must be found to which they can migrate without creating the problem with which you are occupied here. Such a problem does not arise if a home is found that is legally recognized as Jewish. And I submit that the Commission should not fail to take this solution into account and to favor it with its valuable judgment. So far as the Jews are concerned, I have no hesitation in maintaining that the solution is practical and feasible. Above all it is welcome to the unfortunate Jews themselves and would receive their most serious cooperation, because their hopeless misery is the cause of troubles with which both they and this Commission are at present confronted.

Herzl must be envisioning territory that is open to unrestricted Jewish immigration, regardless of Judaic practice, and over which control is held by Jews. This would eliminate enclaves of Jews in such countries as the United States or Argentina, since ultimate control of any such enclave would remain with the host country; therefore, continuous unrestricted immigration could not be guaranteed. In 1902, when he spoke these words, the aim of the Zionists to return to Palestine was no secret. By speaking out at a hearing of the Royal Commission on Alien Immigration, Herzl was making a plea to the English government specifically to honor his organization's objective. This was fortunately timed because the English were to become the protectors of Palestine when the Ottoman Empire finally failed during the First World War.

In October 1902, Herzl's book entitled *Altneuland*, (Old-New Land) which laid out his vision for the development of the Jewish colony in Palestine twenty years hence, was published. "Old-New Land" had been written by Herzl over a period of three years. Its Utopian view of an imagined 1923 Palestine was based on four primary assumptions: open immigration with the full consent of the protectorate power, no interreligious differences, no political parties, and peace with the indigenous peoples. Written as a thinly disguised work of fiction, it was on the mark with many predictions. Herzl's motto for the book was, "If you will it, it is no fable." It is interesting to note that the person who translated the book into Hebrew gave it, by a play on words, the title *Tel Aviv*, which became the source for naming the first all-Jewish Israeli city in 1909.

Herzl's vision for the new state was, incongruously, not so much that of a new state arising from uniquely Jewish underpinnings, but rather a copy of an idealized European state for Jews. Culturally in this respect, it was secular, cosmopolitan, and pluralist. In order to prove that his envisioned state was attainable, Herzl cited these three driving factors: the reality of Jewish distress, the self-interest of the world, and the technology of the times. Herzl was indifferent, or at times opposed, to the religious aspects of the return. He foresaw the new Israel as a country like any other country.

But Herzl's vision is exactly what Judaism is *not*. Israel is commissioned to be God's servant people mediating on behalf of God to the nations of this world. Therefore, the political aspects of Zionism must be weighed in light of the covenant duty of the Jewish people. *Old-New Land* is idealistic Herzl not inspirational Herzl, as was *The Jewish State*. In this book, Herzl speaks for himself, not for God. As a result, and in consideration of his declining health, *Old-New Land* is not of the same caliber as TJS.

Ahad Ha'am railed against the vision of Herzl in *Old-New Land* which would, in his mind, have moved to duplicate the Gentile society and culture of Europe. His vision was for a renaissance of Jewish culture and spirit through a carefully regulated center in Palestine. As a result of the publication of *Old-New Land*, the differences between the Political Zionists and the Cultural Zionist of Ahad Ha'am were accentuated. Ahad Ha'am and his supporters, Weizmann and Buber, also ridiculed the idea of peaceful coexistence between a foreseen Jewish majority and the native Arab minority. Ahad Ha'am remarked that with millions of Jews expected to reach Palestine there would be no way to accommodate them without depriving the Arabs of land. On this score they were certainly proven correct.

As things turned out, differences between Arabs and Jews arose early on even before the millions arrived. The new Jewish immigrants of the first *aliyah* (1882-1903) and the second *aliyah* (1904-1914) were committed to the vision of a new Jewish society based on Jewish labor alone in order to insure the creation of a socialist agricultural basis for the future Israel (the *kibbutzim*). They looked down upon those Jews already present who used Arab labor to cultivate the land. The new breed excluded Arabs. This was particularly unfortunate since history has clearly shown that the Jews should be working cooperatively with the native population for the greater good of the territory they share.

One of the major differences between Herzl's vision and the reality of the new Israel was the profound effect that vernacular Hebrew played in Israel's cultural development. Herzl had not foreseen a common language for the new country. He envisioned speakers of most European languages: preferably German, and Yiddish as well. Eliezer ben-Yehuda was the single driving force behind the use of vernacular Hebrew. He recognized while still a young man that in order to have our own land and political life, it is also necessary that we have a language to hold us together. Newly married in 1881, b. Yehuda and his wife immigrated to Palestine vowing to speak only Hebrew for the rest of their lives. By 1916, forty percent of the Jewish population in the settlements spoke Hebrew as their first language. Thereafter, Hebrew became the first language in most of the secular schools.

Hebrew had the virtue of not being in common usage as well as the significance of millennia of use by the Israelite/Jewish people for liturgical purposes. It was in essence a "high" language resulting from its identity with the Bible and the liturgy. The change from any of the languages spoken by the early settlers to Hebrew impressed upon those of the early *aliyot*, the importance and historical significance of their position as the new Israelites.

The conflict between the secular-proposed adoption of vernacular Hebrew and its preeminent position as a high biblical and liturgical language in the Orthodox view, was moderated by their realization that its use in the synagogue was far preferable to the translation of the traditional liturgy into one or more of the settlers' languages. Nevertheless, this basic question remains: is the new Israel a nation state or a religious state? The use of Hebrew in social intercourse helped bring the people of the *yishuv* into the framework of a nation state, and diminished the significance of biblical/liturgical Hebrew.

Herzl, in *The Jewish State*, discussed the possibility of sites other than Palestine, in a chapter entitled Palestine or Argentine:

> Shall we choose Palestine or Argentine? We shall take what is given us, and what is selected by Jewish public opinion. The Society will determine both these points ... The Argentine Republic would derive considerable profit from the cession of a portion of its territory to us.

Although seemingly open to colonization in Argentina, Herzl had written in *The Jewish State:* "Palestine is our ever-memorable historic home. The very name of Palestine would attract our people with a force of marvelous potency." Of course, the attraction of Palestine, or more specifically Jerusalem, is well-embedded in the Bible. In addition to the Isaiah passage describing the end times, when *"instruction shall come forth from Zion, The word of the Lord from Jerusalem"* (Isa. 2:2-4), there are many references in the Psalms.

Pray for the well-being of Jerusalem; May those who love you be at peace.
(Psalm 122:6)
Blessed is the Lord from Zion, He who dwells in Jerusalem. Hallelujah.
(Psalm 135:21)
If I forget you, O Jerusalem, let my right hand wither... (Psalm 137:5)
The Lord rebuilds Jerusalem; He gathers in the exiles of Israel. (Psalm
147:2
If I forget you, O Jerusalem, let my right hand wither... (Psalm 137:5)

The word "Jerusalem" appears more than six hundred times in the Hebrew Bible.

Still fighting for a homeland in Palestine, Herzl convinced the British foreign office of the possible use of the Sinai Peninsula for this purpose. The scheme advanced to the appointment of an inspection committee which Herzl selected. The tour was conducted in January 1903. The commission, however, reported the site unsuitable for lack of water, although the real reason may have been Arab and resident British opposition. Meanwhile, great numbers of Jews in Eastern Europe were abandoning the Pale as the result of an infamous pogrom in Kishinev on April 19, 1903. Herzl was particularly concerned about finding a place for these refugees.

Land in Africa

At the same time as the Kishinev pogrom, Joseph Chamberlin (father of Neville), who was then Colonial Secretary, offered Herzl an opportunity to acquire land in British East Africa (Uganda). Herzl was then embroiled in negotiating with the Russians, unsuccessfully as it turned out, for the constructive release of Jews, and for the government's cooperation in achieving the objectives of the Zionist Organization (ZO). As a result, Herzl left the British offer to his English lieutenants. They drafted an agreement with the aid of an attorney auspiciously chosen — David Lloyd George — who would become Prime Minister thirteen years later. Shortly after submitting the agreement to the Foreign Office, a definitive offer of land in Africa was made to the ZO. This in itself was a momentous matter. The English government was, in essence, dealing with the ZO as a government in exile with full diplomatic powers to negotiate for the well-being of dispossessed Jews.

Herzl recognized the political significance of the British offer and chose to present it to the Sixth Zionist Congress which convened in Basel in August 1903. (There was no congress in 1902.) Although the initial reaction to the offer met with enthusiastic applause based on the recognition given the Zionist movement, subsequent concerns that Palestine was being de-emphasized, and fears that the movement would founder in Uganda (two thousand miles from the Promised Land), made many heart sick. After three days of debate a motion was passed to investigate the proffered land by a vote of 295-178 with ninety-eight abstentions. The Russian delegation then left the floor. It took all of Herzl's cajoling and assurances that Palestine remained the prime objective to get them back to the floor of the Congress.

The Russian delegation was the group that best represented the Religious Zionist viewpoint. From that perspective, resettlement of exiled Jews in any country other than Palestine could only be a temporary solution. Indeed the site proposed by the British came to be called a "night refuge" which in our vernacular would be a "homeless shelter." The mission of the new Judaism in the eyes of the Russian rabbinate was the return to the holy land, there to renew the sacred covenant with God. Why, they must have asked, were the Jews released from the ghetto, and why was the secular Herzl chosen to lead this mission. If the return to Palestine was not prominent in the mind of Herzl, then he was a false prophet, and the entire mission of the ZO was not God-directed as many of the Orthodox had feared.

The deep implications of the Uganda resolution were not foreseen by Herzl from his secular perspective. In defense of his proposal to investigate an alternative site, Herzl spoke to the dissent group during an adjournment of the Congress as follows:

> I have always stood, I still stand, upon the Basle Program; but
> I need your faith in me, not your distrust. And one thing
> more I must tell you: in this achievement which I have given
> to you, I have always left a retreat open: the possibility of
> descending from the tribune at a moment's notice. You may
> drive me out if you wish; I shall return without complaint into
> the longed for tranquility of my private life. I have only one
> wish for you: may no one accuse you with justice of having
> misjudged my motives and rewarded me with ingratitude.

By offering his chairmanship of the ZO to placate the Russian delegation, Herzl probably opened the old false-Messiah wound still prominent in the minds of those Russians whose ancestors had suffered a significant messianic disappointment two centuries before. This was not the most productive use of Herzl's remaining time.

Meanwhile Herzl's African adventure drew considerable press both in London and New York. Opposition came from both sides: the English already in the East African protectorate and the Zionists who were intent on Palestine. Herzl wrote in his journal that an alternative site cannot be ignored for the sake of the unfortunate refugees:

> The ultimate goal has not been reached and cannot be
> reached within a foreseeable time. But an intermediate result

lies within grasp: a land in which we can settle our suffering masses on a national basis with the right of self-government. I do not think that for the sake of a beautiful dream or for our true banner we are entitled to withhold this relief from the unfortunate. But I recognize that the choice has led to a decisive cleavage in our movement, and that the rift is centered about my own person. Although I was originally in favor of a Jewish state no matter where, I later lifted up the flag of Zion and became myself a "Lover of Zion." Palestine is the sole land where our people can come to rest. But hundreds of thousands crave immediate help.

Then speaking to the Sixth Congress, Herzl said:

Zion this certainly is not, and can never become, *i.e.,* Uganda. It is only a colonizational auxiliary or help— but, be it noted, on a national and state foundation. This will not give the sign to our masses to set themselves everywhere in motion. It is, and must remain, an emergency measure which is intended to come to the rescue of our helpless philanthropic enterprises and prevent the loss of these detached fragments of our people.

However heartfelt the pleas Herzl expressed regarding his intent to remain a Zionist of Zion, the issue remained divisive in the Zionist movement. Yet nobody saw or perhaps wanted to see what a great moral achievement it was that the greatest European power openly recognized the Zionist movement as a political factor with which one could conclude contracts and negotiates the cession of territory. Nothing comparable to these events had taken place in the fifteen hundred years of the exile.

But about the same time, the financial efforts were bearing fruit. The Jewish Colonial Trust, which had started in London in 1902, yielded its first interest payment amounting to £6,000. An offshoot of the bank, with a capital of £50,000 was established in Jaffa in 1903, under the name Anglo-Palestine Company. The name was later changed to the Anglo-Palestine Bank which, in turn, evolved into the largest bank in Israel now known as Bank Leumi (National) le-Israel with branches throughout the world. At the same time as the establishment of the Anglo-Palestine Company, the Jewish National Fund reported it had raised £18,668 towards the goal of £200,000 for the purchase of land in Palestine.

The last productive event of Herzl's life was his effort to patch the differences caused by the African colonization motion. Following are excerpts from the talk which he made to the Greater Actions Committee in April 1904:

We want the continuous growth of Zionism, we want Zionism as the representative of the people. Why do we want this? Because we believe that we cannot achieve our goal without great forces, and these great forces are not to be found in a federation of little societies. Such a federation you had twenty years ago, and you are always telling me that you were already Zionists twenty and twenty-five years ago ... But what do you prove thereby? What could you achieve as long as you did not have political Zionism? You lived in little groups and collected money. Undoubtedly your intentions were magnificent, your idealism unchallengeable. Nevertheless you could not achieve anything because you did not know the path to the objective. This path is the organization of the people, and its organ is the Congress. That is why you must submit to the Congress, even though you may be utterly dissatisfied with its decisions.

In the course of time I learned a great deal. First and foremost, I learned to know Jews, and that was sometimes even a pleasure. But above all, I learned to understand that we shall find the solution of our problem only in Palestine ... If today I say to you, "I became a Zionist, and have remained one, and all my efforts are directed toward Palestine," you have every reason in the world to believe me.

One of the first entries made by Herzl in his diary is, essentially, his description of being called to his ministry.

In this city of Vienna one day I tore myself loose from the whole of the circle in which I had lived, from all my friends and acquaintances, and, as a lonely man, devoted myself to that which I considered right. I don't feel the need of any majority. What I need is only that I shall be in harmony with my own convictions.

In his dairy for January 24, 1902 he wrote,

Zionism was the Sabbath of my life. I believe that my influence as a leader is to be attributed to the fact that I, who, as man and writer, have and had so many faults and committed so many mistakes and stupidities, was of a pure heart in the Zionist cause and quite selfless.

Herzl passed away on July 3, 1904. Israel Cohen wrote after Herzl's passing, "he was mourned by the entire Jewish press, not only by Zionist papers but also by non-Zionist ones which had formerly criticized or attacked him but which now acknowledged the greatness of the man who had aroused the conscience of the world to the existence of the Jewish problem and earned the esteem of the heads of governments in his undaunted attempt to deal with it."

> *Then Moses went up from the plains of Moab to Mount Nebo, to the top of Pisgah, which is opposite Jericho, and the Lord showed him the whole land ... The Lord said to him, "This is the land of which I swore to Abraham, to Isaac, and to Jacob, saying: 'I will give it to your descendants'; I have let you see it with your eyes, but you shall not cross over there. Then Moses, the servant of the Lord, died there ... at the Lord's command.* (Deut. 34:1-5)

Herzl in his last testament asked to be laid next to the coffin of his father, "and to remain there until the Jewish people shall transport my remains to Palestine." On August 17, 1949, "the earthly remains of the spiritual founder of the State of Israel, were transferred from Vienna to Israel ... in the presence of members of the Government, of the Rabbinate, and of thousands of representatives of all sections of the people from all parts of the country, and in an imposing and moving ceremonial befitting the historic event ... were laid in their last resting-place, on a hill west of Jerusalem, the highest point of the Holy City, forever afterward to be known as Mount Herzl." As Moses was buried on Mt. Nebo overlooking the Promised Land so Herzl was buried on the highest place in Jerusalem overlooking the sacred City.

As revealed by his directed energies and his writings, it is apparent that Herzl was a prophet. Clearly, his prophecy was: prepare for the worst, save a remnant of Judaism. This was God's message to him, and in true prophetic fashion, his message in turn to all of Judaism. Herzl was not a Messiah; Messiah brings peace to the world. Having given his life to secure the return to the Holy Land, it became the responsibility of those who did return to carry forward God's word to all humanity and to minister to the world to insure the coming of Messiah.

Meanwhile in Palestine following Herzl's death the Jewish population grew to almost 100,000 prior to the First World War, and to more than 500,000 prior to the Second World War. One of the immigrants of that later *aliyah* was Dan Vittorio Segre who, in his autobiography, describes his arrival in Palestine and how the Jewish nurse at the reception center "almost choked when I asked her who the bearded gentleman was looking at me with sad eyes from the wall.

"'Theodor Herzl,' she growled, 'the founder, the Prophet of Zionism.'"

> *Whether they hear or refuse to hear ... they shall know that there has been a prophet among them. Ezekiel 2:5*

Less we forget, the covenant played a role in this episode. God will not desert His chosen in the scrimmage between those who are committed to the terms of the covenant and those who are not. This is the primary battle in our convulsive world.

Notes for Chapter Thirteen

As Herzl struggled with the diverse interests of the various factions involved in the return to *Eretz Israel,* he carefully parceled out his remaining days. Over the years, he had put together a strong cabinet which carried on the dream for forty-three more years until it became a reality. A few more supplemental books were added to the reading list, but basically the books in Chapter 11 written by those who were by his side still tell the story best. The added books are:

Smith, Charles D. *Palestine and the Arab-Israeli Conflict,* Bedford/St. Martins, 2001.
Segre, Dan Vittoro, *Memoirs of a Fortunate Jew.* Dell Publishing, 1985

Chapter Fourteen
German Jewry

[If] Franz ever becomes leader of his party, one of the most
important points of his program will be, "How can all these
Rheinbergs, Wassersteins, yes, even these Jacobs be
oppressed, driven from all positions, and annihilated?" His
excuse will be that popular sentiment compels him to do what
he is doing.

Theodor Herzl, *The New Ghetto*

Before we approach the study of German Jews, we should look at the
historical background of central Europe. During the expansion of the Roman
Empire into Western Europe in the first years of the new millennium, the
Roman army clashed with Frankish and Germanic tribes. Although they were
able to subdue the Franks, the Romans were defeated by the Germans in 70
CE. German tribes continued to dominate the forests until the beginning of
the Holy Roman Empire about 800 CE. Jewish settlement can be traced to the
ninth century in Aachen, and to a dozen municipalities, including Frankfurt,
Mainz, Worms, Cologne and Metz, in the following century.

In Jewish lives during the same time period, the Talmud was
completed about 800 CE, and reached the diaspora about a century later. In
the 11th century, the great Talmud scholar Rashi made clear many talmudic
passages. In the 12th century, Rashi's his son-in-law and three grandchildren
initiated new schools on the basis of Rashi's finely edited glosses. A new epoch
of Jewish learning based on Talmud yeshiva study began.

Jewish families were expelled from central Europe starting about 1425
and continuing to about 1510. About half settled in Poland and became known
as Ashkenazim Jews. This move was fortuitous because the Black Plague was
sweeping over Europe but was very limited in Poland. In 1576, the plague
killed four thousand in Berlin.

Some Jews returned to Germany from Poland in the 16th century, but
were treated with contempt, demonized, and confined to squalid ghettos. On
hearing this, the rest remained in the east until the late 17th century, returning
only after the Thirty Years War (1618-1648). At that time, Jews were

readmitted selectively by German municipalities. The money lenders and the traders were often welcomed back for financial and business reasons and given full rights of citizens when they could be of aid to royalty, but the bulk of Jews were near destitute, and generally limited to peddling, rag picking, retailing, lending, and begging. By the mid-19th century, about 200,000 Jews lived in Germany.

Enlightenment

The 19th Century was the beginning of the modern age. Democracy was sweeping through the Western world, and scientific study was starting to create new jobs for the people. In the early Enlightenment period during the second half of the 18th century, Austrian Emperor Joseph II of the House of Hapsburg permitted all non-Catholics to be free and equal citizens. This edict spread to other Germanic areas, particularly Bohemia and Prussia where Jews were allowed to move into non-restricted neighborhoods, enter vocations, and attend public schools and universities. Jews were, in turn, obliged to use the German language and to Germanize their names and dress.

Germany however, was still a political anachronism, a network of hundreds of city-states, and in no position to take advantage of the growing industrial age as had England in the 1780s. Germany was shaken out of its lethargy by Napoleon in 1805-06, when his army conquered the Prussians and the Austrians. Germans then looked toward a unification that could make their country a power in Europe. But the German people had little or no background in self-reliance and personal responsibility. They lacked the training to create a country with a constitutional government like those of France and America. Accustomed to being a door mat for conquers since the Thirty Years War, Germans had an ingrained respect for constituted authority and a suspicion of liberal government.

At the beginning of the 19th century, only about 20 percent of the Jewish population were comfortable. About 1820, business men began to create new industries and to grow the German economy through entrepreneurships, financial acumen, and managerial ability. Textiles, farm equipment, clothing, railway gear, chemicals, and machinery were in high demand as the industrial revolution accelerated; subsequently, electrical machinery was required as well. German Jewish businessmen placed themselves in leading economic positions through ownership of banking and credit institutions, assuring good press by owning newspapers and magazines. As the Jews achieved unrestricted rights, their share of the new economy increased rapidly, and a well-to-do Jewish middle class began to emerge. The more orthodox continued to maintain their own tight communities, customs, religious observances, and Jewish practices.

Uprising of 1848

At this time, the proletariat was inclined to seek an authoritarian government over one that insured freedom for all. Therefore, a conflict arose between the masses and the younger generation who saw the opportunities that could arise in a modern world of industry, science, and culture through free expression. Resident German Jews, who had millennia to develop strong independent personalities and a keen sense of group dynamics, joined the protectors of individual rights. The status of Germany at the time struck these young people, both Christian and Jewish, as basically unfair to them and stifling to the development of all Germany. Thus, in 1848, they demonstrated in behalf of a unified democratic nation.

Those who took to the streets were students and men who on average were in their early thirties. Not surprisingly, Jews were represented in percentage terms several times more than their number in the general population. The majority of revolutionary acts occurred in the larger northern cities of Germany, where the rebels moved quickly to demonstrate their viewpoint and bypass rural areas. The ability to move about quickly and thereby avoid Prussian troops was due in no small part to the connection of many German cities by railroad. This in itself was a demonstration of the benefits of incipient industrialization. But considering that the linking of the entire German rail system depended upon the whims of hundreds of independent governmental entities, the prospect of a fully unified industrial society was dim indeed.

In reaction to the liberal demonstrations, peasants in hundreds of rural localities primarily in southern Germany, looted and destroyed Jewish property and synagogues. Driven by poor harvests which resulted in near famine, the peasants also struck out at manor houses, feudal rent offices, and church rectories. These counter-demonstrations were a protest against the growing economic gap between the developing middle class and the lower economic class, as well as an expression of the old German suspicion of democratic government.

The demonstrators were never a very large group, numbering from the hundreds to perhaps thousands. They were supported by sympathetic nonparticipants, in particular about eighty percent of Jewish journalists, doctors, and other professionals. The revolution caused havoc throughout Germany for more than a year until it was finally crushed by the Prussian army. One aftermath of the uprising was a large increase in the emigration of energetic young men from Germany to America.

A second outcome was the formation, in May 1848, of a National Assembly at Frankfurt which included seven Jews and ten recent converts. It remained in almost continuous session until June 1849, when it was shut down by Prussian troops. The assembly had by then drafted a constitution for a united Germany. A century later, in 1949, West German parliamentarians incorporated key sections of this draft, including its bill of rights, in the new federal constitution. Unfortunately for the 1848 dreamers, the government that finally unified the country was a militant Prussian monarchy.

The draft constitution discussed at Frankfurt was true to the modernism paradigm, stipulating separation of church and state. This prompted rabbinic sermons greeting the revolution as a truly messianic event as quoted by Elon from the Jewish magazine *Der Orient*: "The savior for whom we have prayed has appeared. The fatherland has given him to us. The Messiah is freedom. Our history is concluded. It has merged with the universal." Then, with obvious disregard for their brethren in the Pale of Russia, " ... autonomous Judaism now lives only in the synagogue and in science." The statement, "our history is concluded," is rather curious, as is the mention of science in which Jews must have already been prominent. The writer probably meant the history of the Jews as a secular ethnic group not the history of Judaism the religion of (some) Jews.

Assimilation

Ludwig Philippson, Rabbi of Magdeburg and the editor of the *Allgemeine Zeitung des Judentums* (Current News of the Jews], wrote in 1848 in defense of German-Jewish brotherhood.

> No longer will we consider ours to be a special case; it is one with the cause of the fatherland: together the two shall conquer; together they shall fail. We are and only wish to be Germans! We have and only wish to have a German fatherland! We are no longer Israelites in anything but our beliefs — in every other aspect we very much belong to the state in which we live.

This passage succinctly summarizes the rapid movement of assimilating German Jews from a religious community to a national citizenry, while presciently stating that "together the two shall conquer; together they shall fail." But the German Jews, like their coreligionists belong primarily to the Jewish nation as Herzl recognized. So we must ask whether the German Jews, still part of the diaspora, were suggesting that they had resigned from that assignment. The situation in France was similar.

The unification of essentially all German states started in Prussia under Bismarck in1866 and included all residents no matter what their religion. This was confirmed five years later in a new Constitution when the country was finally unified. The Jews, at last, felt confirmed in their bid for full citizenship.

It was not, however, as thorough as it sounded, as the Germans were not yet ready to give the Jews a free hand in their economy.

As the eager, educated young Jewish men found outlets for their ambitions in the society of their adopted country, Jewish participation became a noticeable factor in trade, law, banking, medicine, publishing, teaching, and science. This sense of well-being was buttressed by the community's material advances. According to taxation figures, that probably understated the real situation, more than 60 percent of all Prussian Jews were now in the "secure middle-class."

No major city in Europe grew as quickly as Berlin in the mid-19th century. In 1800, the population of Berlin was about 172,000, and there were fewer than three thousand Jews in the city. By 1860, the city had grown to about 500,000, and the Jewish community had grown to about twenty thousand, about four percent of the population. When Berlin became the capital of Germany in 1871, the city population grew to about 850,000, with a Jewish population of about 45,000.

By 1895, Berlin's population had more than doubled once again, to 1.7 million. In 1905, the population reached about two million and Berlin became one of the three largest cities in Europe, boasting one hundred daily newspapers, sixty theaters and twenty-five railroad stations.

In Germany's major cities, most Jewish children were no longer instructed in the intricacies of talmudic law, and parents made sure that their children received a secular education through university. The orthodox rabbinate denounced secular education as undermining the Jewish way of life. but by 1867, 14.8 percent of high school students in Berlin were Jews, three or four times the total percentage of Jews in the city's population.

As citizens of the Reich, Jews were able to run for political office. Between 1871 and 1878, thirty-six Jews (including twelve converts) were elected to the Reichstag. During the 1880s, four Jews — Paul Singer, Eduard Bernstein, Hugo Haase, and Ludwig Frank — worked together to introduce and shepherd through significant social legislation. Singer, a well-to-do manufacturer of women's coats, was the leader of this group.

With the blessing of Bismarck, who could envision personal political advantage in Singer's initiative, they witnessed the passage of a Sickness Insurance Law in 1883, an amended Accident Insurance Law in 1884, and, most significantly, an Old Age and Disability Insurance Law in 1889. The last named became a model for social security insurance in all industrial nations. It would be about fifty years before essentially the same law was passed in this country. Singer continued to serve in the Reichstag until his death in 1911." More than one million German workers attended his funeral." This was a historic demonstration of the ability of a handful of covenant Jews to improve the lives of a vast number of Gentiles. It was also a rebuttal to those who said the Jews were parasites.

Although the *haskala* was a boon to European Jewry in general, the astonishing speed with which the educated and spirited Jews rose economically became a competitive and economic threat and a provocation to the Gentile community not only in Germany but in Hungary, Austria, Russia, and the Balkans as well. The resurgent Jews had become major players in the markets and financial institutions, as they had been in the Ottoman Empire during its heyday.

God had permitted them to enjoy the wealth of the nations and revel in their riches, but had cautioned them not to glory in wisdom, strength and wealth, but only in devotion to God. (Isa. 56:2, Jer. 11:4, Eze 5:7, Hos. 6:7, Mic. 6:8). God had also warned them not to amass wealth by unjust means (Jer. 17:11) and not to accumulate more wealth than the native people.

Anti-Semitism gained momentum from the association of Jews with liberalism and capitalism in the 1870s and 1880s. Following the stock market crash of October 1873, many accused the Jews of criminal economic manipulations.

Early Life of Hitler

Adolf Hitler was born in Braunau, Austria on April 20, 1889. What is known about Hitler's childhood is that he was self-righteous and intolerant of the opinions of others and could react with outbursts of temper. He was not indifferent to most matters. Everything aroused his interest and often disturbed him. He seemed to be at odds with the world and frequently found injustice, hate, and enmity there. On the other hand, he demanded everything from his companions; but was always prepared to do everything for them. But deep down in his nature there was an element in his personality into which he would let no one penetrate.

Of particular interest was Hitler's fascination with his favorite book *The Saga of the German Heroes*. As a boy he could not read enough about them. His familiarity with the sagas was by no means a passing fad. It was essentially the thing which captivated him. In his historical and political considerations it was never far from his thoughts, for this was the world in which he felt he belonged. This fact remains everything in his life. Hitler's personality dwelt only in the beliefs to which German heroic sagas had introduced him. He sought his own world, and found it in the origins and early history of his own species.

Hitler had a great depth of feeling for music. When Richard Wagner entered Hitler's life and gave form to the Nordic gods, he saw not only a confirmation of his path of "transmigration" into early German history, but also the idea that this long-gone era must have something of use for the future. When he listened to Wagner he was a changed man. His violence left him, he became quiet, yielding and tractable. As if intoxicated by some hypnotic agent, he slipped into a state of ecstasy and willingly let himself be carried away into that mystical universe which was more real to him than the actual work-a-day world. He was transported into the blissful regions of Germanic antiquity, that ideal world which was the lofty goal for all his endeavors and where nothing counted but German ways, German feeling, and German thought. With true fervor he clung to the people of his origin, and nothing on Earth did he place higher than his love for what was German.

What does this mean for the Hitler's program as Reichs Chancellor? Professor Edward O. Wilson has written in his book *The Social Conquest of Earth* that people must have a tribe. He goes on to say that: "To form groups, drawing visceral pride and comfort from familiar fellowships and to defend the group enthusiastically, these are among the absolute universals of human nature and hence of culture. Our bloody nature is ingrained because group-versus-group was a principal driving force that made us what we are. In prehistory, group selection lifted hominids that became territorial carnivores, to heights of solidarity, to genius, to enterprise, and to *fear*. Each tribe knew with justification that if it was not armed and ready, its very existence was imperiled."

In the 1890s, native Germans began to witness cultural changes in Berlin. Writing in the first decade of the 20th century, the social and economic historian Werner Sombart portrayed the Jews as incorrigible, an Asiatic clan bent on insinuating themselves through the ploys of urban civilization and subverting the culture and life of the native population. The attitude of German nationals was that the Jews were a nation: not just a religious community, but an alien nation without defined borders which exploited its hosts' economic system to its advantage (*i.e.*, parasites). The Zionist movement, which celebrated the "Jewish nation," was to the assimilationists a grave provocation to their security and safety. The assimilationists were in a particularly dangerous situation.

As Zionism progressed, restrictions on Jews in Germany became more oppressive. In the secular area, for example, Jews were unable to seek employment as teachers in universities or secondary schools and could not be licensed as lawyers. In essence, they were excluded from leadership roles in society. This was particularly true in Prussia, where two-thirds of the German-Jewish population lived. In the religious area, the rabbis who ran schools for the education of Jewish children were loath to hire Jewish university graduates whose viewpoint regarding religious orthodoxy would likely be in variance with theirs.

Germans who felt most aggrieved by the *nouveau riche* Jews were those who had the most to lose: the aristocracy. As the leading Jewish business men became increasingly successful, they bought ancestral country estates and palatial townhouses in the cities. These prominent life styles were derided by the aristocracy as "vices" when displayed by Jews.

Military Service

As Europe rearmed in the first decade of the 20th century, German Jews served time in the army in essentially the same percentage as their numbers in the total population. However, Jews in the army were not privy to the same advancement opportunities as Jewish converts and Gentiles. The high command felt it was unthinkable for Jews to lead Germans. When war came in 1914, the pride of German-Jewry rose to the defense of their adopted fatherland.In 1916, a census of Jews serving in the army was taken ostensibly in response to allegations that Jews were shirking military service. The census was intended to show how many Jews served on the front lines as opposed to those serving in the rear. The census confirmed that Jews may even have been over-represented. More than 100,000 Jewish men served in the military, and twelve thousand were killed in battle during the war, equal to the percentage of deaths among Germansoldiers.The First World War clarified the position of the Jews in the army and in Germany. Their dream of becoming one with the "community of ordinary German folk" (the *Volk*) simply by "professing to be part of it" was an illusion. This reality enforced their awareness of the Jewish condition and their rootlessness in the world.

The war brought many Jewish soldiers into direct contact with the Jewish *shtetl* communities of Eastern Europe. This encounter with unassimilated Orthodox Jews served as a catalyst for a return by some German Jews to more traditional forms of Jewish expression.German Jewish leadership began to turn towards their coreligionists sorely pressed in the East. This process was led by Martin Buber through his publication *Der Jude,* shortly after the end of the war. He used his forum to present Eastern European Jewish issues and thereby refocus German-Jewish concern eastward. He also advanced his case for a new Jewish community in Palestine.

A dilemma that confounded the purveyors of anti-Semitism that the first generation of Russian Jews entering Germany after 1881 was their alien appearance. Fully bearded, wearing a long black kaftan and a distinctive hat from their home town, they were easily recognized and avoided. Two or three generations later, they were clean shaven German speakers who were educated, dressed appropriately for local society, intermarried, often converted, and fully assimilated. Often they were unrecognizable as people of Jewish origin. Whereas they were originally alien and threatening in appearance, they had become one with the native population. Which then was the more dangerous situation, identifiably alien or apparent sameness? From the viewpoint of the anti-Semite, it was the Jews who had managed to insinuate themselves so deeply into Germany society that they could be identified only by their lineage. In other words, look back far enough through the generations and find the man with the distinctive hat.

Philipp Stauff, a German anti-Semitic publicist, took a broad view of Jewish identity:

> Anyone whose great-grandfather a century earlier had
> converted to Christianity and married a Gentile remained as
> much a Jew in his eyes as a recent arrival from the *shtetl*, and
> was more dangerous because he might pass as authentically
> German. But with equal fervor he denounced Gentiles who
> had married Jews and those who worked for a Jewish
> publisher or who had Jewish friends. Either as deluded
> victims or as men who had sold out, he charged, they
> belonged to a vast conspiracy which propagated one form or
> another of a diseased modernism that expressed international
> rather than national values.

Germany had been bled dry by the cost of the war in 1914-1918 and then ravaged by reparation payments which triggered a massive inflation in 1921-23. This was followed by the Great Depression.

As the Nazi party gained strength and members in the mid-1920s, the accusations about Jews became more pointed and unfounded. Consider the German viewpoint. The flood of strange Russian/Polish refugees into Central Europe stamped the German mind with an indelible aversion to Jews. When these people partook of education in the universities of their new homeland, and then rose to dominate banking, finance, law, medicine, science, and the arts, the feeling of having been consumed by alien people became endemic in a portion of the native population. In the end, the fact that the Jewish people were being uprooted and returned to the east from whence they had come, must have made perfect sense to much of the German population.

Culture

Jews had rushed to participate in secular education and take their place in the society and commerce of the host country. Their hard work, good education, and unique intellectual abilities resulted in rapid inroads into commerce, science, and the arts. Determination and persistence based on centuries of despair and persecution motivated Jews to succeed and to reject a return to poverty. Security was the first order of business and assimilation became the second order. Religion was not a high priority.

Through their striving, Berlin in the early 20th century became the most important theater city in the world and also the first in music. To a similar degree, this was true in the sciences, arts, journalism, and literature — all endeavors in which Jews abounded. By 1913, more books were published in Germany than in any other country in the world. The cultural benefits were unparalleled on the continent. Before and after the First World War, progress in technology, commerce, science, and the arts raised Germany to a position of world recognition as the epitome of western civilization, justly praised as "a nation of poets and thinkers."

Here again, we should note that one of God's marching orders to the covenant people was beware of enriching yourselves beyond that of your host. We can extend this now from financially to culturally.

Science and Industry

Even though Jews were now a shrinking minority, representing only 0.9 percent of the population, due mainly to declining birthrates, they continued to be primary contributors to the industrial and commercial strength of the nation. In scientific research, German universities surpassed those of other European countries. "The contribution of the Jews to this preeminence was enormous; in some fields it was overwhelming." German Jewry and the excellent German education system produced talented scientists to a degree far exceeding their Jewish numbers.

At the Kaiser Wilhelm Institute in Berlin, the four major units of which were head by Jews and supported by Jewish philanthropy, that substantive advances in the hard sciences were made which were soon turned into technological advances including: the direct photography of colors, the synthesis of tar derivatives, distillation of hard coal, electroforming, wireless telegraphy, the radio tube, the microphone, early pregnancy detector, aspirin, etc. Based on these discoveries, Jews founded entirely new industries producing chemicals, forming metals, delivering electrical power, providing new medical devices and drugs, and synthesizing carbon based products.

In addition, Jews were also responsible for establishing the first German aircraft factory, the Hamburg-American shipping line, and the electrical industry. Jewish financing made much of this possible through farsighted banks such as the Reichsbank, the Deutsche Bank, the Dresdner and Darmstätter banks, all of which were founded by or were still run by Jewish directors. And, of course, all of these commercial and industrial innovations insured employment for the German workforce.

Much has been made of Jewish predominance in Nobel Prize awards for the hard sciences (medicine, chemistry and physics). The exact figures vary, depending on how one answers the question, "Who is a Jew?" For the following survey, reliance has been placed on the definition on the Internet site, *Israel Science and Technology*.

This list includes only Nobel laureates who are Jewish by the strict definition of *halakhah* (interpretation of the laws of the Hebrew Scriptures) that requires being born to a Jewish mother or formal conversion to Judaism.

Definition of being Jewish is similar to nationality and independent of personal beliefs.

The last sentence means that what counts, excluding conversion, is Jewish blood, not Judaic observance. There is no data that would permit a comparison to persons of different blood lines, and certainly no data to compare with persons of other faiths. In fact, the "faith" of the Jewish Nobel scientists, as reported in their autobiographies, varies from observant Jewish, through atheist, to observant Christian.

The following tabulation includes all science laureates since the first Nobels were awarded in 1901 through the group in 2013. Each person receiving an award is included in the tabulation including those who shared the prize, a common occurrence. Regarding Germany pre-1933, and this includes Austria, persons of Jewish blood by this standard claimed 35 percent of the German science awards. Considering that Jews were never more than one percent of the population at the start of the 20th century and were less than eight-tenths of one percent in 1933, this is an astonishing figure.

As the Nazis pursued their self-destructive racial policies, seventeen Jewish scientists who were either laureates or would be so honored, were forced to leave. Of this group eleven came to the United States, five to England, and one to Sweden. Two others had emigrated with their families in the late 19th century; both came to the United States. Two other laureates not included above because they were not from Germany but were from German-occupied countries, made their way to the United States as well. It is not difficult to see the torch passing to America when fifteen incipient Nobel laureates landed on our shores. Many of these scientists had a major hand in the American war effort, the physicists being most prominent in that respect.

Surely the most important study for the future of the world was that which was conducted by the quantum physics pioneers between 1905 and 1930. Of the ten most prominent, half were of Jewish parentage: Albert Einstein, Niels Bohr, Paul Ehrenfest, Max Born, and Wolfgang Pauli. All but Ehrenfest were Nobel Prize winners. The Jewish laureates at Los Alamos, many of whom were pupils of the pioneers, included: George de Hevsey (German), Eugene Wigner (Hungarian, educated in Germany), Emilio Segré (Italian), and Hans Bethe (German). In addition, there were brilliant Jewish scientists who did not receive a Nobel including: Theodor von Kármán (Hungarian, educated in Germany), Michael Polyani (Hungarian researcher in Germany), Leo Szilard (Hungarian, educated in Germany and researcher there for thirteen years), John von Neumann (Hungarian, mathematics lecturer in Germany for three years), and Edward Teller (Hungarian, received university training in Germany, completed Ph.D. in physics under Werner Heisenberg in at University of Leipzig).

The bottom line is the percentage of awards to Jewish scientists worldwide over the history of the science Nobels in medicine, chemistry, and physics. That figure is 26 percent. Thus people of Jewish blood over the one-hundred and twelve year period from 1901 to 2013 inclusive, made significant contributions to the world body of scientific knowledge far, far beyond their portion of the population. Of course, there were many more outstanding medical achievements by Jewish scientists not honored by Nobels. Throughout this span, Jews worked to improve the lot of all people in fulfillment of their covenant charge.

The Arts

Regarding the world of art in its many forms, Jews had for countless generations tended to their crops, studied Talmud, and protected their families, but the study of art was unheard of. The patronage of the arts in Germany was an outcome of the break from strict Orthodox Judaism and its ban on creating "graven images." Finding beauty in the world, and seeking new ideas and concepts from the artistic presentation of paintings, music, theater, film, etc. was so new in Judaism that there was no distinctive word for "art" in the Hebrew language until the early 20th century. Embracing the new culture while in Germany not only constituted a rejection of tradition, but also a search for expression of a new Jewish identity.

German Jewry, especially in Berlin, was the primary driver for creating the most exciting epoch in German intellectual history. Prominent Munich Jews helped financed the construction of Wagner's concert hall and residence in Bayreuth. Of the National Gallery's thirty-one key benefactors prior to the first war, twenty-eight were Jewish. In Austria, almost all of the Viennese art and culture recognized and admired by the world was promoted, nourished, or created by Jews. The new art arrived on the cultural scene with a rush that must have left much of Germany breathless, and certainly left many citizens spinning in its wake. Incongruously, the children and grandchildren of rabbinic scholars and impoverished peddlers now found themselves at the forefront of European arts and letters.

The new art began with the painter Max Liebermann, who was a founder and central figure in the Secession movement, a breakaway group from traditional art. For fourteen years after its opening exhibition in 1899, the Berlin Secession was a major institutional force in German Modernism. From 1920 to 1932, when modernism had become acceptable, Liebermann was president of the Prussian Academy of Arts. In 1927, he was made an honorary citizen of Berlin. One Jewish couple stood at the center of the modern art movement: Herwarth Walden (né Georg Lewin) and his first wife, Else Lasker-Schüler, whose artistic output included poetry, drama, prose works, and paintings. Walden promoted the new art and literature through his journal *Der Sturm* ("The Storm") and mounted art exhibits at his gallery

The perception that Jews alone were responsible for modernism in art resulted in many non-Jewish modernists being labeled "Jewish" so long as they associated with modernists. Most of the artist, including Beckmann, Dix, Grosz, Kandinsky, Klee, Klimt, Kokoschka, Marc, Macke, and Schad were not Jewish. Of the Jewish painters Meidner, Steinhardt, Chagall and Feininger are well known. But it is true that most of the patrons and buyers were Jewish, and practically all the great art collections were formed by Jews. However, Jews and non-Jews worked closely together both professionally and personally to bring the new art to a wider public. Museum directors, pivotal in making modern art acceptable in Germany were Gentiles. The excitement of theater, concerts, art, film and other aspects of culture must have been an attraction to non-Jews as well as Jews. But even though the cultural scene penetrated many of the smaller cities, much of the rural and working population would have been puzzled at best, and alienated at worst, by what was going on in Berlin.

Movies and Stage

Jewish pioneers in the film world included the innovative directors Otto Brahm (né Abrahamson) and Max Reinhardt (né Goldmann). Ernst Lubitsch was in the vanguard of early films as were the directors Fritz Lang and Josef von Sternberg. Reinhardt was closely linked with Hugo von Hofmannsthal (librettist for many of Richard Strauss' operas: *Electra, Aridane auf Naxos, Der Rosenkavalier*, etc.) and Felix Salten (né Salzmann), who founded one of the first cabarets and is well known today for his children's books including *Bambi*. Lubitsch cut his teeth as a director transposing Yiddish stage to Yiddish film. He made forty films in Germany beginning in 1913, and then left for Hollywood in 1922, where he successfully made thirty-three more. His method in Hollywood was simple: "Write Yiddish, cast British."

Reinhardt produced more than 450 classical plays by writers including the ancient Greeks, Shakespeare, Moliere, Goethe, Ibsen, and Strindberg. Brahm was director of the Deutsches Theater and leader of the modernist movement on stage. Almost all the notable supporters of theater and film came from Jewish families engaged in business or retail, most frequently the textile trades. The theatrical culture of Berlin would have been unimaginable without Jewish participation. What made Berlin Jews, as opposed to Gentile Berliners, even more susceptible to the new theater was the fact that they did not have a long tradition of socialization to German "high" cultural taste. Therefore, Jews entered the cultural realm with open, unprejudiced eyes.

Classical Music

Jewish composers became part of the classical musical scene in Germany and Austria from the time of the opera composer Giacomo Meyerbeer, who was appointed General Music Director of the Berlin Opera in 1842. Following Meyerbeer was Jacques Offenbach, composer of *Tales of Hoffman* and some ninety operettas. Gustav Mahler, a convert to Catholicism later in life, wrote ten symphonies and numerous song cycles while Choir Master at churches in Prague and Leipzig and during his appointment as director of the Royal Hungarian Opera and Director of the Hofoper in Vienna. In the early1860 operetta came to Vienna, and reach its peak in the1870s with the works of Johann Strauss the Younger, who descended from Jewish heritage. The list of Jewish conductors following Mahler includes Bruno Walter (Schlesinger) appointed Director in Vienna by Mahler, Leo Blech, director at the German State Opera, Otto Klemperer and Erich Leiber. On stage were Richard Tauber, operatic tenor, and the most celebrated operetta diva of the 1920s, Fritzi Massary.

Arnold Schoenberg's innovation of the twelve-tone technique was a groundbreaking musical achievement. He also composed the opera *Moses und Aron*. In the realm of show music, Kurt Weill wrote both for the German stage (*Three Penny Opera, Rise and Fall of the City of Mahagonny*) and the American musical stage (*Knickerbocker Holiday, Street Scene, Lady in the Dark, One Touch of Venus*). Cabaret began after the first war as a sort of political burlesque with song, skits, gentle sarcasm, and timely repartée.

Looking back over this extraordinary cultural experience in Germany, one may say that had there been no Jewish leaders, modern art would have made headway in Central Europe, although the process would have been different. Certainly the world was ready for a change from the portraits, landscapes, and heroic paintings of the past to a new imagination that would reflect the major changes rapidly occurring throughout European society. That the Jews were leaders in this movement is not surprising, since they had very little, and for some perhaps nothing at all, invested in the old art. The new art also reflected their abrupt mutation from penniless supplicants in the ghettos to well-to-do burgers. As we look back today on the much loved and admired impressionist painters and the post-war anger of the Fauves and Dadaists, they do not say "Jewish" to us. They say, imagine new things and look for beauty in all forms.

Before 1914, most modern art in Germany was apolitical, although the affinity between Jews and modern culture had been a controversial subject since the last half of the 19th century. The level of Jewish participation in modernist art movements served as a rallying cry for anti-Semites. Nowhere in Europe was the issue of modernism politicized to the same extent as in

Germany. The First World War intensified this tendency, until defining certain kinds of art as degenerate and a threat to the nation's value — usually in anti-Semitic terms — became a political weapon in the struggle against the Weimar Republic.

Although a certain nostalgia still exists for the excitement and creativity of the Weimer period, for most Germans it was a time of great misery with legless war veterans riding the sidewalks on rolling planks to beg for food money, prostitutes (often the widows of fallen soldiers), drug addicts, and fat-necked speculators. Weimar Period artists painted caricatured people in this state for in their view this was what society had become. Indeed, the ideal Nazi type was described as steely, machinelike, and devoid of individual distinction. When the Nazis made barbarism official, these honest artists who depicted the woeful '20s were among the first to go. The artist George Grosz wrote:

> You really begin to wonder how it can be possible that ...
> millions of people exist so mindlessly; so unable to see what is
> really happening, people who have had the wool pulled over
> their stupid eyes ever since their school days, whose minds
> have been stuffed with the attributes of ignorant reaction,
> such as God, Fatherland, militarism.

As for the *Volksgemeinschaft*, the community of ordinary German people, they suffered through the Great War not only on the battlefield, but also on the home front. Kaiser Wilhelm II provided a miserly pension to war widows. Toland reported that people at home were forced to eat dogs and cats. Bread was made from sawdust and potato peelings, and there was almost no milk. As a result, more than 400,000 died of starvation. Hitler, who was devoted to the welfare of the German people, did not forget the experience of the first war when his time came. His basic concern was that the German homeland could not produce enough to feed a growing population. One of his main objectives for invading Russia was to seize the fertile Ukraine soil and make it into a German living environment (*Lebensraum*).

During much of World War II, the *Volksgemeinschaft* were feeling well feed with Dutch cheese and butter as well as Russian produce. Some wore Jewish clothing and lived in Jewish homes often well-appointed with Jewish furnishings. They had no need to wonder what had happened to the former owners.

One can see the widening gulf between Jewish culture and a hardening on the part of the non-Jewish Germans some of whom were moving to reclaim their own culture: one of Nordic heritage and bellicose triumphalism. The former was legendary, and the latter had not existed for some seven centuries before the Prussian uprising. Elon reprinted this historical paragraph by Mortiz Goldstein, a thirty-two-year-old Jewish scholar of German literature who published a revealing statement in 1912 which brought this cultural dispute to a head:

> We Jews are administrating the spiritual property of a nation that denies our right and our ability to do so. Among ourselves we have the impression that we speak as Germans to Germans ... But though we may feel totally German, the others feel us to be totally un-German. We may ... have inspired the German stage to an unanticipated revival or a new poetic style which we may call German, but others call it Jewish. They — reluctantly — feel obliged to acknowledge our achievement, but they wish we would achieve less.

Here we have Jews enthusiastically engaged in displaying a new, rapidly evolving modernist culture without taking more care to draw in native German participation. Ferdinand Avenarius, a nephew of Richard Wagner, noted that the Jewish emergence as the "administrators of German culture" is ultimately a matter of power, and that "wealth is power." This implies that Jewish financiers were imposing the new culture on Germans.

The Nazis

A strong reaction to modernism came with Hitler and his followers when he organized "Great German Art Exhibitions" and an "Exhibition of Degenerate Art" to instruct Germans in Nazi aesthetics. "The whole fakery of a fashionable decadent or diseased and untruthful art has been brushed aside," he declared. "A proper standard has been reached." The "proper standard" celebrated the narcissistic Nordic legend in bland 19th-century tableaux of work and play, with and much exposure of proper German physiques.

An afternote: from the 1920s onward, the American movie business, underwritten by Eastern European Jewish immigrants in the first decades of the 20th century, featured the talents of many German Jewish immigrants, including directors Ernst Lubitsch (*Ninotchka, To Be or Not to Be, Heaven Can Wait, The Shop Around the Corner* and many popular silent movies), Fritz Lang (Catholic-raised *auteur* of *Metropolis, You Only Live Once, The Return of Frank James, Western Union, The Woman in the Window, The Big Heat* and *While the City Sleeps*) and Billy Wilder (*Double Indemnity, The Lost Weekend, Sunset Boulevard, the Seven Year Itch, Some Like it Hot, The Apartment*, and *Sabrina*). Erich Korngold ("the father of film music") composed and scored many great movie backgrounds.

The great German movie studio was decimated by Goebbels, and all Jewish workers in that field were banned from the studios. As well-known

German actors, writers and directors arrived in Hollywood and started to make their mark, they joined together to sponsor and finance the immigration of the people who had made their studios so successful in Germany: the cameramen, the film editors, the sound technicians, the actors and the seconds, etc. In total, more than eight hundred Jewish employees of the German film studios made their way to Hollywood and sanctuary in the German speaking community of Southern California. When the true intent of the Nazis became known, the contrast in life styles between Southern California and Nazi Germany could not have been more stunning.

The Zionist movement did give the Jews of Germany and Poland an escape route which many (mostly the younger) used. About half of German Jews left between 1933 and 1939. As a final note on the new culture in Germany, almost all of the Jewish scientists, composers, and architects disbursed safely to America, England, Palestine, and Sweden. The purveyors of cabaret did not. And the wealthy were forced to bargain to save their lives. According to Elon: Nearly all wealthy German Jews were able to save themselves.

Could it have ended differently in Germany? Germany has a long history of anti-Semitism. About a thousand years ago, it was believed that Jews were to be feared because they had the power to kill the Son of God. It was a simple extrapolation to attribute to the Jews such magical torments as torturing the Host until it bled, sacrificing Christian children for their blood to make Passover matzo. calling on God to bring a plague upon the Christians and poisoning wells. This also justified, in the minds of some Christians, the right to kill Jews.

In 1862, Moses Hess wrote of Jewish assimilation into German society in his book *Rome and Jerusalem*, "Germans as a whole in spite of its collective intellectuality, in its practical and social life is far behind the rest of the civilized nations of Europe." This is due to the German belief in the superiority of the *Volk* (the common folk descended from the Nordic tribes) in comparison to other races especially the Jews. Further, Hess wrote: "We shall always remain strangers among the nations. They may tolerate us and even grant us emancipation, but they will never respect us. The Jew in exile who denies his nationality will never earn the respect of the nations among whom he dwells."

In 1896, Bernhard Cohen, a physician, wrote a publication entitled, *Before the Storm: A Serious Word of Warning to Jews of Germany*. It had limited circulation, but the author minced no words. He advised German Jews to "expect the worst — another St. Bartholomew's Day was in the making," referring to the 16th-century massacre of Huguenots in France.

German anti-Semitism had "method" and was, therefore, more dangerous even than Russian anti-Semitism ... between Jews and non-Jews in Germany there exists, in effect, a state of war. It is no longer a legal question. The demand is not for our defeat or submission — this they have already achieved — but for our destruction.

At the same time as Dr. Cohen warned of a coming slaughter, Theodor Herzl released his Zionist publication *The Jewish State*. These two publications forced the assimilated middle class and wealthy Jews to face certain challenges. Are they determined to stay in Germany even to the extremes of giving up their religion and intermarrying with Germanic people? In effect, changing their way of life perhaps to free themselves from the terms of the covenant with God? All of this in the face of rising anti-Semitism, prohibition against participation in legal professions and teaching, and threat of physical harm.

The Jews had little chance to work in existing German industry or businesses because of discrimination. Therefore they preferred to work for themselves and build privately owned enterprises. Successful owner-owned businesses increased wealth and permitted expansion which produced more wealth. Of course, not every enterprise succeeded, but those that did often did very well. Since most Germans worked at someone else's business, they did not amass wealth. After several generations, it was apparent that Jewish income was an increasing share of German economic wealth. Of course, they were also employing many native Germans.

The growing wealth permitted Jews to partake of the cultural pleasures in theater, music, and art. They did so with great enthusiasm and financial support so that the cultural scene in Berlin became the most exciting in Europe. It also encouraged artists to experiment. The new painting, music, film, and theater turned off many native Germans and raised further fears about the Jews. Many Germans believed that the Jews were taking over their economy and traditional ways and would eventually turn Germany into a Jewish state.

Did the Jews bring this upon themselves? Certainly not intentionally. But they did so without regard to the covenant restrictions. Their accumulation of wealth beyond that of the average family in Germany was a violation of the basic covenant provisions. They may have been aware of this and hoped by supporting the arts and sciences, their donations were sufficient compensation. But the new culture was not shared sufficiently with all Germans. However, the growth of German trade throughout the world increased the economic position of the country and brought many more jobs to Germany. For the most part, Jews were not celebrated for their contribution, and if business slumped, Jews were blamed.

In 1924, Hitler was asked a critical question: "Has your position on the Jewish question been somewhat changed?"

"Yes, yes," Hitler said.

It is quite correct that I have changed my opinion concerning the methods of fighting Jewry. I have come to the realization that I have been far too soft up to now! While working on my book I have finally come to realize that the harshest methods of fighting must be employed in the future if we are to win., I am convinced that this is not only a matter of life and death for our people but for all peoples. The Jew is a world pest.

Of the nine million Jews in Europe before the Holocaust, approximately two-thirds were killed.

"We must recognize, more and more," Heinrich Himmler declared, "that we are engaged in a primitive, original, natural racial battle."
Hitler's grand plan to eliminate the German Jews was, in twisted minds, a return to the heroic age of tribal Germany and the birth of the German *Volk*.

Thus Germany descended into moral turpitude.

Notes for Chapter Fourteen

It is difficult to present a full picture of the rise of German Jewry. These are histories that describe that period.

Gilman, Sander L. and Zipes, Jack, *Yale Companion to Jewish Writing and Thought in German Culture 1096-1996*, Yale, 1997
Sorkin, David, *The Transformation of German Jewry 1780-1840*, Oxford, 1987
Salamander, Rachel, *The Jewish World of Yesterday 1860-1939*, Rizzoli,1991 (Many photographs.)
Craig, Gordon A. *Germany 1866-1945*, Oxford, 1978 (scholarly)
Bilski, Emily D. Gilman, *Berlin Metropolis: Jews and the New Culture 1890-1918*, U. of California, 1999
Eberle, Matthias, *Neue Sachlichkeit ("New Objectivity") in Germany: A Brief History*
Biographies of the Hitler period:
Hitler, *Mein Kampf in English*, 1938 (available through Amazon)
Toland, John *Adolph Hitler*, Doubleday, 1991 (very big book which gathers the facts and lays them out chronologically.)
Kubizek, August, *The Young Hitler I Knew*. MBI Publishing Co., 1953. The author seems not to have written the book. He either jotted down his

notes and/or carried on long conversions with his ghostwriter and translators who might have added their own takes. If you are left scratching your head, check Toland's book.

RELATED BOOKS

Chant, Christopher, *The World's Railroads: The History and Development of Transportation,* Chartwell Books Inc., 1997. Although railroads connected the major German cities, the various principalities could not standardize on rail width.

Jones, Sheila, *The Quantum Ten: A Story of Passion, Tragedy, Ambition, and Science,* Oxford, 2008.

Götz, Aly *Plunder, Racial War, and the Nazi Welfare State,* Henry Holt, 2005
When ordered to board a train headed east, Jews were instructed to bring warm clothing, but all suitcases were loaded in a baggage car. When the train was full and the doors locked, the baggage car was detached and the clothing dropped off at central distribution points.

Chapter Fifteen
Judaism and Vatican II

This people was gathered together and led by God, creator of
heaven and earth. Thus its existence is not a mere fact of
nature or culture ... It is a supernatural fact. This people
perseveres in spite of everything because they are the people
of the Covenant, and despite human infidelities, the Lord is
faithful to his Covenant.

Pope John Paul II, October 31, 1997

Stunned by the German Holocaust and feeling guilty for the past
treatment of the Jews, the Roman Catholic Church under Pope John XXIII
announced its intention to convene the Second Vatican meeting. Vatican I was
convened in 1869 to decide what path to take in order to deal with the
enlightenment (modernism) and the strict division of religion and government.

During the 19th century, new rulers — *e.g.*, Bismarck in Germany and
Victor Emmanuel in Italy — forcibly seized church property, closed Catholic
schools, introduced civil marriage, and circumscribed the powers of the papacy.
In particular, each of the states insisted on having a hand in the selection of
bishops who would represent Catholicism in their country. In Italy, the church
also found that its domain, for millennia the City of Rome, was to be limited
to108.7 acres, the area which now constitutes Vatican City. It was this so called
"Modernist" crisis that forced the Roman Church to take a new dogmatic
position regarding the powers of the pope and the Curia (central administrative
staff).

In order to understand the change in the centuries-old attitude of the
Church toward the Jews, it is helpful to know how the Church evolved in the
late 19th and early 20th centuries. The secular rulers of the nation-states
insisted on administrative control of their government without Church
interference. The Church during this period was divided between the
absolutists (or anti-modernists) who stood for the primacy of the pope, and the
modernists who wanted power spread among the bishops.

Pope Pius IX proclaimed the First Vatican Council in 1869, calling for
strict secrecy on all aspects of Council business, saying that " ... caution appears

necessary since every opportunity is quickly seized by the powerful and destructive forces of wickedness to inspire hateful attacks against the Catholic Church and its doctrine." This internal dispute was put to rest initially when the pope was declared infallible in matters of faith and morals and in the administration of the Church universal, including supreme jurisdiction over the bishops.

Background

Pius X succeeded to the throne in 1903. He was a strict anti-modernist and required all ordinands and priests to swear an anti-modernist oath. A century before this time (1784) the great philosopher Immanuel Kant spoke to the issue of requiring a clerical oath as follows:

> But should not a society of clergymen be entitled to commit itself by oath to a certain unalterable set of doctrines, in order to secure for all time a constant guardianship over each of its members, and through them over the people? I reply that this is quite impossible. A contract of this kind concluded with a view to preventing all further enlightenment of mankind forever is absolutely null and void, even if it is ratified by the supreme power, by Imperial Diets and the most solemn peace treaties. One age cannot enter into an alliance on oath to put the next age in a position where it would be impossible for it to extend and correct its knowledge.

Aware of his untenable assumption of power, the pope sought legal backing. Thus, in 1904, under the urging of the pope, the young priest Eugenio Pacelli (the future Pope Pius XII) began work on what would become the 1917 Code of Canon Law. This document spelled out not only the powers of the pope, but also the right of the Church to control public actions of the laity.

About the same time in Germany, Protestant liberal theologians began to dream of a way between Christian orthodoxy and the Great Separation of Church and State. They had unshaken faith in the moral core of Christianity, despite the religious warfare of the previous four centuries, and faith in the cultural and political progress that Christianity (and one might add Judaism) had brought to the world. Christianity as interpreted by Christian and Jewish philosophers had given birth to the values of individual rights, natural law and universal order, human reason and scientific progress on which life was now based. On this foundation there should be no contradiction between religion and state. The German state (for example) had only to respect Christian institutions, and the "church" would reciprocate by recognizing its political responsibilities.

At the Vatican, Pacelli had become, in effect, the Foreign Secretary of the Holy See, with orders from then Pope Pius XI to employ the new canon to negotiate a settlement (concordat) with the secular governments of Europe. In his singular mission to apply Canon Law to all Catholics in each country, Pacelli used the hold that the Vatican had over its adherents to trade loyalty to the secular government for governmental respect for the Church and all its institutions. By playing all its high cards, the Catholic Church would be able to stem the destructive outcomes (from their viewpoint) of the secularization of Europe. But the new freedom of the Christian proletariat secured through the Great Separation gave rise to unanticipated side effects for the Vatican initiative.

Pacelli had a strong personal investment in negotiating a Germany Concordat. He knew Germany well from his twelve-year residency as papal *nuncio* (1917-1929), and was inclined to favor that country. Further, Germany in the early 1930s was the largest Catholic country in Europe, and Pacelli looked to the negotiation as primary to the achievement of the objectives of the Holy See (the Episcopate Office of the Bishop of Rome) and his work on the Code of Canon Law. With this in mind, and upon the accession of Hitler to the rank of Chancellor in 1933 he returned to Germany to begin negotiations. This step was to lead to removal of the highly active, politically responsible Catholics from the political sector, thereby reordering the national political life of Germany and opening the door for dictatorship.

At the start of Hitler's twelve-year reign, his racial policies were not fully developed nor envisioned as deadly. Catholics in Europe, including those in the Holy See, held the view that the Jews were responsible for their own misfortunes by blindly turning their back on the "truth" of Christianity. Thus, the Vatican was disinclined to take the side of the Jews in Hitler's upcoming plot to suppress world Judaism. Pacelli entered the concordat negotiation with a great deal of personal satisfaction and little concern about the outcome of the burgeoning Nazi racial policies. The resulting document became the instrument by which Hitler was able to appease the very strong political side of German Catholicism and clear the way for his program of racial supremacy.

Pope Pius XII

Pius XI died in 1939, the year of the war, and Pacelli succeeded him as Pope Pius XII. During the course of the war, as it became clear that the Nazis intended to exterminate the Jews, the governments of the Allied Powers as well as Jewish organizations cried for the pope to denounce this outrage in unequivocal terms. Although he made several public statements, usually during his Christmas or Easter radio talks, the pope never specifically named the Jews, nor specifically blamed the Nazis. The pope, however, may have had his private reasons for holding back on German condemnation.

Pacelli had a long standing abhorrence of the Red Russian government going back to its origins in the early 1920s. "In 1995, Alexander Yakovlev, chairman of the Commission for the Rehabilitation of the Victims of Political Repression, claimed that 200,000 clergy had been slain under Soviet rule. In 1922 Lenin had written to Molotov: 'The greater the number of representatives of the reactionary clergy and bourgeoisie we succeed in executing ... the better.'" Thus, the ongoing conquest of Russia by Germany could be seen from his viewpoint as punishment for the chaos Communism had visited upon the Catholic Church.

Could Pius XII have stopped the Nazis by condemning the Final Solution? Probably not, given Hitler's heedless intent to liquidate the Jews. Would the pope's endorsement of the rising global outcry have resulted in harm to himself and his Church? Likely. A plot to kidnap the pope was considered by Hitler near the end of the war, and the destruction of Rome by aerial bombing was a threat from the time that Americans invaded Italy in 1943. Would the good work of German Catholics and those in other European countries including the Vatican itself, clandestinely rescuing and hiding perhaps as many as 100,000 Jews, have been undermined? Certainly, the SS was routinely diverted from other tasks to punish severely those who conducted such activities. So sporadic instances of revenge killings would almost surely have increased.

Still, according to John Toland, the pope secretly addressed the College of Cardinals in June 1943, saying that all his public statements and any work on behalf of the Jews would have to be calculated not to make the situation still more dangerous for the Jews and the Church.

In the end, was the position of the Holy See in relation to the Jews helpful or harmful? Opinions differ, of course, but it seems apparent that the time to strike back was early in Hitler's term before the Germans united behind him in 1940, as his troops marched through Paris. To have done so, however, would have meant a serious and intense scrutiny by the Vatican of the cumulative effect of each turn of the Nazi Jewish inquisition, and "a real sense of urgency and moral outrage." That would have implied an equally intense concern about such issues by the pope who, unfortunately, was then slowly coming down from the "triumphant" high of his concordat policy. There was not a time during the prewar period when those two lines crossed.

Thereafter when events became ever more serious, the power to do something helpful flowed away from the pope, and all he could do was back and fill. Indeed, Cornwell said five years after publication of his book *Hitler's Pope* "that Pius XII had so little scope of action that it is impossible to judge the motives for his silence during the war."

The Second Vatican Council

Pius XII died in 1958, well aware of his failures and seeking God's forgiveness, leaving a depressed and, perhaps, guilty episcopate with growing voices calling for a change in the Roman Catholic Church. He was succeeded by Pope John XXIII who made his position clear from the opening session of Vatican II on October 11, 1962, when he declared: "'The Christian, Catholic and apostolic spirit of the whole world expects a leap forward toward a doctrinal penetration and a formation of consciences in most faithful and perfect conformity to authentic doctrine." This doctrine, he went on to say, was to be studied and expounded "by using modern methods of research and the literary forms of modern thought." The guiding metaphor of the Church of the future was to be the pilgrim people of God ... It was in this heady time that the Second Vatican Council was to seek forgiveness of the Jews for Christian anti-Semitism.

The intent of the Holy See to right its wrong to the Jews was carried through by John XXIII (1958-63), Paul VI (1963-78), and John Paul II (1978-2005). Each one of these popes moved the conversation further along, with John Paul II working with the advantage of prior discussions and proclamations as well as an amicable attitude, making substantial progress. During the papacy of John Paul, the relationship between the two religious bodies had never been better.

Jewish friends of mine at the time said they would have liked to grant him sainthood if only permitted by their religion.

The Second Vatican Council began in 1962, and continued to 1965, during the papacy of Paul VI. Often known by its Latin name, *Nostra Aetate* ("In Our Age," from the first words of the papal proclamation), Vatican II is an exploration of the relationship between Catholicism and non-Christian religions by more than two thousand participating bishops from around the world, and hundreds of theological experts and ecumenical observers. It was the outcome of a series of studies, consultations, and reflections during the course of which and in consideration of the Church's relationship with the Jews, Rabbi Abraham Joshua Heschel was consulted by both Pope John and Pope Paul. The American Jewish Congress contributed significantly to this undertaking as well.

Three major documents of the sixteen produced as a result of this study were promulgated during Vatican II: *Lumen Gentium* ('Christ is the light of the world') in November 1964, *The Church in the World Today*, known as *Gaudium et Spes* for its opening words, "The joys and the hopes...," in December 1965 and, at the close of Vatican II, the summation entitled *The Declaration on The Relation of the Church to Non-Christian Religions* in October 1965. In 1974, Paul commissioned a study on the way Judaism should be understood in Catholic teaching and practice.

In June 1985, Pope John Paul promulgated the Notes on the Correct Way to Present the Jews and Judaism in Preaching and Catechesis in the Roman Catholic Church with this overarching statement:

> Religious teaching, catechesis and preaching should be a preparation not only for objectivity, justice, and tolerance but also for understanding and dialogue. Our traditions [Judaism and Christianity] are so related that they cannot ignore each other. Mutual knowledge must be encouraged at every level. There is evident in particular a painful ignorance of the history and traditions of Judaism, of which only negative aspects and other caricatures seem to form part of the stock ideas of many Christians. That is what these notes aim to remedy.

Analysis of Documents

These four documents — *Lumen Gentium* (LG), *Gaudium et Spes* (GS), *Nostra Aetate* (NA), and *Correct Way to Present the Jews and Judaism* (CW) — form the basis upon which the Roman Church has defined its relationship to the Jews. Specific topics such as the place of Abraham in Christian theology, the meaning of the Exodus, the covenant, the death of Jesus, the role of anti-Semitism in Christian history, the value of reconciliation, and other matters are covered variously among the four documents. It is instructive to compare these subjects across these documents to have a rounded understanding of the church's position on each. However, it is difficult to determine if various shadings on particular issues are indicative of a subtle theological shift or simply the lack of editorial oversight.

Taking the subjects in biblical order, the place of Abraham in Christian theology will be analyzed first. Statements on the role of Abraham appear in NA and CW:

> As the sacred synod searches into the mystery of the Church, it remembers the bond that spiritually ties the people of the New Covenant to Abraham's stock. Thus the Church of Christ acknowledges that, according to God's saving design, the beginnings of her faith and her election are found already among the Patriarchs, Moses, and the prophets. She professes that all who believe in Christ — Abraham's sons according to faith — are included in the same Patriarch's call ... NA:4 Abraham is truly the father of our faith. The patriarchs, prophets, and other personalities of the Old Testament have been venerated and always will be venerated as saints in the

liturgical tradition of the Oriental (Eastern) Church as also of
the Latin (Western) Church. CW II:2

A close reading of the Hebrew Bible with regard to Abraham begins
with a passage in Genesis:

I (God) will make your name great. And you shall be a blessing ...
And all the families of the earth shall bless themselves by you. (Genesis
12:2-3, 18:17-18)
He (God) took him (Abraham) outside and said look toward the
heavens and count the stars if you are able to count them ... So shall your
offspring be. (Genesis 15:5)
"Know well that your offspring shall be strangers in a land not yours,
and they shall be enslaved and oppressed four hundred years; but I will
execute judgement on the nation they shall serve, and in the end they shall
go free with great wealth. (Genesis 15:13-14)
When Abram was 99 years old ... the Lord appeared to him and said
Walk in my ways and be blameless. I will establish my covenant between
Me and you, and I will make you exceedingly numerous. (Genesis
17:1-2, 17:6-7)
As for your wife Sara ... I will bless her indeed I will give her a son by
you. (Genesis 17:15-16)
Then one of the angels of the Lord said: I shall return to you next year
and Sarah shall have a son. (Genesis 18:1-15)

The intent of these biblical quotations (same in the Hebrew Bible and
Christian New Testament) is that all the believing nations descend from
Abraham and Sarah through the patriarchs, Moses, and the prophets. Thus, the
Jewish people and the Christians have the same prehistory, as do also the
Muslims. This is reemphasized in CW II:2. Note that the inclusion of the
phrase, "Abraham's sons *according to faith,*" in NA:4 may be Paul's way of
saying, but not the same racial characteristics.
　　Chronologically the next theological area is the meaning of the Exodus
in the life of Judaism and the Church. This matter is discussed in NA and CW.

... the salvation of the Church is mysteriously foreshadowed
by the chosen people's exodus from the land of bondage. The
Church, therefore, cannot forget that she received the
revelation of the Old Testament through the people with
whom God in His inexpressible mercy concluded the Ancient
Covenant. NA:4
The Exodus ... represents an experience of salvation and
liberation that is not complete in itself, but has in it, over and

above its own meaning, the capacity to be developed further.
Salvation and liberation are already accomplished in Christ
and gradually realized by the sacraments in the Church. This
makes way for the fulfillment of God's design, which awaits
its final consummation with the return of Jesus as Messiah.
CW II:9

The importance of the Exodus experience in Jewish life is the freedom
it represents from slavery and oppression, and worse. It is clear in the minds of
the Jewish people that God meant them to be free, free to do the work of the
covenant in this world. The first statement does not disagree. The second
statement employs metaphor to carry the concept of freedom (*i.e.,* "liberation")
much further. Jews hold that the Christ event does not in any way invalidate
the exodus experience. On the matter of the return of Jesus as Messiah,
Judaism holds in Talmud that the name of Messiah is hidden from humankind.

Remaining in biblical chronology, the discussion of the covenant now
follows. Much is said in the church documents about the covenant, both "old"
and "new." It is directly discussed in NA, LG, and CW. It is mentioned in
passing in many places. The covenant is never very far from the center of
active debate.

God holds the Jews most dear for the sake of their Fathers.
He does not repent of the gifts He makes or of the calls He
issues — such is the witness of the Apostle. NA:4
At all times and in every race, anyone who fears God and
does what is right has been acceptable to him (cf. Acts 10:35).
He has, however, willed to make men holy and save them, not
as individuals without any bond or link between them, but
rather to make them into a people who might acknowledge
him and serve him in holiness. He therefore chose the
Israelite race to be his own people and established a covenant
with it. He gradually instructed this people ... and made it holy
unto himself. All these things, however, happened as a
preparation and figure of that new and perfect covenant
which was to be ratified in Christ, and of the fuller revelation
which was to be given through the Word of God made flesh
... Christ instituted this new covenant, namely the new
covenant in his blood; he called a race made up of Jews and
Gentiles which would be one, not according to the flesh but
in the Spirit, and this race would be the new People of God.
LG II:9.
As Israel according to the flesh wandered in the desert and
was already called the Church of God, so too, the new Israel,

which advances in this present era in search of a future and permanent city (cf. Hebrews 13:14) is called also the Church of Christ (cf. Matt. 16:18). LG II:9.

Those who have not yet received the Gospel are related to the People of God in various ways. There is, first, that people to which the covenants and promises were made, and from which Christ was born according to the flesh (cf. Rom. 9:4-5), in view of the divine choice, they are a people most dear for the sake of the fathers, for the gifts of God are without repentance (cf. Rom. 11:29). LG II:16.

As the sacred synod searches into the mystery of the Church, it remembers the bond that spiritually ties the people of the New Covenant to Abraham's stock. NA:4 (reprised from the Abraham discussion.)

The Church ... cannot forget that she received the revelation of the Old Testament through the people with whom God in His inexpressible mercy concluded the Ancient Covenant. NA:4 (reprised from the Exodus discussion)

This concern for Judaism in Catholic teaching has not merely a historical or archeological foundation ... The Holy Father has stated this permanent reality of the Jewish people in a remarkable theological formula," ... the people of God and of the Old Covenant, which has never been revoked ... " CW I:3.

The Covenant

The matter of the covenant is central to the life of Judaism. It is the reason for being of the Israelites and their descendants the Jews. The meaning of the covenant to Judaism is comparable to the meaning of Jesus Christ to Christianity. Therefore, any move on the part of the Church to tear away the duties of the covenant assigned by God to Israel means, in essence, a life and death theological struggle. This matter cannot be taken lightly. To obtain perspective on these excerpts it is best to review them in sequence, looking at the progressive thought pattern for any shift in the position of the Church.

The excerpts are theologically rich, in the Catholic sense. Yes, God did make a covenant with the Israelites, *but* it was only a preparation for "that new and perfect covenant" with the "new People of God." The use of the word "new," although hardly unique elsewhere, has special meaning in this context. It goes back to the Pauline Jacob/Esau claim that: the "old" will serve the "new." (Rom. 11:9) In NA as well, reference is made to "the New Covenant." But CW, the guide to teaching, carefully steps around the implications of old or ancient covenant versus new, citing only the Apostle Paul in Romans 11:28-9:

"... as regards election they are beloved for the sake of their ancestors; for the gifts and the

calling of God are irrevocable." If the teaching stops there, Judaism is not offended. If, however, it goes on, as did the Apostle Paul to suggest that God may choose who carries the covenant in each generation, *then* there arises a genuine concern which cannot be hidden even from a discerning Christian. John Paul II's 1997 statement, quoted at the start of this chapter, is the latest and strongest statement on the Jews and the covenant. Jews hope it finds its way into the *Correct Teaching.*

Complementary to the covenant issue is the venerable olive tree, the metaphoric Israel, and the Gentiles who have been grafted on to it. This again is a Pauline matter:

> ... *if some of the branches [of the olive tree] were broken off, and you, a wild olive shoot were grafted in their place to share the rich root of the olive tree, do not boast over the branches. If you do boast, remember that it is not you that support the root, but the root that supports you.* (Rom. 11:17-18)

It seems straightforward to say that the olive tree is Judaism from the roots up, and the wild olive shoots grafted on are the "new people of God." It follows then that Judaism is the basis for Christianity. That was surely true in the time of Paul. How does the church look upon this metaphor today?

> The Church is a cultivated field, the tillage of God (I Cor. 3:9). On that land the ancient olive tree grows whose holy roots were the prophets and in which the reconciliation of Jews and Gentiles has been brought about and will be brought about again (Rom.11:13-26) ... Yet the true vine is Christ ... without whom we can do nothing (John 15:1-5). LG I:6.
>
> Nor can [the church] forget that she draws sustenance from the root of that well-cultivated olive tree onto which have been grafted the wild shoots, the Gentiles. Indeed, the Church believes that by His cross Christ, Our Peace, reconciled Jews and Gentiles making both one in Himself ... the Church also recalls that the Apostles, the Church's main-stay and pillars, as well as most of the early disciples who proclaimed Christ's Gospel to the world, sprang from the Jewish people. NA
>
> Jesus was and always remained a Jew, his ministry was deliberately limited to the lost sheep of the house of Israel. (Matt. 15:24) Jesus is fully a man of his time, and of his environment — the Jewish Palestinian of the first century, the anxieties and hopes of which he shared ... There is no doubt

that Jesus wished to submit himself to the law (cf. Gal. 4:4), that he was circumcised and presented in the Temple like any Jew of his time (Luke 2:21-24), that he was trained in the law's observance. He extolled respect for it (Matt. 5:17-20) and invited obedience to it (cf. Matt. 8:4). The rhythm of his life was marked by observance of pilgrimages on great feasts, even from his infancy (cf. Luke 2:41). CW III:12-13.

First off, the declaration that Jesus and the apostles were Jews through and through is a healthy reminder to the faithful, although not exactly news to the Jewish community. That the church has spoken out on this point is commendable.

The statement regarding *"sustenance from the root of the well-cultivated olive tree"* uses this passage to acknowledge that Christianity is indeed an offshoot of Judaism, However, the Christology added to both excerpts carries this metaphor into new territory: the reconciliation of Judaism and Christianity. If reconciliation is taken to mean the restoration of friendly relations, it seems most appropriate. If, on the other hand, it is intended to mean united as a single people, it is not in keeping with Jewish interests. This was emphatically made clear by Jorge Cardinal Mejía, the secretary of the commission that produced *Correct Way,* in the transcript of a lecture he gave in 2004:

> If Judaism can be considered a non-Christian religion, it is not
> so in the same sense as the other religions to which this label
> can be applied. Its relation with the Catholic Church and,
> more in general, with the reality of Christianity is completely
> different ... It was this consideration that led to the decision
> to establish this Commission [for Religious Relations with the
> Jews] within the Department that deals with other Christian
> denominations. Maybe this solution is not the best since it
> might create the misunderstanding that the goal of these
> relations is the establishment of a unity, as with other
> Christians; and this, as is now clear, is absolutely not the case
> with Judaism.

Blame for Crucifixion

Another matter of real concern for Jews is the purported blame in the New Testament placed on their people as a whole for the death of Jesus.

> The formula "the Jews" sometimes, according to the context,
> means "the leaders of the Jews" or "the adversaries of Jesus,"
> terms which express better the thought of the evangelist (the

writers of the Gospels) and avoid appearing to arraign the
Jewish people as such. CW IV:21.

True that the Jewish authorities and those who followed their
lead pressed for the death of Christ, still what happened in
His passion cannot be charged against all the Jews, without
distinction, then alive, nor against the Jews of today.
Although the Church is the new people of God, the Jews
should not be presented as rejected or accursed by God, as if
this followed from the Holy Scriptures. All should see to it,
then, that in catechetical work in the preaching of the word of
God they do not teach anything that does not conform to the
truth of the Gospel and the spirit of Christ. NA:4
Besides, as the Church has always held and holds now, Christ
underwent His passion and death freely, because of the sins
of men and out of infinite love, in order that all may reach
salvation. It is, therefore, the burden of the Church's
preaching to proclaim the cross of Christ as the sign of God's
all-embracing love and as the fountain from which every
grace flows. NA:4

The death of Jesus was not a major event, being one of hundreds (if
not thousands) of crucifixions. His faithful followers numbered perhaps in the
hundreds, essentially all of whom were poor Jews and some of whom scattered
at the time of the crucifixion. No specific reference is made by the Church to
the depiction in Matthew 27:21-23 that the Jews called for the crucifixion of
Jesus and took upon themselves the blame for that demand (*Then the people as a
whole answered, "His blood be on us and on our children."* v.25.)

The historian Philo (c. 20 BCE to 50 CE), a contemporary of Pontius
Pilate and Jesus, wrote that Pilate

"was a man of very inflexible disposition, and very merciless
as well as very obstinate." His habits included "corruption …
acts of insolence … rapine (violent seizure of property) …
insulting people … cruelty … and continued murders of people
untried and uncondemned and his never ending, and
gratuitous, and most grievous inhumanity.

A few years after the crucifixion of Jesus, Pilate rounded up a large
group of Samaritan men on a pretext while concealing his guards, and then fell
upon them slaughtering many. The Samaritans sent an envoy to Rome to
accuse Pilate of murder. He was deposed a few years later in 37 CE . Generally
speaking, Pilate did not need any encouragement to kill anyone.

It is quite doubtful that any of the gospel accounts of the events leading up to the crucifixion depict what occurred. It must be said that the Church, in speaking out against the charge of deicide which has been a pogrom rallying cry for almost two millennia, is taking an important step to dispute the basis for a good deal of anti-Semitism. This is indeed a welcome statement, which the church carries further in the following excerpts:

> Furthermore, in her rejection of every persecution against any man, the Church, mindful of the patrimony she shares with the Jews and moved not by political reasons but by the Gospel's spiritual love, decries hatred, persecutions, displays of anti-Semitism, directed against Jews at any time and by anyone. NA:4
>
> The question is not merely to uproot from among the faithful the remains of anti-Semitism ... but much rather to arouse in them through educational work, an exact knowledge of the wholly unique "bond" which joins us as a Church to the Jews and to Judaism. CW I:8
>
> There is no putting the Jews who knew Jesus and did not believe in him, or those who opposed the preaching of the apostles, on the same plane with Jews who came after or those of today. If the responsibility of the former remains a mystery hidden with God (Rom. 11:25), the latter are in an entirely different situation. Vatican II teaches that "all men are to be immune from coercion ... in such wise that in matters religious no one is to be forced to act in a manner contrary to his own beliefs. Nor ... restrained from acting in accordance with his own beliefs." This is one of the bases on which Judeo-Christian dialogue rests. CW IV:21F
>
> We must in any case rid ourselves of the traditional idea of a people preserved for Christian apologetics. It remains a chosen people, "the pure olive on which were grafted the branches of the wild olive which are the Gentiles." CW VI:25, quoting Pope John Paul II.
>
> The history of Israel did not end in 70 CE following the destruction of the Temple. It continued, especially in a numerous Diaspora which allowed Israel to carry to the whole world a witness — often heroic— of its fidelity to the one God and to "exalt him in the presence of all the living" while preserving the memory of the land of their forefathers at the heart of their hope. CW VI:25

In the last three excerpts, the Church steps away from its policy of seeking to convert Jews and speaks out against forced conversion practices of the church in the past. It also "rids," itself from using Judaism as a permanent counter-example to Christianity's "virtues," as propounded by St. Augustine. The experience of the Jews during the Diaspora is given passing mention regarding the steadfastness of the people while they were often in despair. This has recently been emphasized by Pope Francis when he said:

> Through the awful trials of these last centuries, the Jews have preserved their faith in God. And for this, we, the Church and the whole human family can never be sufficiently grateful to them.

The Church, coming out against anti-Semitism and against coercion of those who may be the object of evangelism, took a very important step to neutralize its prior attitude towards the Jews and Judaism.

Basic Church Tenets

In LG and GS, the Church also stakes out a position on a number of fundamental Christian issues which shows no basic change in theology. In these documents, the Church says, in effect, that whatever agreements may be reached with non-Christians, it must be with full recognition of this theology.

Of most concern to non-Catholics is the Church's claim of inerrancy "in the matters of belief," which is followed by the statement that "Christ is the way of salvation and founder of the Catholic Church"; the passage then declares that those "who know of it and refuse to enter it or remain in it cannot be saved." The Church thus stands between God and God's people in the matter of salvation. The Church holds that John 14:6, the singular way to God, is a foundation stone of the faith; yet it notes that, in keeping with Romans 2:12-16, those "who sincerely seek God," even though they do not know the gospel, may attain salvation as well. Further, the Church assures all that they are free to choose their own religion, albeit with the implication that salvation is not assured. Although the hope of resurrection is offered through Jesus who died for all, no one, particularly a Jewish person, is to be judged as unworthy for having chosen another way.

Belief in God

Another concern is the manner in which people are seeking answers to basic life questions and their awareness of the role that God can play in their life.

> Contemporary women and men are in the process of ... discovering and affirming their rights. The church is entrusted with the task of manifesting to them the mystery of God who is their final destiny; in doing so it discloses to them the meaning of their own existence, the innermost truth about themselves. The church knows well that God alone, whom it serves, can satisfy the deepest cravings of the human heart, for it can never be fully content with the world and what is has to offer. The church also realizes that men and women are continually being aroused by the Spirit of God and that they will never be utterly indifferent to religion. By this faith the church can keep the dignity of human nature out of the reach of changing opinions. GS One: IV.41

This statement embodies the philosophical elements of the Enlightenment as handed down by DaCosta, Spinoza, and Rousseau among others. All religions today carry the burden of secularism, particularly where the temptations of societal wealth are most prominent. As the church points out, life cannot be satisfying if it is not based on other-worldly imperatives. *"God, You are my God; I search for You, my soul thirsts for You, my body yearns for You"* (Psalm 63:2). It is the charge of all Jews to seek out those who yearn for God and help them find a suitable pathway to God. The church makes clear that it does not impose itself between those who by their free choice seek not the gospel but rather a way which speaks to each of them. This is noted in counter-distinction to the Church's claim that "they could not be saved who, knowing that the Catholic Church was founded as necessary by God through Christ, would refuse either to enter it, or to remain in it" (LG II:14). It also counters the gospel assertion, *"Jesus said: I am the way, and the truth, and the life. No one comes to the Father except through me"* (John 14:6).

Jewish-Christian Bible

However, a recent addition to the biblical library could make Jewish-Christian Bible study more meaningful. *The Jewish Annotated New Testament*, edited by Amy-Jill Levine and Marc Zvi Brettler, is designed "to highlight the Jewishness of the New Testament. This includes both the manifold ways in which the New Testament text displays continuities as well as contrasts with Tanakh (the Hebrew Scriptures), and the hermeneutical insights that can be gained from the other roughly contemporary Jewish literature, such as the

Dead Sea Scrolls, Philo, Josephus, etc." An impressive array of scholars from North America, Europe, Israel, and Australia – all of whom are Jewish — contributed to this work.

Vatican II does very little to encourage this type of study. *Correct Way* II:6 notes that:

> ... the Church and Christians read the Old Testament in the light of the event of the dead and risen Christ and that on these grounds there is a Christian reading of the Old Testament which does not necessarily coincide with the Jewish reading. Thus Christian identity and Jewish identity should be carefully distinguished in their respective reading of the Bible. Although this is a worthy goal, it is not easily reached without considerable study by academics of both faiths. And saying further in CW " ... this detracts nothing from the value of the Old Testament in the Church ... " discourages study that can establish mutually agreeable grounds of commonality. And, finally, " ... and does nothing to hinder Christians from profiting discerningly from traditions of Jewish reading." Again, it takes especially well read experts to make the word "discerningly" truly meaningful to the lay reader. CW II:6.

What could be of great value would be a new version of the Hebrew Bible/Old Testament acceptable to both Jewish and Christian scholars with proper annotation explaining the differences. To achieve that ideal, Christians must be willing to reconsider their assumption that the *Old* Testament is superseded by a *New* Testament, and the Jews must be willing to consider that Christianity has much to say about Judaism as it existed almost two thousand years ago.

The matter of supersessionism was not put to rest in Vatican II, although Soulen has pointed out:

> ... some Christian churches (cf. Presbyterians) have concluded that the church's supposed displacement of the Jewish people in God's plan is wrong or at least seriously misleading, and they have affirmed that their church has not superseded the Jewish people in God's plan and that God remains faithful to God's election of the Jewish people.

The supposition that Christianity has superseded Judaism is a theological problem because it threatens to render the existence of the Jewish people a matter of indifference to God. This position throws into doubt God's relationship with this creation. If the promise of God cannot be relied upon, can our personal relationship to God be real? And if that is the case, what is our reason for being, learning, and loving?

The *Correct Way to Present the Jews and Judaism* puts to rest many Christian misconceptions regarding the role of Jews in the world and their relationship to the religion built upon Jesus and the resurrected Christ. It carefully elucidates and, where appropriate, revises Christian thinking on many of the more sensitive areas in this relationship. These include the mythic role of Abraham in the origin of all believing people, the fact that Jesus was a Jew of his time who lived under the law and observed the holidays, and the truth that his apostles all were Jewish as well. Care is taken to dispel the notion that the Jews of the first century acted as a group in opposition to Jesus, where it would be more appropriate to indicate that some Jewish leaders may have done so, and entirely inappropriate to suggest that Jews today were implicit in these ancient disputes or in the crucifixion of Jesus. Finally, Jews remain chosen by God, represent the root stock of all monotheistic people, and must not be viewed unfavorably in comparison to Christianity. All of this is noteworthy and represents a major change in the age-old attitude of the Vatican.

The amazing change in Catholic-Jewish relations is reflected in a statement made by Cardinal Etchegarary in 1983:

> The depth of that change is probably hard for anyone to
> measure who was not personally acquainted with the situation
> before the Second Vatican Council. The impact of Vatican II
> has been felt worldwide on Christianity and Judaism ... Today
> the French, German, Dutch, Brazilian, US and other
> episcopal conferences have all issued pastorals and directives
> urging the faithful to learn to treasure the inheritance they
> have received through the Jewish people and to root out all
> traces of anti-Semitism.

Notes to Chapter Fifteen

This chapter is both long and carefully parsed out. Most of the statements were composed by clerics that intended to justify an apologetic statement regarding relations with the Jews while they were very much aware that there was still an element within the Church that opposed that position because it was to their ears an admission of error. The Church is often cited by the pope as without error.

For those who would like to explore this further, start by reading the Vatican papers that were accepted by the clerics. These are:

Dogmatic Constitution on the Church, *Lumen Gentium,* November 1964
Dogmatic Constitution on Divine Revelation (Dei Verbum) November 1965
Address of Pope John Paul II to a Symposium on the Roots of Anti-Judaism, October 1977
Commission for Religious Relations with the Jews, *Correct Way to Present the Jews and Judaism,* June 1985

Then supplement your reading with the following books and web sites:

Wiltgen, S.V.D., Rev. Ralph M, *The Rhine Flows into the Tiber,* Hawthorn Books, 1967 (He was present at most sessions of Vatican II and took notes for the pope).
Lawrence E. Cahoone, From Modernism to Post Modernism: An Anthology, Blackwell, 1996
Cornwell, John. Hitler's Pope: The Secret History of Pius XII, Viking Press, 1999
Lederer, Thomas G. 2000 Years: Relations Between Catholics and Jews Before and After World War II, www.arthurstreet.com, 1998.
Hasting, Adrian, ed. Modern Catholicism: Vatican II and After, Oxford, 1991.
Fisher, Eugene J, Rudin, A. James, Tannenbaum, Mark H, *Twenty Years of Jewish-Catholic Relations,* Paulist Press, 1986

Chapter Sixteen
Judaism and Christianity Today

> Since time immemorial it has been necessary — as it is also
> for the future — to maintain the principle according to which
> each particular Church must concur with the universal
> Church, not only as regards the doctrine of the faith and the
> sacramental signs, but also as regards the usages universally
> accepted by uninterrupted apostolic tradition, which must be
> observed not only to avoid errors but also to transmit the
> integrity of the faith, because the Church's law of prayer
> corresponds to her faith.

Apostolic Letter *Summorum Pontificicum*, Pope Benedict XVI,
July 7, 2007.

The immediate reaction to the Second Vatican initiative was strong on
both sides. Arab diplomats lobbied against an official Catholic document aimed
at minimizing anti-Semitism and even threatened reprisals against Catholics ...
There were also some very negative reactions from Protestants and Eastern
Orthodox as well. On the Jewish side, Rabbi A. James Rudin likened *Nostra
Aetate* to other historic documents such as the Magna Carta and the
Declaration of Independence, while some Jews were disappointed that the
church made no outright apology, much as those given by the church to
Muslims and Protestants in the past.

However, since the Roman Catholic Church had spoken out so
forthrightly about relations with the Jews, a measured response from the
Jewish community was called for. Hence an interdenominational group of
more than 170 Orthodox, Conservative, and Reform rabbis felt compelled, in
the year 2000, to respond in kind. The prologue of their report, *Dabru Emet
(Speak the Truth): A Jewish Statement on Christians and Christianity*, declares,

> We believe it is time for Jews to reflect on what Judaism may
> now say about Christianity. As a first step, we offer eight brief
> statements about how Jews and Christians may relate to one
> another.

Jews and Christians worship the same God ... We rejoice that, through Christianity, hundreds of millions of people have entered into a relationship with the God of Israel.

Jews and Christians seek authority from the same book. Turning to it for religious orientation, spiritual enrichment, and communal education; we each take away similar lessons.

Christians, as members of a biblically based religion, appreciate that [the land of] Israel was promised — and given — to Jews as the physical center of the covenant between them and God ... We also recognize that Jewish tradition mandates justice for all non-Jews who reside in a Jewish state.

Jews and Christians accept the moral principles of Torah. Central [to which] is the inalienable sanctity and dignity of every human being.

Nazism was not a Christian phenomenon. We encourage the continuation of recent efforts in Christian theology to repudiate unequivocally contempt of Judaism and the Jewish people. We applaud those Christians who reject this teaching of contempt, and we do not blame them for the sins committed by their ancestors. [N.B. There was dissension on this point by a minority group.]

The humanly irreconcilable difference between Jews and Christians will not be settled until God redeems the entire world as promised in Scripture.

A new relationship between Jews and Christians will not weaken Jewish practice. An improved relationship will not accelerate the cultural and religious assimilation that Jews rightly fear.

The closing statement speaks to all ages and religions:

Jews and Christians, each in their own way, recognize the unredeemed state of the world as reflected in the persistence of persecution, poverty, and human degradation and misery. Although justice and peace are finally God's, our joint efforts, together with those of other faith communities, will help bring the kingdom of God for which we hope and long. Separately and together, we must work to bring justice and peace to our world.

Good Friday Prayer

The Church has attempted to bring the Jewish people into the Christian fold for more than fifteen hundred years. Classic Pauline doctrine balanced disappointment that the Jews had not accepted Christ in large numbers with the hope that the Jews would accept the "true" religion. This became the basis of normative Church policy. But, the longer the Jews persisted as an unyielding religious group, the stronger the challenge. Relations between Christians and Jews during the European Diaspora reached a paradoxical point: on the one hand, the grim picture of persecution and humiliation, intolerance and fanaticism, and on the other, the real concern of the Church to protect and preserve the Jews.

Why did the church believe that the Jews must be preserved? As St. Augustine elaborated, should the Jews and, along with them, Judaism ceased to exist, then Christians too might neglect God's revelation and desert the faith. This is best expressed in Pauline theology: if the root of the olive tree dies, how can the branches survive? And, finally, the Church was well aware of humanity's inability to nullify God's purpose: the free yet irrevocable love for the people Israel.

Still, the Church prayed the Tridentine-rite on Good Friday, as authorized by the Council of Trent and instituted by Pope Pius V in 1570, as follows:

> Let us pray also for the perfidious (deceitful, untrustworthy) Jews: that Almighty God may remove the veil from their hearts; so that they too may acknowledge Jesus Christ our Lord. Almighty and eternal God, who dost not exclude from thy mercy even Jewish faithlessness, hear our prayers which we offer for the blindness of that people; that acknowledging the light of thy Truth, which is Christ, they may be delivered from their darkness. Through the same Lord Jesus Christ, who lives and reigns with thee in the unity of the Holy Spirit, God for ever and ever. Amen.

At that time the congregants did not kneel during the prayer for the conversion of the Jews, even though kneeling in silent prayer was prescribed for all other petitions in the Good Friday rite, because, it was said, the Church did not wish to imitate the Jews who mocked Christ before his crucifixion by kneeling before him and reviling him. In 1955, Pope Pius XII instituted kneeling for this petition. In 1960, Pope John XXIII removed perfidious from the prayer. In 1965, Pope Paul VI eliminated the phrase on blindness.

The revised declaration on *The Relation of the Church to Non-Christian Religions* was approved 2,221 in favor, eighty-eight opposed. At the closing of

Vatican II on October 28, 1965, Pope Paul VI proclaimed *Nostra Aetate*, in which nothing was said about converting Jews. After Vatican II in 1970 the Jewish prayer was completely revised to read:

> Let us pray for the Jewish people, the first to hear the word of God, that they may continue to grow in the love of his name and in faithfulness to his covenant.
> Almighty and eternal God, long ago you gave your promise to Abraham and his posterity. Listen to your Church as we pray that the people you first made your own may arrive at the fullness of redemption. We ask this through Christ our Lord. Amen

The 1970 prayer version, which is in the *ordinary* (vernacular) form of the Good Friday Mass, is a true reflection of Vatican II and a very important step in neutralizing the Church's prior attitude towards the conversion of the Jews.

During the discussions that constituted the Second Vatican Council, Rabbi Heschel worked behind the scenes to prevent any injunction to convert Jews and to eliminate language that characterized them as despicable. The key figure in carrying out the emendation regarding the Jews was the German Jesuit Cardinal Augustin Bea. To those in opposition, Heschel's main theological point was: Is it really the will of God that there be no more Judaism in the world? Still, the conservative minority was alarmed. They saw that traditional mainstream understandings were being reversed. Must that not mean that the church had previously been in error? But Bea argued that the church must reflect the love of Christ and the apostles — all of them Jews — for the Jewish people.

Cardinal Bea's opponents objected that St. Paul had spoken not only of the divine election of the Jews and God's love for them "for the sake of their forefathers," but also of their being "enemies of God" as regards the gospel (Romans 11:28-29). A ground swell of anti-Semitism arose among a minority. At this point Heschel made his most forthright intervention, strongly condemning the draft text of the document, which expressed a hope for the eventual conversion of the Jews, "[a] message that regards the Jews as candidates for conversion and proclaims that the destiny of Judaism is to disappear, will be abhorred by Jews all over the world."

In 1978, John Paul II was called to Peter's chair; he served until his death in 2005 and was succeeded by Pope Benedict XVI. The matter of the Jewish prayer remained unchanged during that period. In July 2007, Pope Benedict published an Apostolic Letter (Summorum Pontificum) which encouraged a wider use of the 1962 Latin Mass (Missale Romanum). His accompanying letter posed the question, "Does the wider use of the extraordinary form of the rites of Holy Week reflect a change in the Church's teaching on anti-Semitism?"

> No. The 1962 Missale Romanum already reflected [Pope] John's revision of liturgical language often construed as anti-Semitic. In 1965, the watershed statement Nostra Aetate, of the Second Vatican Council then repudiated all forms of anti-Semitism as having no place within Christian life. When Pope Paul VI issued the Missale Romanum of 1969, the only prayer for the Jewish people in the Roman liturgy was completely revised for Good Friday to reflect a renewed understanding of the Jews as God's chosen people "first to hear the word of God."

In late August 2007, the Vatican Secretary of State publicly acknowledged the concerns of the clergy regarding, among other matters, the effect the revival of the Latin Mass might have on the Church's relations with the Jews. The Secretary suggested that making the 1970 prayer the common text for both missals might be the best solution. Groups and individuals, long associated with efforts at Christian-Jewish understanding after Vatican II, sent messages to the Vatican urging that the Latin version of the 1970 Good Friday prayer be inserted into the 1962 Missal. Concern over the prayer was shared equally by Christians and Jews.

However, on February 5, 2008 the Vatican published Pope Benedict's updated Tridentine Good Friday prayer for the Jews which reads as follows:

> Let us also pray for the Jews. May the Lord our God enlighten their hearts so that they may acknowledge Jesus Christ, the savior of all men. All powerful and everlasting God, you who want men to be saved and to reach the awareness of the truth, graciously grant that with the fullness of peoples entering into your church all of Israel may be saved. Through Christ our Lord. Amen.

The pope decreed that the new prayer must be used in place of the Tridentine prayer in all celebrations of the liturgy of Good Friday in accordance with the 1962 *Missal Romanum (extraordinary)* Latin form of the mass starting with Good Friday 2008.

The new prayer engendered much controversy. Protests came from countries and ecumenical Jewish-Christian groups many of whom had been working steadily over the prior forty years to find common ground. Three points are apparent from the commentary on the Jewish mission:

- There is an eternal covenant between God and the Jewish people.
- The Jews are called to witness to God's faithful love and to prepare the world for God's kingdom.
- Any concerted attempt at conversion of the Jewish people by Christian evangelism would interfere with God's purpose and antagonize the Jewish people.

It is certainly fair to ask why the pope seemed to be undermining the concordat so laboriously worked out with the Jews. During the period 1974 to 2012, Catholic church attendance in the US dropped from 46 percent to 27 percent while attendance at Protestant churches increased from 45 percent to 54 percent. In Europe the situation was worse. In some of Catholic Europe's largest dioceses in Germany, France, Italy, and Ireland, the percentage of Catholics who attend Mass regularly had slipped to as low as 20 percent, and in a few cities, like Paris, reached as low as the single digits, according to figures compiled by the church in 2005. Pope Benedict (2005-2013) considered this to be the greatest problem facing the Church. His approach was to assure that the faithful remained in the pews of the so called "smaller but purer church." The most faithful parishioners were these who attended the Latin mass. It was for this reason that Benedict fashioned the Good Friday prayer to be, at least, familiar to them.

However, this was just a one-time hurried solution. To understand Benedict's reasoned position, we must delve into the Church's view of *all* (Western) religions (including Judaism) and *all* who profess no religious belief. Pope Benedict's position on the Church is detailed in the declaration *Dominus Iesus,* which he wrote as Cardinal Ratzinger in his role as Cardinal Prefect of the Congregation for the Doctrine of the Faith. This document was adopted by John Paul II and released on June 16, 2000. The purpose of this document is clearly stated in paragraph 3:

> The present Declaration seeks to recall to Bishops,
> theologians, and all the Catholic faithful, certain indispensable
> elements of Christian doctrine, which may help theological
> reflection in developing solutions consistent with the contents
> of the faith and responsive to the pressing needs of
> contemporary culture ... [the] purpose ... is not to treat in a
> systematic manner the question of the unicity and salvific
> universality of the mystery of Jesus Christ and the Church,
> nor to propose solutions to questions that are matters of free
> theological debate, but rather to set forth again the doctrine
> of the Catholic faith in these areas, pointing out some
> fundamental questions that remain open to further

development, and refuting specific positions that are erroneous and ambiguous.

In setting the stage for a major statement on the powers of religion, the pope focuses on "unicity" which, in this instance, means *uniting for a unique purpose*, and "salvific" which means *redemption in the sense of the afterlife*. The "truth" rests with the Holy Catholic Apostolic Roman Church. It is against the practices of this church that all other Christian creeds will be measured.

Belief Systems

Before delving into some of the pope's supporting statements, let us first consider that our personal beliefs are just that. And even though there might be a vast group of people holding the same or similar beliefs, and even if it is possible that over time a large majority of the world's people will eventually come to do so, that does not make the belief any more objective (*i.e.*, "real") than if it were held by only a handful or even a single individual. And that is because these beliefs are in fact "subjective" (based upon personal or emotional feelings).There is no objective agreement on, for example, a near-death experience. Many have described what they have seen and felt. But any such description is true in its totality only for the observer. Certainly someone else can question your beliefs but in doing so, they would only make known their own beliefs.

The following paragraph is from a discussion of theological discourse in the life of St. Thomas Aquinas:

> Theological discourse looks like any other discourse and is, needless to say, governed by the common principles of thought and being, but it is characterized formally by the fact that its arguments and analyses are taken to be truth-bearing only for one who accepts Scriptural revelation as true.

Thus, the belief system of any religious body is true only for those who profess that faith.

In *Dominus Iesus,* the pope drew a bright line across which no professed Catholic could cross without endangering personal salvation. Following are the high points of that document. (Citations are to paragraph numbers.)

> 4. The Church's constant missionary proclamation is endangered today by relativistic theories which seeks to justify religious pluralism, not only in fact but also in principle ... uncritically absorbed ideas from a variety of philosophical and theological contexts without regard for consistency,

systematic connection, or compatibility with Christian truth ...
[results in] the tendency to read and to interpret Sacred
Scripture outside the Tradition and Magisterium of the
Church.

The pope minces no words in holding up "relativistic theories" (*i.e.*,
those not absolute in comparison to a standard) which seek to justify religious
plurality, "not only in fact but also in principle." In using the word "fact," the
pope implies that a claim is being made as to indisputability. In a later sentence
he uses the terminology "compatible with Christian truth." As noted before,
generally speaking "truth" is not the issue in religion, rather it is "belief."
However, "Christian truth" probably means, in this context, the Roman
Catholic Church not, for example, a Protestant denomination.
     The pope then sets immutable guide posts.

5. It must be *firmly believed* [italics in original] that, in the
mystery of Jesus Christ, the Incarnate Son of God, who is *the
way, and the truth, and the life.* (John 14:6), the full revelation of
divine truth is given: ... *no one knows the Son except the Father,
and no one knows the Father except the Son and anyone to whom the
Son chooses to reveal him.* (Matt. 11:27); *No one has ever seen God. It
is God the only Son, who is close to the Father's heart, who has made
him known.* (John 1:18) *For in him [Christ] the whole fullness of
divinity dwells bodily.* (Col. 2:9-10) ... Only the revelation of Jesus
Christ, therefore, introduces into our history a universal and
ultimate truth which stirs the human mind to ceaseless effort.

The opening line, "It must be *firmly believed*" leaves little room for
Christian Bible discussion in this the most important aspect of Christianity.
Who is Jesus? Was he really born of woman? Or was he sent by God, The
Father, to clean up the morality system of His Chosen People? Why don't the
Jews believe in the ministry of Jesus? If there is to be real discussion with the
Jews, the "firmly believe" part will not be helpful. The paragraph's last lines,
"the revelation of Jesus Christ ... introduces into our history a universal and
ultimate truth," are also troublesome. If the word *universal* is intended to mean
the cosmos, there is no basis to make that assumption. If the words *ultimate
truth* are intended to mean nothing ever will be more defining, that too is
without objective basis.

13. The truth of Jesus Christ, Son of God, Lord and only
Savior, who through the event of his incarnation, death and
resurrection, has brought the history of salvation to

fulfilment, and which has in him its fullness and center, must
be *firmly believed* as a constant element of the Church's faith.
20. Above all else, it must be *firmly believed* that "the Church ...
is necessary for salvation; the one Christ is the mediator and
the way of salvation.

In these paragraphs we reach an intensely personal issue — whether
salvation (*i.e.*, the prospect of eternal life) rests upon what each of us,
individually, believe or what the Church tells us. This makes many people
understandably nervous about end-of-life issues. Granted, being in a
"believing" church makes salvation more comforting because supplicants can
rely upon each other, but that does not change anything about what lies on the
other side of the curtain.

To this point the text is pointed directly at the clergy and the faithful
laity. And, as such, should be taken by non-Catholics as the Church's
entitlement to specify the precepts of its faith. The next passages, however,
becomes a matter of much greater concern to non-Catholics:

7. Thus, theological faith (the acceptance of the truth revealed
by the One and Triune God) is often identified with belief in
other religions, which is religious experience still in search of
the absolute truth and still lacking assent to God who reveals
himself. This is one of the reasons why the differences
between Christianity and the other religions tend to be
reduced at times to the point of disappearance.

Speaking Magisterium, as one who knows "the truth," it is observed
that "other religions" may base some of its belief on Catholicism, but in doing
so they cannot reach "absolute truth" since, the pope claims, it is only fully
revealed through the Son of God. Given that Judaism was revealed by God to
the Israelites through Moses and the prophets, and Islam was revealed to
Muhammad by God's archangel Gabriel, he must be talking to Protestant
denominations. (Let us stick with Western religions.)

Now speaking directly to the other Christian churches, the Catholic
Church sets out its special place in God's firmament:

16. ... the Church of Christ, despite the divisions which exist
among Christians, continues to exist fully only in the Catholic
Church, and on the other hand, that "outside of her structure,
many elements can be found of sanctification and truth," that
is, in those Churches and ecclesiastical communities which are
not yet in full communion with the Catholic Church. But with
respect to these, it needs to be stated that "they [other

ecclesiastical communities] derive their efficacy from the very fullness of grace and truth entrusted to the Catholic Church."
21. [I]t is clear that it would be contrary to the faith to consider the Church as *one way* of salvation alongside those constituted by the other religions. Which may be seen as complementary to the Church or substantially equivalent to her, even if these are said to be converging with the Church toward the eschatological kingdom of God ... some prayers and rituals of the other religions may assume a role of preparation for the Gospel ... [but] one cannot attribute to these, however, a divine origin ... Furthermore, it cannot be overlooked that other rituals insofar as they depend on superstitions or other errors, constitute an obstacle to salvation.
22. With the coming of the Saviour Jesus Christ, God has willed that the Church founded by him be the instrument for the salvation of all humanity (cf. Acts 17:30-31). This truth of faith does not lessen the sincere respect which the Church has for the religions of the world, but at the same time, it rules out, in a radical way, that mentality of indifferentism characterized by a religious relativism which leads to the belief that "one religion is as good as another." If it is true that the followers of other religions can receive divine grace, it is also certain that, objectively speaking, they are in a gravely deficient situation in comparison with those who, in the [Catholic] Church, have the fullness of the means of salvation. [My bold and brackets]

In fairness to John Paul, it should be noted that soon after signing *Dominus Jesus* he wrote, "This confession does not deny salvation to non-Christians, but points to the ultimate source in Christ in whom man and God are united." He also observed, "The Gospel teaches us that those who live in accordance with the Beatitudes — the poor in spirit, the pure of heart, those who bear lovingly the sufferings of life — will enter God's kingdom." This is helpful, but so far as I can ascertain, these comments have not been written into the basic document. The chance that these side remarks will continue to live, seems slim.

The Rev. John T. Pawlikowski wrote that "the Church has rigidly assumed the role of God's gate keeper and insists on its right to do so." In other words, God parses out His favors in a manner known only to The Church. I would also like to add that to assume "objective reality" for what is a subjective matter is, at best, questionable. No doubt the Church does represent objective reality in its structure: places of worship, pageantry, art, music, parish society, etc., but that does not carry over to theology.

In this next paragraph the pope deals directly with the "Jewish Question."

13. It was in the awareness of the one universal gift of salvation offered by the Father through Jesus Christ in the Spirit (cf. Eph.1:3-14), that the first Christians encountered the Jewish people, showing them the fulfilment of salvation that went beyond the Law and, in the same awareness, they confronted the pagan world of their time, which aspired to salvation through a plurality of saviors.

The Rev. Pawlikowski noted,

The ultimate theological issue: the understanding of God, has yet to receive much reflection from Catholic theologians. Until Christians recognize their own salvific nakedness and stand ready to learn from Judaism, because it is clear that Judaism has preserved aspects of the full biblical revelation better than Christianity, the old theology of mission will not be overcome once and for all. Paragraph 13's assertion that "the first Christians encountered the Jewish people" is fallacious, because the "first Christians" were Jews.

In August 2002, the U.S. Bishops' Committee for Ecumenical and Interreligious Affairs and the National Council of Synagogues representing Conservative and Reform Judaism issued a joint statement the key passage of which was,

A deepening Catholic appreciation of the eternal covenant between God and the Jewish people, together with a recognition of a divinely-given mission to Jews to witness to God's faithful love, lead to the conclusion that campaigns that target Jews for conversion to Christianity are no longer theologically acceptable in the Catholic Church.

One cannot help but smile at the obvious difference of opinion between Rome and its U.S. Bishops. The statement would have been a stretch even for John Paul. For Benedict, it must have been a nonstarter.

The Church states its relation to Christianity's multiple forms in the following excerpts:

17. The Churches which, while not existing in perfect communion with the Catholic Church, remain united to her by means of the closest bonds, that is, by apostolic succession and a valid Eucharist, are true particular Churches. Therefore, the Church of Christ is present and operative also in these Churches, even though they lack full communion with the Catholic Church, since they do not accept the Catholic doctrine of Primacy, which according to the will of God, the Bishop of Rome objectively has and exercises over the entire. On the other hand, the ecclesiastical communities which have not preserved the valid Episcopate and the genuine and integral substance of the Eucharistic mystery, are not Churches in the proper sense; however, those [individuals] who are baptized in these communities are, by Baptism, incorporated in Christ and thus are in a certain communion, albeit imperfect, with the Church ... The Christian faithful are therefore not permitted to imagine that the Church of Christ is nothing more than a collection ... of Churches.

The Church, in the first excerpt, is talking to the Anglicans, Greek and Russian Orthodox, and the Eastern Catholic Church among others. While, in the second paragraph, the Church is speaking to mainline Protestant Churches for the most part. And although the Catholic Church is willing to tolerate these offshoots, more or less, it still holds that the Reformation did not count for much. [The Archbishop of Canterbury of the Church of England is the only outsider that holds a dedicated observer seat at the Vatican.] So far as the faithful are concerned— don't even think of moving to another (perforce lesser) church.

Biblical Truths

Let us turn now to the matter of biblical truths. The position of the Catholic Church is:

The Church's tradition, reserves the designation of *inspired texts* to the canonical books of the Old and New Testament, since these are inspired by the Holy Spirit ... These books firmly, faithfully, and without error, teach that truth which God, for the sake of our salvation, wished to see confided to the Sacred Scriptures.

This particular passage is extracted in part from the First Vatican Council paper *Dei Filius* in 1870, the writings and viewpoint of which were notoriously conservative. The currently authorized version of the Hebrew Bible is not identical in content to the most widely read versions of the New Testament in English, nor is it the same as the versions in Greek used by the

Russian Orthodox Church, the Eastern Catholic Church, and other major Christian denominations. Historically these Bibles all grew along separate paths. Therefore it seems appropriate to conclude that the pope must be alluding to the Vatican edition of the Sacred Scriptures.

The Church first entrusted the preparation of an authorized Latin version to St. Jerome who worked between 382 and 400 CE. He based the Old Testament portion on the then current Hebrew Bible, except that the Psalter was based on Origen's translation. Jerome's translation of the New Testament was subject to much revision before it was first collected into a complete form probably in the sixth century. Other changes were introduced over the centuries until a "standard text" was prepared at the University of Paris in the 13th century. The Council of Trent adopted the only authoritative version in 1546, but that was altered in 1590. That version departed from Jerome's Bible at many points, and an amended version was issued in 1734. In 1908, Pius X appointed a Commission to produce a new authorized edition. A limited edition, non-authorized version was released in 1969.

The English Bible used in Catholic schools is the Douay Rheims version made up of the Hebrew Bible as published by the English College at Douay in 1609 and the New Testament as published by the English College at Rheims in 1582 after the Council of Trent, but, in the case of the New Testament, before the 1590 edition. (Note: The KJV was issued in 1611; however, it would certainly have been ignored by the Vatican.) The New American Standard Bible produced by an independent foundation, and based on the KJV, is currently used by Catholic Churches in America. There is no version as yet authorized by the Vatican although publication was purported to have begun in 1926. So much for "firmly, faithfully, and without error."

Interreligious Dialogue

Bound through the Hebrew Scriptures, Jews and Christians must continue working together toward a mutual understanding through interreligious dialogue. It is important for Christians to understand the distinctive mission of the Jewish people without embracing Judaism so that Christians and Jews can be a blessing to one another.

By providing a living testimony to the hope of Israel and the ancient promise, faithful Jews can inspire and strengthen Christians who share the same hope and promises, though in a new modality. While Christians and Jews understand the messianic hope involved in the perfection of the world quite differently, still, whether waiting for the Messiah — as the Jews believe — or for the Messiah's second coming — as the Christians believe — both share the belief that we live in an unredeemed world that longs for repair.

Pope Benedict's Good Friday prayer for the Jews is contra to John Paul, who had sought to give positive direction to that dialogue. Reminding us that "the links between the Church and the Jewish people are grounded in the design of the God of the Covenant," John Paul had underscored, time and again, the vital importance of collaboration with the Jews for working out the Church's own mission in the world. In addition, the Christian Scholars Group of Protestant and Roman Catholic scholars, historians, and theologians has specifically stated that "Christians should not target Jews for conversion."

Archbishop Piero Marini analyzed the workings of Vatican II from his first-hand knowledge of the liturgical reforms that followed. His book as reviewed is "a wakeup call to contemporary Catholics to sustain the liturgical achievements of the Second Vatican Council" despite the Curia's attempt to limit those reforms. The Curia was opposed by the episcopal (bishops') conferences and remains opposed by certain aspects of the episcopate. (Pope Francis is studying this structure.) Thus, the tide of counter reform was stayed from the end of the council until the papacy of Benedict. The Jewish people needed, at a minimum, assurance that Pope Benedict would not encourage evangelization among them.

But for the faithful at the Good Friday Latin Mass, the Jewish prayer may confirm their prior catechesis and, likely, harden ancient prejudices against the "stubborn" Jews. Unfortunately, the new prayer is not sensitive to the contemporary history of Catholic-Jewish relations. Pope Francis now carries the burden of apostolic tradition from the past two thousand years.

Prior to the change by Benedict in the Good Friday service, Jews and Christians at the leadership levels were continuing ongoing discussions to understand each other and to find common grounds for cooperation. A better understanding of their respective missions has come out of these talks. Over the forty year period 1965-2005, the new mutual understandings were supported by the public statements and actions of Popes Paul VI and John Paul II. As a result Christian-Jewish relations have been on the strongest foundation in the two-thousand-year-old history of the two religions.

However, to build this secure platform, a number of basic Christian-Jewish matters have to be resolved. Among these are:

1. Is Jesus the savior of the world or only the savior of the non-Jewish world?

2. If Jesus is the savior of the world, should this be brought to the attention of the Jewish people?

3. Do Jews have an eternal covenant with God?

4. If Jews do have an eternal covenant, does that complement or interfere with the Christian missionary covenant?

So far as the as the Jewish people may be concerned about the salvific powers of Jesus and the Christian mission to bring all people to him, that is the business of the Church. The Church's missionary work, however, goes beyond those who do not know God to those whose belief system does not include the Son of God. It is here that the leaders of Judaism become concerned. It becomes necessary to counter such conversion initiatives to Jews with concerted action to keep believers in the synagogue. When evangelizers are tempted to bring pressure of any kind on targeted Jews, then the encounters become dangerous not only for those targeted, but also for Jews in general. Major anti-discrimination programs must then be initiated.

At this writing the level of anti-Judaism has been comparatively low in the United States, and the Christian initiatives to convert Jews has not gone beyond the offering stage. True, there are evangelical ministries, but they have not generally targeted Jews. There is a greater concern now that the Good Friday prayer raises the missionary level a notch or two. Will the future bring more concerted efforts to convince Jews?

So far as the Jewish covenant to bring God's name to all people is concerned, ecumenical discussion groups have conceded that there is an eternal covenant with God, and this book has demonstrated how effective it has been. The final question is the most engaging: does the Jewish covenant complement or interfere with the Christian mission? Consider initially that God's charge to the Jews can be put into four primary objectives:

- *first*, to bring people who do not know God to an understanding of God's attributes,
- *second*, to use the gifts God has given the Jews to raise up the living standard of other people and thereby demonstrate God's intent for them,
- *third*, to insure that all people — Jews as well as native people — have the means to participate equally in the work of improving society,
- and *fourth*, to use their God-given gifts to bring all people closer to a knowledge of God's universe.

Christians have brought more than two billion people under the broad umbrella of their faith and continue to evangelize today. Islam has more than 1.5 billion followers, Hindus numbers about 900 million, and Buddhists about 300 million. Despite all of that,16 percent of the world population of about seven billion, or about 1,000,100,000, are nonreligious. And that number continues to grow. That leaves plenty of work to bring the name and attributes of God to them.

As for raising living standards, so much of the world lives in poverty with insufficient food, housing, and clothing and without medical attention and educational advantages. All major religions have vast charitable organizations serving the under privileged worldwide. This charge is certainly not unique to Judaism.

The third objective, to insure that all people have the means to participate in the work of improving society is dependent on the quality of life and the availability of jobs. There is a vast gap in the quality of life among world cities judged by health, pollution, and sanitation standards. Much remains to be done to insure that all people have access to health professionals and are not exposed to disease from untreated sewage. Clean cities can be prosperous cities. And prosperous cities can draw investment capital that creates new jobs. Certainly this is a field in which all religious groups can participate.

The last matter, which some would classify as scientific advancement, deals with our understanding of the universe and our part in it. Here the Jewish people have participated to a much greater extent than their numbers would predict (by a factor of about fifty) based on the annual Nobel prizes. God has provided for us on this planet home all the resources we might need, but to understand how to use them (and not destroy them) we must discern the ecology of this planet and the universal forces that sustain it. This, of course, is a high priority requirement in which the contribution of Jewish men and women is greatly appreciated.

Pope Francis declared that "since the Second Vatican Council we have rediscovered that the Jewish People are still for us the holy root that produced Jesus. Despite the horrors inflicted on the Jewish People by the Shoah, God never abandoned his covenant with Israel, and notwithstanding their terrible suffering over the centuries, the Jewish People have kept their faith. For this, we will never be sufficiently grateful to them as a Church, but also as human beings. In the persistence of their faith in the God of the covenant, they summon all, including us as Christians, to recall the fact that we are awaiting the return of the Lord as pilgrims, and must therefore always remain open to Him and never retreat from what we have already achieved."

It is this bargain between God and the Chosen People that is intended to bring God's peace, love, justice, and charity to this world.

Chapter Seventeen
The Covenant Today

We have completed our historical review of the attention the Jewish people gave to the terms of the covenant. From one historical period to another Judaism rarely made a determined effort to ensure that they were keeping its terms. Christianity, on the other hand, did, but randomly. Concerted and directed attention to God's terms really did not take hold until the people, regardless of religious beliefs, incorporated aspects of the covenant into their generational goals. But now it is time to summarize. What have we learned and what does it tell us about keeping the specific terms of the covenant. Let's start with God's first goal.

Make His name known throughout the world

God wants His name declaimed throughout the world. This is a great change in relationship and in the meaning of the covenant. We generally look upon the covenant as a guide to ethical behavior. This provision to make God's name known makes it clear who is in charge. The opportunity to do so has, from God's viewpoint, finally risen. Just think about the development of the earth and the strange creatures that arose millions of years ago. God may have had a hand in their destruction when it became clear that they had not the slightest interest in developing such remote concepts as ethical behavior. Humans finally appeared about two million years ago.

As humans began migrating, eventually the Neanderthals arrived in the area we now call Europe about sixty thousand years ago. About twenty thousand years later, prototypical humans of contemporary *homo sapiens* arrived and setup local groups to protect themselves from the "different" people already there. Edward O. Wilson in his book *The Social Conquest of Earth* points out that,

> In prehistory, group selection lifted humanoids that became territorial carnivores to heights of solidarity, to genius to enterprise. And to fear. Each tribe knew with justification that if it was not armed and ready, its very existence was imperiled.

Our bloody nature is ingrained because group-versus-group
was a principal force that made us what we are ... The worst
in our nature coexists with the best. And so it will ever be. We
are of two natures, and we all live out our lives in conflict and
contention.

We can see it today in our political parties, religious fables, and gun
clubs. As for the Neanderthals, they were vanquished but they left their mark
and attested to the kinder side of us. Those who can trace their heritage to
ancient Europe are about three percent Neanderthal. Our nature will be an
important issue in our relationship with God.

Making God's name known was, apparently, the first order of business
in how the terms of the covenant were to be carried out. However, the
Israelites of that period were not ready to take action in God's behalf. At the
start of the covenant, the Israelite tribes were loosely related and not
experienced in organizing a joint effort with their neighbors. Besides many of
the nearby non-Israelite tribes were considered to be enemies. No plans to
carry out God's desire were then undertaken. However, when the Hebrew
Bible was translated into Greek for Alexandrian Jews, about eight hundred
years later, it became available to Greek Gentiles as well. As a result of their
interest in the Bible, great masses of Greek-speaking people became devotees
of Judaism or sympathizers of Judaism. Did this great rush to join Judaism
advance the covenant?

The goal of making God's name known throughout the world
certainly advanced when Greek speaking people were able to read the Bible.
This was a step forward, but also a step back. Intermarriage could result in
children who are not compelled to observe the tenets of the covenant. And,
further, the objective was to make God known, not to make Judaism known.
Judaism at this time was a religion that still paid little heed to God's covenant,
and, according to *halakha,* was open only to those who were born of a Jewish
mother.

There were also many other people who were not fluent in Greek.
Eventually, most of the people of the world did have access to a Bible in their
language as a growing belief in God made His name known through various
translators. Because of the doctrinal differences in religions, Jewish translators
would have been called upon to carefully parse out passages in other languages.
In that respect Jews were helping make known God's name. But the hard work
of evangelism was carried on by Christians starting about the ninth century and
continuing to the present. Judaism did not actively pursue evangelism, and the
gains in Jewish followers made when the Bible was translated into Greek were
lost when Christianity became the preferred religion of the Roman Empire.

The Apostle Paul in his letter to the Romans plaintively posed and
answered the primary question of monotheistic theology: *Is God the God of Jews*

only? He answers that God is the God of Gentiles as well. This is the fundamental point that the Jews were charged to teach under their covenant. This is the statement that should have aroused the missionary spirit of Judaism. When a new form of monotheism arises, the first consideration should always be whether God's purpose is being served. Does a new religion advocate love of God and respect for all people?

What did the bargain ask of the Israelites and their descendants the Jews?

Love the Lord and observe His commandments

From the time of the Deuteronomists until the first public reading of the Bible some five hundred years later, most Israelites depended upon worship to other gods. When the five Books of Moses (Torah) was first read to the Israelites (c.440 BCE), some turned to God and made Him their savior. But prior to that time did they keep the commandments?

> *Because there is no honesty and no goodness and no obedience to God,*
> *false swearing, dishonesty, murder, and theft and adultery are rife.*

This excerpt from the Prophet Hosea 4:1-2 (c.750 BCE) makes it quite clear that essentially all the commandments were violated at this time.

Subsequent to the reading of Torah shortly after 440 BCE, the priests were accused in the words of Malachi as follows:

> I will step forward to contend against you, and I will act as a
> relentless accuser against those who have no fear of Me. Who
> practice sorcery, who commit adultery, who swear falsely,
> who cheat laborers of their hire, and who subvert the cause of
> the widow, orphan, and stranger. (Malachi 3:5, c.430 BCE)

Love one another as I love you.

The practice of the covenant by the Israelites, and subsequently the Jews, was something to ponder for a millennium. Then Christianity became noticeable in the second century CE, and a new Bible appeared about two hundred years later. It became clear that many of those things God called upon the Jews to observe in the covenant were repeated by Jesus. Although Jesus in his lifetime spoke to Jews, his words were folded into the New Testament where they also spoke to Christians. Examples follow of covenant terms that Christians have adopted from the Hebrew Bible; all are from the mouth of Jesus as recorded in the New Testament:

> *Just as I have loved you, you also shall love one another.* (John 13:34)
> *You shall love the Lord your God with all your heart, with all your soul, with all your mind, and with all your strength.* (Mark 12:30)
> *If you love me, you will keep my commandments.* (John 15:15)
> *Do unto others as you would have them do unto you.* (Matt. 7:12)

Jesus also said:

> *Love your enemies, do good, and lend expecting nothing in return.* (Luke 6:35)

Love was the basis for living out the Christian life. During the plague years in the mid-second and third centuries, the Christian communities saved many lives by their loving care. The Jewish and Gentile communities had no effective way of coping.

Love your neighbor as yourself

The Christian New Testament also contains the saying: *Love your neighbor as yourself.* (Mark 12:31) Over time, and with great care to respect their neighbors, the Jews in continental European diaspora (c. 800 CE) were accepted for extended periods. The virtues of the anachronism to love your neighbor became known to the Jews in reality.

What were the lessons the Jews learned in the Ottoman Empire in the 15th through 19th centuries? Help all people by giving them an opportunity to participate in economic growth. The Ottomans probably would not have looked kindly on this suggestion with regard to the resident Christians, never-the-less the Jews should have tried. Had they pursued the inclusion of the Christian residents, the Ottoman Empire may have become a contributor to European culture and serve to make their Empire a productive part of the new industrial revolution. It would also have spread the wealth among many more people.

Share what you have with those in need

At the onset of the Great Depression in the late 1920s and until the Second World War, Jewish families and singles, especially in New York City, received aid from the Jewish Social Service Association (JSSA) and the Hebrew Shelter and Immigrant Aid Society (HIAS). The former a German-Jewish group, could look back to the late 1880s when refugees fled from Russia to sanctuary in America via Germany. At the height of the depression, more than three million meals were served daily in the city with Jewish aid societies doing their part. Locally funded public assistance was also available from The Municipal Shelter program in New York City since 1896.

American Jews, especially those in the movie industry, sponsored and paid all expenses for German Jews to leave Germany and settle in America between 1933 and 1939. Other families in this country sponsored relatives as well as business friends. Carl Laemmle, a founder of Universal Pictures, was fully involved in bringing Jews to America whether they were relatives, friends, or ordinary people. In total it is believed he sponsored about three hundred people. Approximately 100,000 German Jews did emigrate in the 1930s, escaping Hitler's persecution despite facing restrictive immigration laws elsewhere.

Beyond financial aid, there remained many opportunities to work with the poor, the sick and the oppressed. When German Jews flooded into New York and ended up in the East Side slums (1899-1914), Jewish women from financially comfortable homes trained as nurses and established medical clinics to aid the sick.

Today the Jewish communities of America uphold their covenant obligations in part through charitable organizations. The B'nai Birith started its charitable work in America in 1844. But Jews have been happily settled in the United States since 1750, when seventy-five families joined to build the first synagogue in New York City.

Jewish Charities of America today continue the work to feed the hungry, heal the sick, shelter the displaced, and pursue justice, freedom, and peace for all humanity in America, Israel, and around the world. Included in this philanthropy is the great support that American Jews give to the arts as well.

The Chronicle of Philanthropy in its annual report of the largest four hundred non-profits show many Jewish charities rank from 25th (Jewish Federation of America), 54th (American Jewish Joint Distribution Committee, New York), 74th (United Jewish Appeal of NYC) to 86th (Jewish Federation of Metropolitan Chicago) are some in the first hundred alone. [This list is dominated by secular institutions especially colleges.] Of course, many Christian charities, whose church membership is many times the number of Jewish adherents, contribute to this bounty. Now philanthropy is well established as an obligation for all who can afford to contribute to organizations that work for the needy. (The Salvation Army and the Catholic Charities rank among the top five in the United States.)

Do unto others what you would have them do unto you.

As prior discussions were about respect and love for God, this category deals with equity among people: that is, with the quality of being fair and impartial as opposed to seeking revenge. The subtitle of this paragraph is known as the golden rule, and it is a part of most world religions. In this group of human traits, God asks all of us to respect each other and seek peaceful outcomes for all disputes, speak the truth and deal loyally and compassionately with one another, and share what we have with those in need. There is a great need for these social attributes in our times, and many groups support them.

Professor Edward O. Wilson has dealt extensively with these social issues, *e.g.,* the difference between right and wrong, in the paradigm of evolution. Wilson has written that:

> There is a principal to be learned from the study of biological origins of moral reasoning. It is that outside of the clearest ethical precepts, such as the condemnation of slavery, child abuse, and genocide which all agree should be opposed anywhere without exception, there is a large grey domain inherently difficult to navigate. The declaration of ethical precepts and judgments made from them requires a full understanding of why we care about the matter one way or the other. And that includes the biological history of the options engaged. This last inquiry has not often been done.

Europe, including Russia, was totally Christianized by the year 1200 and had a population between four and five million. With the necessity to absolve sin, a culture gradually built up in the confessional over the years based on one's relationship to God.

Judaism does not have a systematic procedure to confess sin on a regular basis. On the day of Atonement (Yom Kippur) Jews can pray for transgressions against God. But for transgression against another human being, it does not atone unless that person's pardon has been obtained. Jewish societal influence could only have been displayed to Christians by their manner of living. They had no central organization that could dictate good mores to all Jews, but this was available to them in Torah.

> *Mark, the heavens to their uttermost reaches belong to the Lord your God.* (Deut. 10:14)
> *I behold your heavens the work of your fingers, the moon and stars that you have set in place.* (Psalm. 8:4)
> *You who have covered the heavens with your splendor.* (Psalm 8:2)
> *The heavens declare the glory of God, the sky proclaims his handiwork.* (Psalm19:2)

The six Jewish pioneers of quantum mechanics, of the original ten, gave us the formula for mathematically deriving the probability of finding an electron in a given region of space. Judaism in its most important contribution to the covenant reaches out to the heavens, the glory of God, and turns minds to the understanding of God's creation.

How long will this covenant last?

If these laws should ever be annulled by Me ... declares the Lord ... only then would the offspring of Israel cease to be a nation before Me for all time. "For all time" in God's words probably means so long as humans reside on this planet. There will always be Jewish people in the planetary racial mix advocating for God's way and searching God's universe to understand the wonders of creation. But will these people represent a living body of Judaism? Let's look at the future of Judaism in light of intermarriage today.

> *You shall not intermarry with them (other nations): do not give your daughters to their sons or take their daughters for your sons. For they will turn your children away from Me to worship other gods.* (Deut. 7:3-4)
> *However, a captive woman can be taken for a wife.* (Deut. 21:10-14)

Professor Wilson tells us -

For the immediate future, emigration and ethnic intermarriage have taken over as the overwhelming dominant force of micro evolution by homogenizing the global distribution of genes. The impact on humanity as a whole is an unprecedented dramatic increase within local populations around the world. The increase is matched by a reduction in differences between populations.

In a much-discussed 2011 survey of New York-area Jews, nearly three-quarters of those for whom being Jewish was "very important" said they would be upset if one of their children married a non-Jew. Among the synagogue-affiliated, the same strong preference for endogamy (marriage within a specific group as required by custom or law) was expressed by 66 percent of Conservative Jews and 52 percent of Reform Jews; for Orthodox Jews, the figure rose to 98 percent. Similar patterns have surfaced in a national survey of Jewish leaders, including younger leaders who are not yet parents, but paternal attitude does not frequently alter offspring intentions.

Intermarriage does indeed loom large for American Jews who are justifiably concerned about the transmission of Jewish religious culture to the next generation. And yet, when we place intermarriage in the context of broader trends in American society, we see a more pervasive problem. Jewish intermarriage is just one current amidst a sea change in patterns of familial formation in the United States.

From the 1960s until today, the prominence of heterosexual two-parent endogamous families has receded as diverse household models have increased. Skeptical American singles continue to view marriage and parenthood as abridgements of personal options. Partnered or single men and women, among them some number of gay and lesbian couples, who eagerly pursue religious marriage ceremonies and the legal entitlements of conventional families, create households with single mothers and fathers, two mothers, or two fathers.

At present there are two major debates regarding intermarriage among scholars and activists in the U.S. Jewish communities: that between assimilationists and transformationists. The former group believes that intermarriage will eventually eliminate the Jewish people. The transformationists see aspects of ongoing change and accommodation to modern America. At what rate has intermarriage in America been moving?

TIME PERIOD	INTERMARRIAGE
1900-1920	2.0 percent
1921-1930	3.2
1931-1940	3
1941-1945	6.7
1946-1950	6.7
1951-1955	6.4
1956-1960	5.9
1961-1965	17.4
1966-1972	31.7
1980-1984	38
1985-1995	43
2013	58

In 1939, Core Jewish population worldwide reached its peak of seventeen million, or 0.8 percent of world population. That number declined to eleven million in 1945 because of the Holocaust and war. It returned to 13.9 million in the 1970s, but had not grown for some twenty years since because of low birth rates and assimilation. Since then the growth rate has resumed growing due to the large family sizes in Israel of the ultra-orthodox Haredi and Hasidim sects; the total Jewish population is currently about 6.4 million. The growth rate in 2013 was 0.78 percent. Current world wide Jewish population is now 13.3 million or 0.25 percent of world population.

In the U.S. where current Jewish population is 6.5 million or 2.2 percent, there are five major Jewish categories as follows: Reform 35 percent, no affiliation 30 percent, Conservatives 18 percent, Orthodox 10 percent and Reconstructionists 7 percent. Essentially all intermarriage in the U.S. is between Jews who have no synagogue affiliation and non-Jews, as well as between Reform Jews and non-Jews. Neither Conservative Jews nor the Orthodox permit intermarriage, but Conservative rabbis can perform such marriages outside their synagogue.

Israeli law does not permit marriages between members of different religions within its borders. But intermarriage occurs occasionally in as many as one in ten Israeli marriages. Such ceremonies must be conducted out of the state, and, upon return, the non-Jewish partner is often subjected to second-class treatment by the state. The children of the majority of these couples are not considered Jewish according to *halakha* and, therefore, they cannot be married in Israel.

Conservatives have resolved that in the past, intermarriage was viewed as an act of rebellion, a rejection of Judaism. Jews who intermarried were essentially excommunicated. But now, intermarriage is often the result of living in an open society. If our children end up marrying non-Jews, we should not reject them, Conservatives say. We should continue to give our love and by that retain a measure of influence in their lives. Life consists of constant growth and our adult children may yet reach a stage when Judaism has new meaning for them. Controversy still exists on intermarriage in the Conservative faith and these disagreements have turned some members from this branch of Judaism.

That is the situation as it currently stands in both the U.S. and Israel. But surprisingly attendance at Jewish day schools has picked up remarkably in the U.S. And Jewish studies have likewise increased at the collegiate level. However, about one-third of Americans marry across religious, ethnic, and racial lines today producing a new generation impatient with census questionnaires and with a single box for ethnicity. Meanwhile, conventional family life has been periodically subjected to scathing critique in the academic press and the popular media. Against the backdrop of these sweeping changes, intermarriage between Jews and non-Jews is often regarded as just one more family construction among many. The larger battle is for marriage itself.

And this brings us back to Professor Wilson's statement at the start of this discussion.

For the immediate future, emigration and ethnic intermarriage have taken over as the overwhelming dominant force of micro evolution by homogenizing the global distribution of genes. The impact on humanity as a whole is an unprecedented increase within local populations around the world.

That describes societal trends in the U.S. which will bear heavily on Reform, Conservative and Reconstructionist Jews in the future. Israeli Jews will not be seriously affected by these influences, and Judaism worldwide will live on.

What will be the outcome if the Jews keep the covenant?

You shall prosper in peace and security, enjoy the wealth of the nations and revel in their riches; but do not glory in your wisdom, strength, and riches but only in devotion to God. (Eze. 37:25-8, 39:36, Isa. 61:6, Jer. 9:22-23, Micah 6:8, Mal.3:5)

This warning in respect to the covenant is very important. The situation in Germany was unsustainable for the Jews. From the beginning of their incorporation into the social and economic spheres, the Jews worked hard to increase jobs for native Germans by starting new businesses, but, apparently, backed them with their own resources. In a fairly short period of time they had become well-to-do. Take for example these figures: At the beginning of the 19th century, most German Jews had been paupers, but by 1870 only about five percent still were. According to taxation figures, which probably understated the real situation, more than 60 percent of all Prussian Jews were now in the "secure middle-class." At the turn of the century, of about the two hundred wealthiest Prussian families, forty (or 17 percent) were said to be Jewish. This failure to become a cooperative element in the German economy working beside the existing structure lent truth to the intense propaganda that the Jews were an economy inside of their economy determined to take over the long existing structure. A comparable situation existed in the world of art.

Have the Jews carried out their end of the bargain?

Israelites of the biblical millennia paid no attention to the covenant, even as the prophets bombarded them with biblical warnings. It was only when Christianity took root in the second century CE did they become concerned. The actions of the Christians in establishing religious communities coalesced and strengthened their bonds. Meanwhile the Jews were losing their hold on the land given to them many centuries before and went into diaspora.

Living in unfamiliar lands starting about 800 CE, the Jews had to tread very carefully to avoid offending their neighbors. Around the same time the Christians began a great evangelical movement to bring all Western Europe and Russia into the Catholic Church. As a result God's name became known to a significant portion of the civilized world. And a charge to the Israelites was assumed by the Christians. Several hundred years thereafter the Roman Catholic Church took up the cudgel of teaching ethical behavior and thereby incorporated into the behavior required by God, the more important part of the covenant of Moses.

It was the original writing of the Babylonian Talmud that gave the Jews another role in God's world. By study of the Talmud, Jews increased their analytical skills and rose to principle roles in the study of God's universe. They also used these skills in economic and social fields. So as we look back over the millennia, we see the world changing largely due to the efforts of the Christian Church which adopted many of the rules for ethical behavior that had been part of the original Israelite covenant. But as of today, the exploration of God's universe, also part of the original covenant, has been a leading role for Jewish scientists.

It has been a long journey for the Israelites and the Jews. Their early years in the service of God were not productive and their debates with the growing ranks of Christianity were overwhelmed by ridicule and scorn. But they never admitted failure to keep their promise to God, and Christianity never made good on its claim that they were now the inheritor of God's covenant.

Judaism settled down to a quiet, cooperative life even though the Christians at times imposed harsh terms on them. Then opportunities arose in Muslim Spain and in Ottoman Anatolia that raised their abilities to be successful in economic terms. But the latter venture did not speak directly to the terms of the covenant and the former did not work to love their neighbor.

The turning point was the acceptance of Jews in America which became the fertile ground upon which they could put their mind to work on God's universe. And also to work energetically to display loyalty and compassion and justice with one another and share with those in need. They, of course, were not the only people who carried out the ethical rules, but the Jewish persistent efforts were a model for many others. And American Jews today occupy many important positions in government, in the courts, in the financial world, and generously support the arts and social life as well.

Does the covenant still have meaning today?

Of course, the covenant carries the same rules it had from the time of Moses, rules still not observed by many in this world. Only through our own sensibilities and actions can we convince others of the resilience of God's covenant. It will always present to us what God expects from each of us and what God demands from his Chosen People. So neighbors, Jews and Christians, let us work together to save the world.

Tikkum Olam

Chapter Eighteen
Is There A God?

Let us start this chapter with a discussion of our relationship with God. I understand your impatience with the title of this chapter, since the name, G-O-D, is displayed throughout the book. But that word is commonly used with little thought to its deeper meaning. The universe from our viewpoint is immense and those in charge have a seemingly endless job. Are they doing their best for us?

A current Harris poll found that 74 percent of U.S. adults say that they believe in God. That's strong but down from 82 percent in 2009 and continues a downward slope. Organized religion today is losing adherents at a significant pace. In a recent Gallup poll 40 percent of American say they attend church, synagogue, or mosque regularly, but that figure is estimated to have been doubled when poll takers counted the actual number of adherents present.

In the United States, the Roman Catholic Church reported Sunday attendance dropped from 1542 in 1970 to 845 in 2008, a decline of 45 percent. The percentage of Jews attending synagogue at least once per month has dropped to17 percent in Reform and 34 percent in Conservative congregations, while Orthodox attendance has increased 74 percent. Though the latter gain is impressive, only ten percent of Jewish worshipers in the United States are Orthodox.

Why are we losing our love for God and our belief in the miracles of Jesus' ministry? To a certain extent, we seem to be influenced by the scientific explanations of the workings of the universe. Take, for example, the following from Rabbi David W. Nelson in his book *Judaism, Physics and God,* Jewish Lights, 2005:

> [If] we think of physics as the human effort to understand the workings of matter in space and time in a systemic fashion, we conclude that the big bang singularity was the point at which the entire structure of matter, space, and time had its origin, then science does not appear to be of much use in finding the reason for that singularity.

Without knowledge of what came before the big bang, we assume that in some way God is synonymous with the big bang. Here we can envision, as would have Michelangelo, God overspreading the new universe as the firmament begins the task of converting the pure force of the big bang into time and matter, as well as energy. We can now include Albert Einstein in this diorama overseeing in rumpled slacks, shirt and sweater. But we are saying, in effect, that God *is* part of the big bang, by virtue of having been expelled at the birth of the new universe, and Einstein, somewhat later, by virtue of his symbiotic understanding.

Included in this expanding, churning, thundering new universe are wildly different energy points of varying surface temperatures, emission spectra, and appetites. We presume that God is assisting in sorting out matter that can eventually develop into rational, thinking beings who, when situated on a rocky planet, can nourish intelligence and spread the key word— love. But which planet will God choose? The firmament is seemingly chock full of them. The only one of which we have full knowledge is us our own dear planet Earth somewhere in the lower part of the universe, as presently pictured.

Of course our astronomers are reviewing the firmament and counting the other planets that might sustain life as we know it. At this writing there are 4175 so called extrasolar planets, or exoplanets identified upon the retirement of the satellite Kepler. That is a planet which orbits a star other than our sun, and therefore belongs to a different planetary system. Estimates of exoplanets in our universe can run much higher. This reminds us that we yearn to visit another civilized planet and discuss our development with theirs.

Before we make that trip, consider this scenario: Our physicists become so skilled that they can solve one conundrum after another, but for each problem they solve, a star disappears from the firmament. After several years, many stars are gone, and we find that we will soon be alone in the universe. As I wrote this down, I was overtaken with a feeling of intense and all-encompassing loneliness. This is not right; we are intended to share with the hominids of the universe!

Keep this in mind as I relate two personal stories.

Samuel was twenty-five when he married Paula who was 21. Samuel died at sixty-eight after forty-three years of marriage, and Paula lived on in her son's household for many years, but became a burden to handle and was placed in a nearby nursing home. There she lived a sedentary life into her mid-eighties. She remained in reasonably good health, and her son visited several times a week.

One morning twenty-one years after Paula's husband had died, her son got a call from the nursing home saying his mother had died right after breakfast. He went over immediately and talked to the nurse who had been present when she died. The nurse said that Paula had eaten her usual breakfast and was reading the morning paper while rocking on the porch, when all of a sudden she jumped to her feet and exclaimed: SAM! and died.

The image of my grandfather, apparently distinctly seen by my grandmother, was most likely sent from our-heaven to bring my grandmother home. It seems quite unlikely that it came from exoplanet 3999, for example, where, most likely, they know nothing of our existence. Therefore I attribute this story to our God.

I am well aware, as I am sure you are, that we are delving into God's world where, perhaps, we have no business going. As St. Paul said about his own near-death experience: *"(I) heard things that are not to be told, that no mortal is permitted to speak "*(II Cor. 12:4), but I hold that we are not likely to discern anything that God wants to withhold from us. Nor do I suppose that we are taking a Jobian viewpoint in this study either. That is, approaching it supremely confident that we can figure out what God has wrought. *"Then the Lord answered Job out of the whirlwind: 'Who is this that darkens counsel by words without knowledge?'"* (Job 38:1-2) So, let us proceed with the firmly held conviction that God loves us and wants us to understand the heavenly kingdom. As the 17th-century philosopher Spinoza wrote, "Love of God is our understanding of the universe, our virtue, our happiness, our well-being and our salvation."

But is there really a heaven that we, each one of us, can profess? And if there is such a home, does it have a down side as well. I cannot answer that question directly but I can give you some insight.

It was about three months after I was baptized in the Episcopal Church that we received the phone call. A couple with whom we were friendly lost their only child, a son, to a drunk driver, during his first year in college. It was a shattering event for them. We had seen their boy play football for his high school team the prior fall. Like his father, he was very athletic and intelligent.

When the trial was scheduled, our friends were asked if they would like to attend and make a statement. They were uncertain and asked us what we thought. I prayed about that and came up with the firm conviction that they should go, and we offered to drive them.

The father of the boy had been a star football player in college and was well known in the region where the trial was to be held. The circumstances had attracted considerable local press interest. The loss to the parents was very difficult for them to resolve, and the father's main feeling was vengeful at the start of the trial.

We anticipated that the driver who had driven drunk that night was an irresponsible alcoholic of limited means. But the reality was quite different. He was a business man who appeared at trial well kempt in suit and tie. The hearing was before a judge, no jury. Both our friend and the driver were permitted to make a statement after which the judge recessed to consider the evidence.

We stepped outside the courtroom while the press moved in to interview the parents. The defendant and his attorney stood some distance from us. At that point I was told, telepathically, to go the defendant. It was almost impossible for me to refuse. But I had no idea what to say or do when I reached him. As I walked over there, I understood that I would be told what to say. When I stood in front of the driver I said something that would never have occurred to me before I was baptized: "We love you too."

I was then freed to return to our friends. When I did, I noticed the press turn toward the defendant who was walking toward our friends. When the defendant reached them, he told the parents of the boy how sorry he was and how much it meant to him for them to know that. He offered his hand in forgiveness to the father who took it. This act released the father from his dark intentions and, more than that, it gave the defendant the chance to atone for his act.

Afterward, we four left and ate lunch and talked about their son. All the tension that had existed before the trial was gone, and they were able to relax and speak freely. I thanked God for using me as an instrument of His love.

As I look back on this experience, I have no doubt that this simple act of mine was directed by an agent of God. That our friends were of more than ordinary concern to heaven speaks of their devotion to God, family love, and service to society.

But, you may very well ask, why didn't the agents of God warn the young man not to go out that night?

The answer to that very pertinent question, in all likelihood, is they couldn't because from their viewpoint the accident had already happened and once done it became part of the space-time network. But why do events on our planet happen later than they do in heaven? Apparently, time slows down in the presence of a gravitational field such as that of the Earth. This has been verified by Gravity Probe B which gave physicists renewed confidence that the strange predictions of Einstein's theory are indeed correct, and that these predictions may be applied elsewhere in the universe.

Then Earth's heaven is some distance away, where the gravity is less than that on Earth to nonexistent. To sum up this effect, we can say that time flows more slowly in a gravitational field; the stronger the gravity, the slower the flow of time. The theory with all its details enumerated is quite complex.

The overseers of this planet must continually monitor the passing events and know when to initiate a counter event. They probably have five to ten minutes to do so.

The fact that heaven cannot change one's prospects after the fact may prompt you to say: "Then I'll do it myself!" Which, of course is exactly what heaven wants us to do. We are here to find a place in society that advances the morality on Earth. All of the mores that God has set forth for us to follow are listed (and illustrated) in the prior chapter.

God is and has always been concerned about us— and by "us," I mean all life, all plants, and all the protective atmospheric coverings that swathe this small planet. What meaning does a poll have that registers 80 percent or 70 percent of us believe in God while God loves all of us? Rejoice in the marvels of life on Earth and bring an appreciation to those who have no inclination to do so.

These philosophical meditations lead to the following conclusions: First, a respect for God, God's ordered universe, and God's love for this earthly creation. Second, the nature of this planet follows the attributes of God as ordered by God. Third, human society should follow a natural order as well in which all people are equal. As for the nature of God, we can only say that God permeates the whole of our civilization and is ever present within us. God is the pervasive and sustaining cause of all that exists, and nature is that which flows from the necessity of God's attributes.

As for the premise that God oversees just this planet, that seems unlikely. But to believe that God oversees and reacts to stories on 4175 (or more) other planets, is also difficult to believe. If we believe that God is the purveyor of the solemn commitment that constitutes the covenant with the Jewish people, then we must believe that God expects us to love Him and to love each other, and to deal with one another on this planet in a fair and impartial manner.

This speaks of an ideal society. Obviously, we are not there yet. If other societies are working toward the same objectives, and we suggest a joint visit, they would view our planet with a good deal of trepidation. Perhaps the goal of this immense universe is peace and love for all people, a universe free of sin. What does this all mean and what does it tell us of the nature of God?

Consider the important components of this chapter: stories of God's presence in my life, our yearning to visit another civilized exoplanet and the apparent existence of an overseeing group that monitors life on this planet to evaluate our progress towards God's goal. There is still one more condition to consider, and that is the enigmatic status of the covenant itself.

Why would God offer the covenant to Moses with all its conditions and all its rewards?

After all, Moses represents a poor, and relatively unorganized group of people often at war or religious dispute with nearby communities. Can they even find time to give the demands of the covenant some thought?

Based on the fact that there appears to be an overseer group concerned with our progress on the covenant, we should ask then, what is God doing? My answer is offering the same covenant to all other developing exoplanets, the list of which is probably growing, and setting up overseers for those who accept it. Consider the tribal experience of early settlers on Earth. What did they do as their immediate area became overrun? The next generation picked up and found new land on which to farm and hunt.

We can surmise that ten thousand years from now, when a planet becomes too crowded to support the founding group, the next generation will pick up and find another unoccupied planet. Each time that occurs, God's burden is increased.

Let's return to us now struggling to carry out the terms of the covenant. Our major failing, well recognized by our overseers, is the propensity to kill each other. The chance to visit another civilized planet while we practice mass murder is, essentially, zero. We are beginning to study manned space flight in earnest. If we really want to travel to another occupied planet, we must forego war. To truly prepare for this momentous trip, we have to live God's covenant and respect each person on Earth with whom we interact.

But what of our ingrained propensity to protect our group and insure that we have the armament and trained guardians to withstand, and, possibly, retaliate against any attack on us by means of armament, electronics, acts of terrorism, sabotage of infrastructure etc. Proceeding logically let us determine how many conflicts actually occurred since the end of the second world war (1946) and until to 2005 a period of sixty plus years. Overall there were 173 conflicts of various stripes: state vs state, revolution, ad-hoc group(s) vs state, civil war, rebellion, and invasion. This averages close to three wars beginning about every year and, of course, many prior ones running concurrently. There seems to be war somewhere on this globe, essentially, all the time.

God must have known this when the covenant was offered to Moses. But that was a while ago and the global population was considerably less than it is today. The situation gets worse with each passing billion. So why has God stuck by us? There could be numerous reasons, but consider first that no other planet has done a much better job than we have. That would imply the occupied universe is far from the ideal loving home for all present. But it also implies that God has that objective in mind, and will continue monitoring and demonstrating what a peaceful existence is like.

What implications can we draw from this scenario? It seems that people on other planets might have had basically the same developmental experiences that we have had. This doesn't mean that they look like us or could intermarry with us. If Darwin is correct, and most archeologists believe he is, we are exquisitely bred to satisfy our needs using the resources of the home planet, meaning not only the plant and animal life for food, but the energy sources required to fuel our economy, travel, communication and entertainment. We may find that the appearance or life style of the exoplanet residents is abhorrent to us or the atmospheric makeup is incompatible. But their prehistoric history is similar and their Bible, when translated, tells much the same story as ours. Did God send messengers like Jesus to other planets?

All we can say at this point is, if it happened here it could have happened elsewhere.

Our Bible can be considered a concealed code, part of God's plan to give us a firm base to understand who we are and what we have pledged to do. The Bible also tells us directly what the plan is for all of us:

> *Obey God and observe the terms of the covenant.* (Isa. 56:2, Jer.11:4 18:24, Eze. 5:7, Hos. 6:7, Mic. 6:8)
> *They shall never again know war.* (Isa. 2.4, Micah 4:3)

We also learn from Torah/Talmud that it is God's intention to see a just and righteous universe under a messianic leader whose values are God's own.

> *The Messiah, son of David, will come when all people perfectly keep the Covenant.* (*The Babylonian Talmud*, Sanhedrin 97a)

July 22, 2015

Glossary

Macc	Maccabee books (Apocrypha books)
Mal	Book of Malachi (in the Prophets)
Mic	Micah (in the prophets)
Neh	Nehemiah (in the Writings)
Num	Numbers (fourth book of the Bible)
Prov	Book of Proverbs (in the Writings)
Ps/Pss	Psalms (in the Writings)
Sam	Book of Samuel (in the Prophets)
Sir	Ecclesiasticus (a/k/a Ben Sira or Sirach)

Other Sources (Jewish)

Aleppo Codex	Oldest Bible copy about 500 years old; partially destroyed
Bavli	Babylonian Talmud
Leningrad Codex	Ancient Bible copy upon which contemporary copies are based
Mishnah	Book of oral tradition
Sefer Bahir	"Book of Light," anthology of kabbalistic methods
Sefer Zohar	"Book of Splendor," the classic work of Jewish
Tanya	mysticism.
Torah	Book on messianiasm
Yerushalami	Five Bible books of Moses, Palestinian Talmud

Christian Sacred Books

Acts	Acts of the apostles
Col	Epistle to the Colossians
Gal	Epistle to the Galatians
Heb	Letter to the Hebrews
Jn	Gospel of John
Lk	Gospel of Luke
Mk	Gospel of Mark
Mt	Gospel of Matthew
Rom	Epistle to the Romans

Words in Hebrew and Other Languages

akedah	proposed sacrifice of Issac (Hebrew)
al-Azhar	world's oldest university located in Cairo (Arabic)
Amoraim	explainers (Hebrew)
arba'turim	four columns (Hebrew), refers to rabbinic breast plate
b a'alei ha-tosafot	supplementers (Hebrew)
baraita	extended form of Mishnah commentary (Hebrew)

b__it	covenant (Hebrew)
Beth Din	High Court (Hebrew)
Bet midrashi	High Academy (Hebrew)
convivencia	great revival of ancient documents by Jewish, Christian, and Arabians working together (Spanish)
dhimmís	alien residents (Arabic)
Die Welt	The World (German)
Eretz Israel	the Holy Land aka Palestine (Hebrew)
exilarch	Leader of Jews in exile (Hebrew)
galut	dispersion (Hebrew); diaspora (Greek)
Gemara	study or learning (Hebrew)
gematria	assigning a number to each (Hebrew) letter
Geonim	Experts (Hebrew)
ghiy_r	Distinctive dress required of dhimmís (Arabic)
halakah	law (Hebrew)
Haram al-Sharif	mosque on the former temple mount (Arabic)
haMashiach	the Messiah (Hebrew)
haredi	ultra-Orthodox Jews (Hebrew)
haskala	the enlightenment movement (Hebrew)
Hatikvah	Israeli national anthem (Hebrew)
hilfsverein	aid association (German)
jizya	tax on aliens (Arabic)
kodashim	holy things (Hebrew)
leshonoh haboh	next year in Jerusalem (Hebrew)
b'rooshaolayim	b'rooshaolayim
maskilim	supporters of the enlightenment (Hebrew)
Mo'ed	Festival (Hebrew)
nashim	women (Hebrew)
nasi	patriarch (Hebrew)
nezikin	damages (i.e. costs) (Hebrew)
nasi	patriarch (Hebrew)
pharisee	set apart, e.g. rabbis (Hebrew)
quntresim	notations ((Hebrew)
Qur'án	sacred book (Arabic)
religio	religion (Latin)
rezon ha-bore	the will of the Creator (Hebrew)
sedarim	orders, as in defining distinction (Hebrew)
sefirot	a channel of divine energy or life force (Hebrew)
sharia	law (Arabic)
Shavuot	spring food gathering (Hebrew)
shtetls	towns (Russian)
sifrè	book (Aramaic)
sukkot	fall harvest (Hebrew)

superstitio	superstition (Latin)
sura	chapter (Arabic)
suyga	topic (Hebrew)
synagogue	place of assembly (Greek)
tagblatt	daily newspaper (German)
tahrif	fabrication (Arabic)
tallit	an upper body undergarment (Hebrew)
Tannaim	teachers
Tefillin	small leather boxes encasing Torah passages strapped to the arm and forehead before morning prayers (Hebrew)
tikkum olam	rebuild the world in God's image (Hebrew)
Tosefta	Supplement (Hebrew)
volk	native Germanic people (German)
volksgemeinschaft	community of native Germans (German)
Yahudiler	Jews (Arabic)
Zera'im	seeds (Hebrew)

Definitions

Definitions

Am Olam	Russian organization that advocated communal agrarian settlement in the United States by Jews (Hebrew)
converso	Jews who chose to convert (Spanish)
Essenes	sect that wrote accusatory prophesy in Bible (Hebrew)
God-fearers	followers of Judaism (Gentile-Jews)
Hibbat Zion	lovers of Zion (Hebrew)
Kabbalah	Jewish mysticsim and demonology (Hebrew)
Ladino or *Judezmo*	Spanish-Jewish languages (Spanish)
marrano	Spanish Jews who were forced to convert (Spanish)
messianism	believers in the coming of the Messiah
Mizrahi	acronym from (Hebrew) words *merkaz ruhani* meaning "spiritual center"
responsa	rabbinical board's reply to a religious question (Hebrew)
Rishon le-Zion	first Jewish settlement in Palestine (now fourth largest city) (French)
Sadducees	strict followers of Bible law only (Hebrews)
Sefer ha-Mivhar	Karaite commentary on the Bible (Hebrew)
sefirot	Channel of divine energy or life force (Hebrew)
Yiddish	Language of middle European Jews, based on German and Polish
yishuv	Jews living in Palestine before Israel's creation (Hebrew)
volk	native Germanic people (German)
volksgemeinschaft	community of native Germans (German)
Zera'im	seeds (Hebrew)

Bibliography

Abraham, Pearl. *The Seventh Beggar*. Riverhead Books, 2005.

Aharoni, Yohanan. *The Macmillan Bible Atlas*. Macmillan Publishing, 1993.

Alon, Gedalahah. *The Jews in Their Land in the Talmudic Age*. Magnes Press, 1980.

Alter, Kacyzine. *Polyn. Jewish Life in the Old Country*. Metropolitan Books, 1999.

Arott, Peter. *The Byzantines and Their World*. St, Martin's Press, 1973.

Avrohom, R. *The Wisdom of the Fathers*. Noble Book Press, 1995.

Barks, Coleman. *The Essential Rumi*. HarperSanFrancisco, 1995.

Barnavi, Eli. *A Historical Atlas of the Jewish People*. Schocken Books, 1992.

Bein, Alex. *Theodore Herzl, A Biography*. Jewish Publications of America, 1941.

Berger, David. *The Jewish-Christian Debate in the High Middle Ages*. The Jewish Publication Society, 1939.

Berlin, Adele. *The Jewish Study Bible*. Oxford U, 2004.

Bilski, Emily D. *Berlin Metropolis: Jews and the New Culture 1890-1918*. U. of California and the Jewish Museum, 1999.

Bokser, ben Zion. *The Talmud Selected Writings*. Paulist Press, 1989.

Brown, Nancy Marie. *The Abacus and the Cross: The Story of the Pope Who Brought the Light of Science to the Dark Ages*. Basic Books, 2010.

Brown, Michele. *In the Beginning: Bibles by the Year 1000*. Freer Gallery of Art & Sackler Gallery of Art, 2006.

Buhle, Paul. *From the Lower Eastside to Hollywood: Jews in American Popular Culture*. Verso, 2004.

Burkes, Shannon. *God, Self and Death: The Shape of Religious Transformation in the Second Temple Period*. Leiden, 2003.

Butwin, Julius. *Favorite Tales of Sholom Aleichem*. Frances Butwin (trans). Avenel Books, 1993.

Cahoone, Lawrence. *From Modernism to Post Modernism: an Anthology*. Blackwell, 1991.

Chambers, Simone. *Alternate Conceptions of Civil Society*. Princeton University Press, 2002.

Chant, Christopher. *The World's Railroads: The History and Development of Transportation*. Chartwell Books, 1997.

Childs, Brevard S. *The Book of Exodus: A Critical Theological Commentary*. The Westminster Press, 1974.

Cohen, Shay, J.D. *From the Macabees to the Mishnah*. Westminster, 1989.

Cohen, Abraham. *Everyman's Talmud*. Schocken Books, 1949.

Cohen, Israel. *Theodor Herzl, Founder of Political Zionism*. M W Books, 1959.

Cohen, Jonathan. *The Origins and Evolution of the Moses Nativity Story*. E. J.Brill, 1993.

Cohen, Mark R. *Under Crescent and Cross: Jews in the Middle Ages*. Princeton, 1974.

Coogan, Michael D,. *Canaanites: Who Were They and Where Did They Live?*. Bible Review, June 1993.

Cornwall, John. *Hitler's Pope: The Secret History of Pope Pius*. Viking, 1999.

Craig, Gordon A. *Germany 1866-1945*. Oxford, 1978.

Cross, Frank Moore. *Understanding the Dead Sea Scrolls*. Random House, 1992.

Darling, Linda. *Revenue-Raising and Legitimacy: Tax Collecting and Finance Administration in the Ottoman Empire, 1560-1660*. Brill, 1996.

Davies, Philip R. *The Complete World of the Dead Seas Scrolls*. Thames & Hudson, 2002.

Davis, R. Avrohom. *Pirkei Avos, The Wisdom of the Fathers*. Noble Book Press Corp, 1998.

Diefendorf, Elizabeth. *Books of the Century*. Oxford Press, 1996.

Dorff, Elliot N. *Conservative Judaism: Our Ancestors to our Descendants*. United Synagogue of Conservative Judaism, 1998.

Dotham, Trude and Moshe. *People of the Sea: The Search for the Philistines*. Macmillan Publishing Co., 1992.

Dupré, Judith. *Churches*. Harper Collins, 2001.

Durham, John I. *Word Biblical Commentary*. Word Books, 1987.

Eisenberg, Ellen. *Jewish Agricultural Colonies in New Jersey 1882-1920*. Syracuse University Press, 1995.

Elazar, Daniel J. *The Other Jews: The Sephardim Today*. Basic Books, Inc., 1988.

Elon, Amos. *The Pity Of It All: A History of Jews in Germay 1743-1993*. Henry Holt & Co., 2002.

Epstein, Dr. R.I. *The Babylonian Talmud, Seder Mo'ed*. Soncino Press, 1935.

Eugene, Ulrich. *The Dead Sea Scroll and the Origins of the Bible*. Wm. B, Eerdmanns Publishing Co., 1999.

Evans, Helen C. *Byzantium: Faith and Power (1261-1557)*. The Metropolitan Museum of Art & Yale University Press, 2004.
The Glory of Byzantium: Art and Culture (843-1261). Metropolitan Museum of Art, 2004.

Fine, Stephen. *Did the Synagogue Replace the Temple?*. Bible Review, April 1996.

Fischer, Eugene J. *Twenty Years of Jewish-Catholic Relations*. Paulist Press, 1986.

Fox, Everett. *The Five Books of Moses*. Schocken, 1983.

Freedman, David Noel. *The Anchor Bible Dictionary*. Nahum Sarna. Doubleday, 1996.

Fretheim, Terence E. *Exodus Interpretation*. John Knox Press, 1991.

Friedman, Richard Eliot. *Who Wrote the Bible*. Summit Books, 1987.

Gaber, Neal. *An Empire of Their Own: How the Jews Invented Hollywood.* Anchor Books, 1988.

Garthwaite, Gene R. *The Persians.* Blackwell, 2007.

Gedaliah, Alopn. *The Jews in Their Land in the Talmudic Age.* Magnus Press, 1980.

Geis, Francis & Joseph. *Daily Life in Medieval Times.* Black Dog & Leventhal, 1990.

Gilman,Sander L. *Yale Companion to Jewish Writing and Thought in German Culture 1096-1996.* Yale, 1997.

Goldberg, David. *To The Promised Land.* Penguin, 1996.

Goldfarb, Michael. *Emancipation.* Simon and Schuster, 2009.

Goldstein, Nathan. *I Macabees.* Doubleday, 1987.

Götz, Aly. *Plunder, Racial War, and the Nazi Welfare State.* Henry Holt, 2005.

Grossman, Maxine. *Reading for History in the Damascus Document.* Brill, 2002.

Gunther., W. *The Torah: A Modern Commentary.* Union of American Hebrew Congregations, 1987.

Ha'am, Ahad. *The Jewish State and the Jewish Problem.* www.zionistmonthlyweb.org, first printing 1897.

Halbertal, Moshe. *People of the Book: Canon, Meaning and Authority.* Harvard UniversityPress, 1997.

Hanson, Paul D,. *Isaiah 40-66.* John Knox Press, 1995.

Harries, Jill and Wood, Ian, *The Theodosian Code.* Cornell University Press, 1993.

Hasting, Adrian. *Modern Catholicism: Vatican II and After.* Oxford, 1991.

Hazony, Yarom. *The Jewish State: The Struggle for Israel's Soul.* New Republic, 2001.

Heilman, Samuel. *Defenders of the Faith: Inside Orthodox Jewry.* University of California, 1991.

Hertzberg, Arthur. *Jews the Essence and Character of a People.* HarperSanFrancisco, 1998.

Herzl, Theodor. *The Jewish State.* Dover, 1988.

Heschel, Susannah. *Abraham Geiger and the Jewish Jesus.* University of Chicago Press, 1998.

Hess, Jonathan M. *German Jews and the Claims of Modernity.* Yale University Press, 2002.

Hezser, Catherine. *Jewish Literacy in Roman Palestine.* Mohr Siebeck, 2001.

Hirsch, Ammiel. *One People, Two Worlds.* Schocken Books, 2002.

Hitler, Adolf. *Mein Kampf (in English).* Amazon, 2009.

Hoberman, J. *Entertaining America: Jews, Movies and Broadcasting.* Princeton, 2003.

Howe, Irving. *World of Our Fathers.* Harcourt, Brace, Jovanovich, 1976.

Hunter, James Davidson. *Culture Wars: The Struggle to Define America.* Basic Books, 1991.

Japhet, Sara. *I & II Chronicles: A Commentary.* John Knox Press, 1993.

Jones, Sheila. *The Quantum Ten: A Story of Passion, Tragedy, Ambition, and Science.* Oxford, 2008.

Karabell, Zachary. *Peace Be Upon You.* Alfred A. Knox, 2002.

Khan, Dr. Muhammad Mushi. *The Noble Qur'an.* Darussalan, 1999.

King , Philip J. *Life in Biblical Israel.* Westminster Joh Knox Press, 2001.

Knowles, David. *Augustine: Concerning the City of God Against Pagans.* Penguin Books, 1972.

Kolatch, Alfred J. *Complete Dictionary of English and Hebrew First Names.* Jonathan David Publishers, 1996.

Kubizek, August. *The Young Hitler I Knew (in English).* MBI Publishing, 1953.

Lazarus, Emma. *An Epistle to the Hebrews.* Jewish Historical Society of New York, 1987.

Leach, Margaret. *Dictionary of Folkore and Legend.* Funk & Wagnalls, 1950.

Lederer, Thomas G. *2000 Years: Relations Between Catholics and Jews. Before and After World War .* www.arthurstreet.com, 1998.

Levine, Lee I. *Judaism and Hellenism in Antiquity.* Hendrickson, 1999.
The Nature and Origin of The Palestinian Synagogue. Periodical, 2012.

Levy, Avigdor. *The Jews of the Ottoman Empire.* The Darwin Press, 1994.

Lilla, Mark. *The Still Born God: Religion Politics and the Modern West.* Alfred A. Knopf, 2007.

Lowenthal, Marvin. *The Diaries of Theodor Herzl.* The Dial Press1956.

Makiya, Kanan. *The Rock.* Pantheon Books, 2001.

Mann, Vivian B. *Convivencia: Jews, Muslims, and Christians in Medieval Spain.* George Braziller in association with The Jewish Museum, 1992.

Martin, Richard C. *Islam: A Cultural Perspective.* Prentice Hall, 1982.

Massie, Robert K. *Dreadnought: Britain and Germany and the Coming of the Great War.* William Morrow & Co, Random House, 1991.

Masters, Bruce. *Christians and Jews in the Ottoman Arab World.* Cambridge, 2001.

McGinity, Keren R. *Still Jewish: A History of Women and Intermarriage in America.* Brown University, 2005.

Meek, H.A. *The Synagogue.* Phaidon Press Limited, 1995.

Mendes-Flohr, Paul. *The Jews in the Modern World.* Jehuda Reinharz. Oxford University Press, 1995 (second edition).

Meyers, Carol. *Exodus.* Cambridge University Press, 2005.

Muhsi, Dr Muhammad. *The Noble Qu'ran.* Darussalam, 1999.

Neuhas, John. *What Really Happened at Vatican II .* First Things Magazine. October 2008.

Neuser, Jacob. *Dictionary of Judaism in the Biblical Period 450 to 600 BCE.* Hendrickson, 1996.
Formative Judaism: Religious, Historical and Literary Studies. Scholars Press, 1982.
Introduction to Rabbinic Literature. Doubleday, 1994.
The Tosefta Moed. KTAV Publishing, 1981.
Yerusalmi, Talmud of the Land of Israel. University of Chicago, 1971.

Noble, David F. *The Religion of Technology: The Divinity of Man and the Spirit of*

Invention. Alfred A. Knopf, 1998.

Patai, József. *Star Over Jordan: The Life of Theodore Herzl.* Philosophical Library, 1946.

Paul, Mendes-Flohr. *The Jew in the Modern World: A Documentary History.* Jehuia Reinharz. Oxford, 1995.

Pawlikowski, The Rev. John T. *New Trends in Catholic Religious Thought.* Paulist Press, 1986.

Purvis, James D,. *The Samaritan Pentateuch and the Origins of the Samaritan Sect.* Harvard University Press, 1968.

Reuven, Hammer. *Sifre. Deuteronomy.* Yale University Press, 1986.

Richarz, Monika (ed.). *Jewish Life in Germany: Memoirs From Three Centuries.* Indiana University Press, 1991.

Robbins, Harry Wolcott. *Western World Literature.* Coleman, Williams Harold. Macmillan, 1938.

Robinson, James M. *The Nag Hammadi Library.* Harper & Row, 1988.

Rosen, Joe. *Lawless Universe.* Johns Hopkins University Press, 2010.

Sacher, Howard A. *A History of Israel from the Rise of Zionism to Our Times.* Alfred A. Knopf, 2001.

Sacher, Howard M. *The Jews in the Modern World.* Alfred A. Knopf, 2005.

Sacks, Jonathan. *Arguments for the Sake of Heaven. Emerging Trends in Traditional Judaism.* Jason Aaronson, 1991.

Salamander, Rachel. *The Jewish World of Yesterday 1860-1938.* Rizzoli, 1991.

Sarna, Nahum. *The JPS Commentary: Exodus.* The Jewish Publication Society, 1991.

Schiffman, Lawrence R. *Encyclopedia of the Dead Sea Scrolls.* James C. Vandercamp. Oxford University Press, 2000.

Schimmel, Annemarie. *Islam: An Introduction.* State University of New York Press, 1992.

Schor, Esther. *Emma Lazarus.* Nextbook/Schocken, 2006.

Segal, Eliezer. *Varieties of Orthodox Judaism.* University of Calgary.

Segre, Dan Vittorio. *Memoirs of a Fortunate Jew.* Dell Publishing, 1985.

Seyyed, Hoissein Nasir. *Ideals and Realities of Islam.* Aquarian, 1994.

Shavit, Ari. *My Promised Land: The Triumph and Tragedy of Israel.* Barnes and Noble, 2012.

Shayne J.D., Cohen. *From the Macabees to the Mishnah.* Westminster Press, 1989.

Shimoni, Gideon. *Zionist Ideology.* Brandeis, 1995.

Smith, Charles D. *Palestine and the Arab-Israel Conflict.* Bedford/St. Martins, 2001.

Smith, Mark S. *The Early History of God.* HarperSanFrancisco, 1990.

Soloveitch, Joseph B. *The Lonely Man of Faith.* Doubleday, 1992.

Sorkin, David. *The Transformation of German Jewry 1780-1840.* Oxford1987.

Soulen, R. Kendall. *The God of Israel and Christian Theology.* Augsburg Fortress Press, 1996.

Stark, Rodney. *The Rise of Christianity*. Princeton, 1996.

Steinsaltz, R. *The Talmud, Steinsaltz Edition*. Random House, 1989.

Stemberger, Günter. *Introduction to Talmud and Midrash*. T&T Clark, 1991.

Stow, Kenneth R. *Alienated Minority: The Jews of Medieval Europe*. Harvard U., 1992.

Strauss, Richard. *Time Lines in Jewish History*. Self-published, 2009.

Thorn, John. *New York 400*. Melanie Boweer. Museum of the City of New York, 2009.

Toland, John. *Adolf Hitler*. Doubleday, 1991.

Trautman, Donald W. *A Challenging Reform: Realizing the Version of Liturgical Renewal by Archbishop Piero Marini*. Liturgical Press, 2007, America 2008.

Tyerman, Christopher. *Fighting for Christendom: Holy War and the Crusades*. Oxford University Press, 2004.

Ulrich, Eugene. *The Dead Seas Scrolls Bible*. HarperSanFrancisco, 1999. *The Dead Seas Scrolls and the Origins of the Bible*. Wm.B Eerdmans Publishing Co., 1999.

Untermeyer, Louis. *Rubáiyát of Omar Kháyyám*. Random House, 1947.

Vermes, Geza. *The Complete Dead Sea Scrolls in English*. Penguin Books, 2004.

Vryonis, Speros, Jr. *The Decline of Medieval Hellenism in Asia Minor and the Process of Islamization from the Eleventh Through the Fifteenth Century*. University of California Press, 1971.

Weinfeld, Moshe D. *What Makes the Ten Commandments Different?* Bible Review, April 1991.

Whiston, William. *The Works of Josephus*. Hendrickson Publishers, 1987.

Wigoder, Geoffrey (ed). *The New Encyclopedia Of Judaism*. New York University Press, 2002.

Wilson, Robert R. *Prophecy and Society in Ancient Israel*. Fortress Press, 1984.

Wilson, Edward O. *The Social Conquest of Earth*. Liveright, 2012.

Wiltgen S,V,D., Rev. Ralph M. *The Rhine Flows into the Tiber*. Hawthorn Books, 1967.

Wistrich, Robert S. *Demonizing the Other: Antisemitism, Racism, and Xenophobia*. Harwood Academic Publishers, 1999.

Wright, N.T. *What St. Paul Really Said*. William B. Eerdmans, 1997.

Yonge, C.D. (trans.). *The Works of Philo*. Hendrickson, 1993.

Yoseloff, Thomas. *The Founder of Political Zionism*. MW Books, 1959. *Theodor Herzl Founder of Political Zionism*. MW Books, 1959.

Yual, Israel Jacob. *Jews and Christians in the Middle Ages*. Academic Publishers, 1997.

Zangwill, Israel. *Dreamers of the Ghetto*. Harper & Brothers, 1898.

Index

About the Author

Born to Jewish parents, Robert F. Strauss had minimal Jewish education, but retained a deep interest in the history and meaning of Judaism. He also felt a calling from God which, later in life, spurred him to study Christianity.

Strauss served for two years in the US Navy during the Second World War. Educated as a mechanical engineer, he majored in aeronautics at the New Jersey Institute of Technology. He worked with German engineers, including Wernher von Braun, to develop rocket engines for the first manned space vehicle, and participated in the launching of the prototype shuttle system at Cape Canaveral. His experience is part of the audio library at Marshall Space Flight Center.

For the next decade, he was a partner in a technology corporation and served his community as a school board member and as an officer in the county and state school boards association. He then worked with his wife, attorney Judith Esmay, to develop policies and regulations for public school districts. As the founders of Strauss/Esmay Associates, they served several hundred school districts in New Jersey for two decades, preparing bylaws, policies and regulations consistent with law, state regulations, and court decisions.

Robert Strauss was baptized in the Episcopal Church twenty-five years ago, and has been a faithful church member ever since. Orthodox Jewish theologian Michael Wyschogrod wrote that "the acid test of the [Christian] church's theological posture is its conduct toward Jews who have been baptized. For if the church acknowledges the abiding reality of Israel's election, it will expect baptized Jews to maintain faithfully their Jewish identity."[1] As an active member of St. Thomas Episcopal Church in Hanover, New Hampshire, Strauss has always maintained his Jewish identity. His upbringing in Judaism and his experience as a committed Christian has helped him see the Jewish-Christian struggle from both sides.

---

[1] Soulen, Kendall. *Michael Wyschogrod and God's First Love*. The Christian Century, July 27, 2004, 22-7.

Made in the USA
Middletown, DE
17 October 2017